INTERPRETIVE RESEARCH DESIGN

Research design is fundamental to all scientific endeavors, at all levels and in all institutional settings. In many social science disciplines, however, scholars working in an interpretive–qualitative tradition get little guidance on this aspect of research from the positivist-centered training they receive. This book is an authoritative examination of the concepts and processes underlying the design of an interpretive research project. Such an approach to design starts with the recognition that researchers are inevitably embedded in the intersubjective social processes of the worlds they study.

In focusing on researchers' theoretical, ontological, epistemological, and methods choices in designing research projects, Schwartz-Shea and Yanow set the stage for other volumes in the *Routledge Series on Interpretive Methods*. They also engage some very practical issues, such as ethics reviews and the structure of research proposals. This concise guide explores where research questions come from, criteria for evaluating research designs, how interpretive researchers engage with "world-making," context, systematicity and flexibility, reflexivity and positionality, and such contemporary issues as data archiving and the researcher's body in the field.

Peregrine Schwartz-Shea is Professor of Political Science at the University of Utah. **Dvora Yanow** is Visiting Professor in the Faculty of Social and Behavioral Sciences at the University of Amsterdam and in the Communication Sciences Department, Faculty of Social Sciences, at Wageningen University. Together they are co-editors of *Interpretation and Method: Empirical Research Methods and the Interpretive Turn,* and they created and run the "Methods Café" at both the American and Western Political Science Associations' annual meetings.

Routledge Series on Interpretive Methods
Edited by:
Dvora Yanow, University of Amsterdam and Wageningen University
Peregrine Schwartz-Shea, University of Utah

The *Routledge Series on Interpretive Methods* comprises a collection of slim volumes, each devoted to different issues in interpretive methodology and its associated methods. The topics covered will establish the methodological grounding for interpretive approaches in ways that distinguish interpretive methods from quantitative and qualitative methods in the positivist tradition. The series as a whole engages three types of concerns: (1) *methodological issues*, looking at key concepts and processes; (2) *approaches and methods*, looking at how interpretive methodologies are manifested in different forms of research; and (3) *disciplinary and subfield areas*, demonstrating how interpretive methods figure in different fields across the social sciences.

Approachable yet authoritative, the volumes are especially useful for graduate students looking for sources that lay out the reasoning and terminology of interpretive methodologies. Academic and independent researchers writing research plans for grant applications or sabbaticals can use these volumes to support the systematic procedural character and rigorous argumentation of interpretive research. Instructors teaching research methods courses will find the books valuable in providing an explanation of the differences between interpretive research methods and those of "traditional" positivist research. These may also be useful volumes for journal editors and reviewers of manuscripts who are not familiar with these differences.

Interpretive Research Design: Concepts and Processes
Peregrine Schwartz-Shea and Dvora Yanow

Elucidating Social Science Concepts: An Interpretivist Guide
Frederic Charles Schaffer

Interpreting International Politics
Cecelia Lynch

Postcolonial Theory and Analysis in Political Studies
Kevin Bruyneel

Ethnography and Interpretation
Timothy Pachirat

Analyzing Social Narratives
Shaul R. Shenhav

Frederic Charles Schaffer
University of Massachusetts, Amherst

Edward Schatz
University of Toronto

Ronald Schmidt, Sr.
California State University, Long Beach

James C. Scott
Yale University

Samer Shehata
Georgetown University

Diane Singerman
American University

Joe Soss
University of Wisconsin, Madison

Camilla Stivers
Cleveland State University

John Van Maanen
MIT

Katherine Cramer Walsh
University of Wisconsin, Madison

Lisa Wedeen
University of Chicago

Jutta E. Weldes
Bristol University

INTERPRETIVE RESEARCH DESIGN

Concepts and Processes

*Peregrine Schwartz-Shea and
Dvora Yanow*

Routledge
Taylor & Francis Group

NEW YORK AND LONDON

First published 2012
by Routledge
711 Third Avenue, New York, NY 10017

Simultaneously published in the UK
by Routledge
2 Park Square, Milton Park, Abingdon, Oxon OX14 4RN

Routledge is an imprint of the Taylor & Francis Group, an informa business

Library of Congress Cataloging in Publication Data
Schwartz-Shea, Peregrine, 1955–
   Interpretive research design : concepts and processes / Peregrine Schwartz-Shea
   and Dvora Yanow.
   p. cm.—(Routledge series on interpretive methods)
   Includes bibliographical references and index.
   1. Science—Methodology. 2. Experimental design. I. Yanow, Dvora. II. Title.
   Q175.S4144 2011
   001.4'34—dc23
   2011033462

ISBN: 978–0–415–87807–4 (hbk)
ISBN: 978–0–415–87808–1 (pbk)
ISBN: 978–0–203–85490–7 (ebk)

Typeset in Bembo
by Swales & Willis Ltd, Exeter, Devon

DEDICATION

This book is dedicated to Howard Becker, Bud Duvall, Murray Edelman, Richard Fenno, Clifford Geertz, Egon Guba, Yvonna Lincoln, Lloyd Rudolph, Susanne Rudolph, Jim Scott, to name but a few, and others in many fields who have walked these paths before us; to our colleagues and students who walk them with us now, leading us to new ways of seeing, knowing, and thinking about these matters; and to the leaders of those directorates within the US National Science Foundation which have begun to grapple with some of these issues, in the hope that they, along with their counterparts in other states' funding organizations, will pave new paths in the near future.

CONTENTS

ILLUSTRATIONS

Figures

Tables

ACKNOWLEDGMENTS

Many of the ideas contained herein were worked out in teaching contexts, whether in classroom settings or in conversations with our respective students and colleagues. We thank all of them in their several settings: the Political Science Department at the University of Utah; the 2006–2009 "Meaning and Methods" course in the Culture, Organization, and Management Department at VU University, Amsterdam, and the Netherlands Institute of Government "General Methodology" course, co-taught with Markus Haverland; the 2009 National Science Foundation Workshop on Interpretive Methodologies in Political Science; and methods courses, workshops, and seminars of various sorts at Vienna's Institute for Advanced Studies, Erasmus University Rotterdam's Institute for Health Policy and Management's Healthcare Governance Group, Charles University-Prague's Center for Social and Economic Strategies, and the Methods Cafés at the Western and American Political Science Association meetings. In particular, we are grateful for the extraordinary collegiality of members of our extended interpretive research community—Robert Adcock, Lee Ann Fujii, Patrick Jackson, Xymena Kurowska, Cecelia Lynch, Ido Oren, Tim Pachirat, Fred Schaffer, Ed Schatz, Joe Soss, Merlijn van Hulst, and Dorian Warren—who have never stinted on advice and critical input. What we have learned from our ongoing conversations with them is reflected in the pages of this book, even as the usual and customary caveats concerning ultimate responsibility apply. We also thank Eric Blanchard, Matthew Burbank, and Jennifer Yim for comments on earlier drafts of the manuscript; Lee Ann Fujii, in particular, for bringing her strict eye for formal writing to a line by line reading of much of the previous draft; and Akiko Kurata for last-minute graphic design help. The conversations initiated through the vehicle of detailed comments received from our four reviewers have helped us shape the book into its present form, challenging us to better articulate our reasoning and views. In addition, Dvora Yanow would like to thank the Faculty of Social and Behavioral Sciences, Political Science Department, at the University of Amsterdam, and especially Mark Rutgers, John Grin, and Frances Gouda, for creating a hospitable setting in which to write this book.

It is not only colleagues who enable research and writing. Given that we speak in Chapter 4 of the relational character of research and the support field research often requires, we want also to acknowledge the trans-collegial relationships whose emotional and other support enabled the writing of this book: Dave Gelici, at the Coffee Connection in Amsterdam, and the friendly baristas at Salt Lake Roasting Company and The Coffee Garden, both in Salt Lake City, where each of us has spent many hours thinking through the issues discussed here; Juraj Fabus at Health City, Amsterdam, and the many yoga instructors who brought that discipline to the US, who helped each of us keep body and soul together in ways that enabled long hours glued to the desk chair; and Tim Shea, who has been unstinting in his support over many years.

INTRODUCTION

[Such research is characterized by an] intensive focus on the empirical world; on seeing and understanding behavior in its particular and situated forms. Data that do not stay close to the events, actions, or texts being studied are always suspect. There is a hostility to generalizations at any level that are not connected to description, to immersion in substantive matter. . . . The preference for descriptive material and observation made us suspicious of . . . material torn from the context of their creation. Action was too situated, too contextual to be understood at the high levels of much macroanalysis. Meanings were often not assuredly understandable without an experience with those we were describing.

—*Joseph R. Gusfield (1995, xii)*

How does one begin to design an empirical research project? Many scholars across the social sciences, socio-cultural anthropology perhaps excepted, would reply with the steps associated with "the scientific method": articulate your hypotheses, define your concepts, operationalize these in the form of variables, establish the relationships among the latter, and then plan to test them in your research setting, checking for validity, reliability, and generalizability. This is the formula for research design found in most methods textbooks. And yet this way of proceeding does not describe very well a whole segment of scientific research: that conducted under the heading of interpretive social science, a term increasingly being used in some disciplines or fields of inquiry to refer to qualitative social science in the Chicago School tradition. This is research that, similar to 1920s–1960s anthropology and sociology field research conducted at the University of Chicago, focuses on specific, situated meanings and meaning-making practices of actors in a given context, as described in the epigraph by Joseph Gusfield, reflecting on his own experiences and role there, then (see also Calhoun 2007: 26–33). It is to address this missing conversation that we have written this book.

Given the increasingly inter- and cross-disciplinary research and publishing practices within the social sciences, what it means to do interpretive empirical research needs articulation and development such that scholars from various epistemic communities can appreciate the full extent of its practices and, in particular, their methodological underpinnings. This volume lays out the grounding for the design of research projects that build on interpretive methodological presuppositions, with such scholars, among them newer researchers, as our imagined readers. Notable within this group are those reviewing interpretive research, whether for thesis, dissertation or ethics committee assessments (such as Institutional Review Boards, IRBs, in the US), funding or publication reviews, or promotion and tenuring evaluations.

Research design is about making choices and articulating a rationale for the choices one has made. As a term, "design" evokes expectations of a carefully formulated plan. Many elements are common across research designs, whatever ontological and epistemological presuppositions inform the specific work. But these seemingly common elements can mask significant differences in approaches to research. We engage here both those elements that are shared and those that are clearly distinctive to interpretive research designs. If this distinctiveness is not understood, an interpretive research design may be judged by those unfamiliar with its premises to be weak, sloppy or underdeveloped, rather than adequate, well-developed or even "strong." In attending to and articulating the differences between design forms, it becomes crucial at times to explore other terms for design concepts that are well known, but which inadequately express ideas that are central to *interpretive* research processes. Other vocabularies make these differences clear, and they articulate the design concepts' underlying ideas in ways that more closely fit interpretive presuppositions. Engaging alternate terms can help both interpretive researchers and reviewers of various sorts from other epistemic communities understand the philosophical grounding of interpretive research and its design requirements.

In writing this book, then, we had three broad readerships in mind. One of these is graduate students, who in particular need information about interpretive concepts and processes so that they can do empirical research that genuinely allows for an interpretive approach without having their confidence undermined at this stage of the game by uninformed critiques. These include, for instance, comments that suggest that interpretive research does not stand on its own, being useful only as a preliminary stage to generate information that can serve as the basis for a quantitative study; or criticisms that inquire about the variables used in the study, misunderstanding the purposes of interpretive research, which is not variables-based. The treatment of interpretive research design presented here counters prevailing misinformation about the methodological grounding for "qualitative" methods (even among research methods textbook authors) and the widespread ignorance of interpretive methods. The volume discusses interpretive method-ologies' and methods' distinctive concepts and processes and the reasoning that underlies them in ways that enable students to think and talk about the particulars of the interpretive research designs they are developing or conducting. In several places, discussions of interpretive approaches are situated adjacent to discussions of positivist approaches to the same topic, especially when methodological concepts from the latter are widespread and commonly used. Through that contrast, we hope to make clear the claims and processes of both approaches.

Second, we are writing for more experienced researchers—academics, policy analysts, independent scholars, and consultants—who apply for funding, for research-related release time, and/or for other resources to conduct such research (e.g., entrée/access to field settings). They will find here a way to talk about interpretive methodologies and methods that can be useful in those applications. Such research-speak is needed in order to explain the rationale behind the more flexible, open-ended approach to research design that is common in this sort of empirical research, manifest, for example, in the lack of formalized hypotheses and random sampling. More flexible approaches and the absence of hypotheses, variables, and sampling are commonplaces in social or cultural anthropology, where interpretive methodologies have received their fullest expression in the conduct of research. When used in disciplines in which other methodological approaches are dominant, these commonplaces often are treated as outliers, and even as signs of poorly designed research. As a result, the research proposal, as well as subsequent manuscripts, is often found wanting. Yet these characteristics of interpretive research designs are neither haphazard nor sloppy, but systematic (i.e., "rigorous") in their own right, as we explain in Chapters 1–6 of the book.

Third, those teaching research methods courses will find the book useful, for the same reasons, for curricular purposes. Most treatments of research design across the social sciences (social-cultural anthropology excepted) take a variables-based, hypothesis-testing, (quasi-)experimental approach to the topic that is quite different from the word-based, abductive, field and archival research approach common to interpretive empirical work. Most methods textbooks, even when presenting and discussing qualitative methods, lack a full understanding of the ways in which many kinds of qualitative research design, let alone interpretive ones, are different from "traditional" research designs—the latter influenced by the forms and logic of inquiry dominant in economics, psychology, and other fields that follow "positivist"-inflected methodological argumentation (which is not to say that those fields do not have their own forms of interpretive research; see, e.g., McCloskey 1985 in economics, Giorgi *et al.* 1983 or Wertz 2005 in psychology).[1]

Our approach is informed by a science studies or sociology of knowledge perspective that sees scientific work as a practice—and one that seeks to per-suade others of the "goodness" of its findings. As such, we are asking ourselves, constantly, about the political (or power) dimensions of what scientists do, including social scientists. Although this statement is strongly reminiscent of Foucault's engagement with the intersections of knowledge and power (1984), we are influenced more by ethnographic analyses of various kinds of natural and physical scientific practices (see, e.g., Latour 1987, Latour and Woolgar 1988, M. Lynch and Woolgar 1990, Traweek 1992) and by the utility of bringing such a perspective to bear on the practices of social scientists (see, e.g., Brandwein 2000, 2006, Büger and Gadinger 2007, Woolgar *et al.* 2009, Yanow 2005).

Some points of clarification concerning concepts that run through this volume are in order. First, the discussion rests on a distinction between *methodology* and *methods*. Methodology commonly refers to the presuppositions concerning ontology—the reality status of the "thing" being studied—and epistemology—its "know-ability"—which inform a set of methods. It might be thought of, in a way, as applied philosophy. If methodology refers to a *logic* of inquiry, the conduct of the inquiry itself might be thought of in terms of the particular tools—the methods—with and through which the research design and its logic are carried out or enacted. So, in this sense, interviewing might be seen as a tool—a method; and it is one that can be informed by different, and often conflicting, methodological presuppositions.

A researcher can interview based on the belief that she is going to be able to establish "what really happened" in a setting. This reflects a realist–objectivist methodology that rests on three things: faith in the existence of an objective *social* world that is external to the researcher; knowledge of that world which can be achieved through observation from a point outside it; and the belief that this knowledge can yield an understanding of what the researcher holds to be the truth of that external world, an understanding that mirrors that world. Or a researcher can interview based on the belief that there are multiple perceived and/or experienced social "realities" concerning what happened, rather than a singular "truth." In this view, the researcher would assume that event narratives are likely to vary depending on the perspective (political, cultural, experiential, etc.) of the persons being interviewed. This approach reflects a constructivist–interpretivist methodology that rests on a belief in the existence of (potentially) multiple, *intersubjectively* constructed "truths" about social, political, cultural, and other human events; and on the belief that these understandings can only be accessed, or co-generated, through interactions between researcher and researched as they seek to interpret those events and make those interpretations legible to each other.[2]

Attending to their methodological underpinnings makes it less reasonable to think of any method as an item in a "tool box," a metaphor commonly found in textbooks that do not distinguish between methods and methodologies (if they discuss methodology or philosophy of science issues at all). Underlying the tools metaphor is an assumption of neutrality among methods: the researcher is methodologically—philosophically—agnostic as to whether she picks up an open-ended interview or a survey instrument to use in her research. Yet no method is methodologically neutral: each one—modeling, ethnomethodology, modes of interviewing, "styles" of participant observation—rests on the choices that researchers make when they enact their ontological and epistemological presuppositions. These are "pre-"suppositions less in time than in logic: they typically are part of researchers' tacit knowledge (in Polanyi's, 1966, sense), such that instead of being able to declare them at the outset of a research career, it is only when researchers reflect on research already conducted, and perhaps even published, that their knowledge of their own presuppositions becomes explicit (often when a colleague or reviewer points out the ontological and epistemological ground on which the research stands). This understanding leads us to focus, instead, on the language of methodological *"approaches"* and choices among them, rather than of tools, the second point. Referring to approaches emphasizes the inevitable intertwining of the many choices that a researcher makes in bringing research question, methodology, and methods together. These choices give expression to, or enact, the methodological approach—interpretive, positivist, critical realist, or some other—informing the work that a researcher carries out.

Third, we draw a distinction not only between quantitative and qualitative research and their attendant designs, but among *quantitative, qualitative,* and *interpretive* research. The older, and still widely known and used, two-part taxonomy developed at a particular point in time to demarcate University of Chicago–style observational and interview-based research from the kind of quantitative and survey-based research developed at Columbia University and the University of Michigan. As survey research instruments, statistical science, and the computer hardware and software that could process ever greater quantities of data further developed, along with behavioralist theories, "quantitative" research ascended over "qualitative" research in many social science departments and/or disciplines.[3] As a consequence, researchers using qualitative methods came under increasing pressure to adopt the evaluative criteria central to quantitative ones. Qualitative research continues to use one or more of three common data generating methods: observing, with whatever degree of participating; talking to people (a.k.a. interviewing); and the close "reading" of research-relevant materials. But in many fields, it has grown to resemble less and less Chicago-School–style field research, drawing increasingly, instead, on analytic methods that enact positivist philosophical modes of scientific knowing (e.g., a realist ontology, the possibility of objective knowledge, generalizing universal laws). The bipartite "quantitative–qualitative" taxonomy of *methods* has, more and more, come implicitly to stand in as proxy for a distinction between positivist and interpretivist *methodologies.*

In many fields, the dual taxonomy has increasingly lost that sense of methodological difference, although in some, such as parts of sociology and educational studies, "qualitative" still carries its older meaning intact. In other fields, reflecting the "interpretive turn" that took place across the social sciences in the 1970s–1990s (see, e.g., Geertz 1973, Rabinow and Sullivan 1979, 1985, Polkinghorne 1983, 1988, Hiley *et al.* 1991), Chicago-School–style qualitative methods resting on a phenomenological hermeneutics that privileges local, situated knowledge and situated knowers has increasingly become known as "interpretive" research. This yields a three-part taxonomy of research approaches: quantitative–positivist methods drawing on realist–objectivist presuppositions, qualitative–positivist methods drawing on similar presuppositions, and qualitative–interpretive methods drawing on constructivist–interpretivist presuppositions.[4] Properly speaking, then, we should use those three compound adjectives when describing methods; but to make the language simpler, we will use quantitative, qualitative, and interpretive, instead. In some places, where qualitative and interpretive methods are similar in their approaches to a topic, we use them together. In others, in order to emphasize interpretive design's distinctiveness, we contrast it with positivist design elements found in both qualitative and quantitative approaches.

In part because of this history, what gets included or counted as "interpretive *empirical*" research can be confusing. Does it include analyses interpreting theoretical texts, such as those seeking to understand the implications of Weber's writings from a feminist perspective (Ferguson 1984),[5] for example, or of some other writer whose work is considered canonical or otherwise central to a discipline? Clearly, analyzing documentary materials, whether historical or contemporary, draws on similar methods of text-treatment and thought. This was precisely Taylor's (1971) argument: that in studying human actions, researchers render them as "text analogues" for purposes of analysis (see also Ricoeur 1971). And it is equally clear in how interpretive empirical scholars approach physical artifacts, such as governmental buildings and other built spaces in which acts of research interest take place (see, e.g., G. Mosse 1975, Yanow 2006a).

In political science, where we are most familiar with these issues and debates,[6] the interpretation of theoretical texts is often explicitly framed as "non-empirical" research, leading political theory graduate students in some programs to be exempted from research methods courses required of all others (Schwartz-Shea 2003). But this understanding of textual analysis rests on meanings of "empirical" that are narrowly cast and increasingly contested. Political theorists interview (Bellah *et al.* 2007 [1985]), for instance; work in archives on contemporaneous materials in ways that parallel historical research (especially social history; see, e.g., Darnton 1984, 2003, Davis 1983) situating correspondence, diaries, paintings, and other texts and text-analogues in contemporary social, political, and cultural contexts (e.g., Ferguson 2011, Bellhouse 2011); and analyze college catalogues (Kaufman-Osborn 2006) or methodological practices (Norton 2004).[7] In emphasizing that this book engages "interpretive empirical" research, we also have these kinds of work in mind (although we also note that the manuscripts reporting on such research often have a rather different "voice" from those reporting on field observations, likely due to different intended audiences and dissemination outlets, including conferences, journals, and book publishers).

Fourth, although it is itself something of a misnomer, we use the *shorthand* "positivist research" to refer to those forms of research that rest on realist ontological and objectivist epistemological presuppositions,[8] in order not to have to repeat what is a linguistic and conceptual mouthful every time we want to refer to that kind of research; we do the same with "interpretive research."[9] Likewise, we use the phrases "positivist researcher" or "interpretive researcher" as shorthand references to the approach a researcher uses in a particular project. We do not intend thereby to equate a research approach with an individual's identity or to reify this link, as some researchers choose to move between approaches, depending on the research question they are engaging. Some researchers do specialize in one approach or another; for them, personal identity and research identity may be more intertwined than for others who are more ambidextrous, so to speak. The possibility and ease of such movement depends on an individual's inclination toward and specialization in certain forms of research, as well as on the breadth or narrowness of graduate methods training and what is made available to students as they are socialized to their discipline's practices. It can be challenging, for instance, to develop a "research ear" for both metaphor analysis and formal modeling and to master the technical intricacies of both. The ability of a single researcher to "mix" methods or methodologies—so-called mixed methods research—is related to this point. We defer a consideration of such mixing to Chapter 8.

Fifth, we make reference at times to *phases of a research project*, distinguishing "fieldwork" (which we use in reference to archival research as well as to its more traditional participant observer, ethnographic, and interviewing designation) from "deskwork" (more focused analytic activities, typically away from the field) and "textwork" (the more focused preparation of the research report).[10] We do so in full recognition of the fact that these activities are intertwined: although fieldwork itself may be separate in both time and space from the other two phases, analysis often begins in the field, if not beforehand, and continues through the preparation of the research manuscript or presentation; and chunks of text may come directly from notes prepared in the field or from the research proposal. Still, we find it useful for heuristic purposes at times to mark and use this distinction.

Lastly, one of the things that makes the topic of research design so fraught with tension and miscommunication is that various epistemic communities often use the *same word to mean different things*—without recognizing those differences and, therefore, without understanding the reasons for the miscommunications that ensue. For instance, an experimentalist's understanding of what makes research *valid* differs from validity's meaning in other research approaches, reflecting different modes of thinking about the way(s) in which research is done. To take another example, in some cases, *naturalist* has been used to describe research on biological and physical topics in the understanding that those scientists can conduct their studies from positions outside the research domain. There, the "behaviors" of plant cells, bacteria or rock and mineral formations are "natural" and indifferent to such observation and to the results of the study (e.g., Bevir and Kedar 2008; for an in-depth analysis of this latter point, see Oren 2006a). But a large section of the qualitative–interpretive research world uses naturalist to refer to precisely the opposite kind of research, in which the researcher is firmly positioned *within* the community and setting under study (e.g., Schatzman and Strauss 1973, Lincoln and Guba 1985, Erlandson *et al.* 1993, Athens 2010)! This research is "naturalist" in that the researcher engages in activities that are naturally occurring in such set-tings—e.g., observing people, talking to them, and/or taking part in the course of their everyday, "natural" activities in their own, "natural" settings, much as "ordinary" members of that setting would comport themselves.

In yet another instance, *constructionism* and *constructivism* are used in different disciplines, or even in different subfields of the same discipline, with different meanings. International Relations, for instance, has developed its own historically grounded use of these terms with their own particular meanings and reference points (see, e.g., Green 2002, Hopf 2002, P. Jackson 2002: 258, n. 12); but that field's use of these terms is often at odds with the broader methodological and methods literature. Similarly, experimentalists and others use the term *subject* in reference to persons who are the objects or units of study; whereas in other types of research, "subject" is seen as denying persons agency, and the terminology has shifted to "research participants."[11] Researchers working with these terms need to make themselves aware of such differences, as conversations often develop in which scholars end up speaking past each other because they assume that scholarly terms are being used to mean the same thing, when this is, in fact, not the case.

This discussion of language and nomenclature in the methods and methodo-logical literature links to a different question: the meaning of "design" in this book's title. It has two; they are intertwined; and we have already been using them interchangeably and will continue to do so. On the one hand, *interpretive* research design—imagine the stress on the first word—could mean the outline of the steps a researcher would follow in planning a research project using an inter-pretive approach. This is the sense that marks much of Chapter 1; it is design as object, as noun. At the same time, interpretive research *design*—where the noun has almost the quality of a gerund—is somewhat more dynamic, emphasizing the thought processes and ensuing strategies that go into designing interpretive research. This is the meaning that informs much of the book and lies at the root of its subtitle—*Concepts and Processes.* If the reader finds our discussion of design-ing for interpretive research more narrative in its treatment by contrast with the typically more stepwise, procedural approach of traditional textbooks, it is due to these dual meanings and our emphasis on the second of the two.

The one area of interpretive methods that receives short shrift in this book is the more "creative" side of the methodological family: methods drawing on poetry, play-writing and performing, painting, and other artistic endeavors. Given our own empirical engagements in the political sciences (specifically, with public policy, public administration, political sociology, and feminist and gender studies) and in organizational studies, where research engagements tend to be rather tradi-tional and such methods are not commonly found, we have not included specific examples of them, nor do we engage the particularities of the kinds of designs and justifications they require. The journal *Qualitative Inquiry* is a major source for such work, and we happily refer readers interested in such methods to the articles there and to their references.

In sum, researchers in the social sciences across the board need more effective preparation for designing research projects, whether in the field or in archives, that are shaped and supported by phenomenological, hermeneutic, and allied methodological presuppositions and argumentation. We hope the volume engages readers across the full spectrum of these disciplines, at both undergraduate and graduate levels, as well as those in "applied" or professional degree programs: educational studies, nursing and allied health studies, organizational studies, public administration, public policy analysis, urban and regional planning, and others too numerous to list. Because of the specific orientation we take, we anticipate that intersectionality scholars and feminist researchers, many of whose approaches intersect with and overlap interpretive ones, will also find the book speaking to their concerns.

A Sketch of the Book

As the first volume in the *Routledge Series on Interpretive Methods*, this book treats concepts and processes in interpretive empirical research design, and the methodological issues they raise, looking across methods of generating and analyzing data. Although it engages some very practical issues, such as the structure of research proposals, it is not a how-to volume, as many methods—especially of data analysis (e.g., ethnomethodology, semiotics, metaphor or category analysis; Feldman 1995, Yanow 2000)—follow specific logics of inquiry and require specific designs. We discuss some topics in an overview fashion, relying on other volumes in the series to flesh these out, each in ways appropriate to its own method.

Chapter 1 is devoted to the whys and wherefores of research design, and Chapter 2 then explores the logic of inquiry of interpretive research, with particular attention to where research questions come from. It sketches out abductive ways of knowing before turning to the methodological underpinnings of interpretive research: the ideas from hermeneutic and phenomenological philosophies that are enacted in various forms of meaning-focused, context-specific, interpretive research methods. Research designs, however, require not only a specification of a research question and a theoretical domain; they also need a specification of planned sources of evidence relative to that research question and domain, as well as a sense of how those data will be analyzed. Chapters 3, 4, 5, and 6 engage the kinds of issues that inform choices of data sources: contextuality, its several implications (e.g., for concept development, access, forms of evidence), and, finally, issues in evaluating the trustworthiness or "goodness" of an interpretive research project. Chapters 7 and 8 then take up issues that situate research designs in a broader context.

The rationale underlying the middle section of the book requires a bit more explanation. The design parts of an intended research project are often articulated in the context of a research proposal, as discussed in Chapter 1 and outlined there in Table 1.1. Most textbook discussions of research design explore it in linear fashion, following the contours of the completed outline of such a proposal. Because we are interested in the concepts and processes that go into thinking about interpretive research and what distinguishes it from other research approaches, we take a different tack in Chapters 3 to 6. We engage, instead, the kinds of issues a researcher thinking interpretively would need to consider in carefully formulating the steps of a plan. In doing so, we note the elements that are common to research proposals whatever their epistemological and ontological presuppositions. But we pay close attention to the significant differences that arise when one takes an interpretive approach.

Due to the practice, begun in the early 1970s, of requiring statistics courses in social science curricula, most, if not all, researchers today are familiar with the kind of research design that is typical of a positivist methodology, with its attendant concepts. Most methods textbooks, many of them required reading in graduate and some undergraduate coursework (see Thies and Hogan 2005), lay out its presuppositions, often designated "the" scientific method (as if there were only one). Many design concepts and terms, such as operationalization, sampling, and falsifiability, are, therefore, second nature to most researchers, who are not aware that these are grounded in positivist research methodologies and, therefore, less appropriate for other research approaches.

Because of the prevalence and dominance of these and other terms, positivist researchers, and even those doing interpretive research, may have difficulty recognizing this misfit. In Chapters 3 to 6, because of many researchers' greater familiarity with positivist-informed concepts, we have situated our discussion of interpretive research characteristics and criteria in close proximity to those on the whole more familiar terms. This enables us to show where and how interpretive methodologies part company with those terms and to explain the ways in which interpretive researchers think about related concepts and processes. Interpretive researchers need a language for responding, for instance, to questions and comments that emerge from a positivist paradigm, such as: What is your independent variable? How did you operationalize that concept? Is that a falsifiable proposition?[12] In articulating the reasons that those terms are not good fits for interpretive research design elements, we argue for certain concepts that are more directly linked to interpretive presuppositions and whose use helps surface those differences. In some cases, other concepts and terms better connect to and reflect interpretive presuppositions and extant research practices. We take this up at length in these four chapters.

Specifically, Chapter 3 explores the implications for designing research of the central characteristic that distinguishes meaning-focused inquiry from other approaches: the role of context. In interpretive research, meaning-making is key to the scientific endeavor: its very purpose is to understand how specific human beings in particular times and locales make sense of their worlds. And because sense-making is always contextual, a concern with "contextuality"—rather than "generalizability"—motivates research practice and design. In this chapter, we explain this concern and take up its implications for concept development and understandings of hypothesizing and causality. The three of these play out differently in interpretive research because of its emphasis on context and on the situatedness of both researchers and "researched."

Context has further implications for the character of evidence: where and how am I going to find "my data," what will those data look like, and, when I am interacting with research participants, what sort of researcher role will I assume as I co-generate those data with them? What emerges from this discussion is a fuller understanding of the necessity for flexibility in interpretive research design. These matters are explored in Chapters 4 and 5. The ways in which evidence is generated, *and* the ways in which such processes are discussed in an interpretive research manuscript, are key to how the trustworthiness of a researcher's knowledge claims will be evaluated by a diverse range of readers. Chapter 6 takes up various processes through which researchers designing interpretive projects can anticipate checking on their sense-making in the field, in data analysis, and in writing.

Chapters 7 and 8 move beyond the details of a research design itself to look at research designs in their broader contexts. In Chapter 7 we take up some of the largely silenced areas of field research: the play of emotions in the field, researchers' sexuality, and, in particular, the "wheelchairedness" and other physical constraints under which some researchers work, all of which might well be anticipated in thinking through a research design but are commonly not spoken of. We also look at two issues gaining attention these days, human subjects protections and data archiving, both problematic from the perspective of interpretive methodologies, whether for procedural or ethical reasons. And we relate elements of a research design to sections of the manuscripts that report on the research. In Chapter 8 we consider "mixed methods" research before turning our attention to still broader issues involved when interpretive research crosses over to other epistemic communities, such as during reviews of various sorts.

To avoid misunderstanding concerning the book as a whole, we add three caveats. First, if some readers are expecting to find polemics here against modes of research other than interpretive ones, they will, we trust, be disappointed. While the contrasts we draw between interpretive and positivist approaches can simplify exposition in the laying out of contrasts between their respective designs, we have been at pains to avoid caricaturing positivist thinking and design, in particular, and we alert readers to possible simplifications where this arises. We do not see positivism as a negative development in the world of ideas or as a derogatory term. In fact, neither of us would be in our present positions or writing this book, for reasons of sex, in both of our cases, and, in one case, of religion, were it not for the heritage of social positivism's emphasis on universality having entered into the social and political world of its day. Both French and American revolutions were fought for *egalité*/equality—for the 1789 *Déclaration des droîts de l'homme* and the statement in the US Declaration of Independence, "We hold these truths to be self-evident, that all men were created *equal*," the political manifestations of positivism's idea of universal scientific laws. Subsequent civil rights movements of all sorts have fought to realize that principle.

We use "positivism" as an umbrella term to refer to many types of research, from experimental research with its hypothesis-testing ideal, which seems to have set the gold standard for ideas about quantitative methods, to survey and other variables-based, statistical research, to studies conceived of as basically "descriptive," including some forms of historical and comparative case study analysis. (See Note 7.) Given the behavioralist orientation dominating many social science graduate programs by the time we got there, both of us were trained in survey research design and/or statistical analyses of various sorts, one of us peregrinating further than the other along that path. Yet we are pluralists in our methodological convictions. While we are, ourselves, more inclined toward an interpretive methodological position, we hold that certain kinds of research questions lend themselves much better to survey research or experimentation, and it would be foolish to undertake, say, semiotic squares or ethnomethodological analyses to address these (e.g., because of time or other resource constraints, or simply because one wants information on a very focused matter across a large number of respondents, rather than in-depth, meaning-focused stories concerning their work or lives).

Our interest here is in laying out the methodological grounding for interpretive methods in the context of research designs, and in doing so in a way premised on the view that different modes of science are characterized by different standards and criteria of evaluation, even if all scientists share, in one way or another, an interest in the procedural systematicity and attitude of doubt that legitimate knowledge claims. Given the over 40-year prominence of behavioralist and statistical approaches to the full range of social sciences, two generations of scholars (at least, in the US) have been trained or educated largely without exposure to that grounding—or, for that matter, to the ontological and epistemological grounding of positivist-informed methods. Those researchers who would have been educated to a different, more pluralist way of looking at the social science world are, on the whole, no longer educating students or reviewing manuscripts, leading to a more monocular view of "science." We would like to recover and build on the broader view that characterized scientific practices of earlier times.

Second, even as we write about the logic of interpretive inquiry, we take to heart cautions against "methodism"—a preoccupation with methods that subjugates the substantive issues under study to the dictates of technical requirements, as if these could somehow ensure the truth of knowledge claims.[13] Graduate students, in particular, may sometimes be paralyzed by the imposed or felt need to conform to such dictates, when it should be their substantive concerns, instead, that motivate their research endeavors. When methodological awareness degenerates into a "check list" assessment process that ignores substantive issues, that is one indicator that methodism has taken over. Such a move should be resisted vigorously, in our view, for interpretive as well as positivist research projects. "How we know" is an essential part of science; but without a deep concern for the "what," research would be a sterile exercise.

Finally, in treating positivist research approaches, we have engaged their representation in textbooks and other discussions, rather than delving into the detailed nuances of research practices such as those found in more sophisticated methodological analyses among positivist scholars (e.g., Brady and Collier 2010, articles in such journals as *Evaluation Research*, *Organizational Research Methods*, *Political Analysis*, *Sociological Methods & Research*) or in actual scientific practices. Our reasoning for doing so is that, on the whole, more students (and perhaps others) are likely to be introduced to research methods through methods textbooks than through the more nuanced methodological literature. And it is these ideas that have taken hold, broadly, often presenting a picture of "the scientific method" and other procedural issues in ways that do not always resemble what practicing researchers do. For example, "replication" is an often cited practice that is said to demarcate "true" science from "pseudo" science. Yet, as Zimmer (2011) reports in discussing publications in *Science* and *The Journal of Personality and Social Psychology*, it does not appear to be much practiced or valued, nor even effectual.

We recognize that the practices involved in the implementation of research designs are complex and that in its execution, research does not always implement initial plans exactly (an issue for IRBs; see Chapter 7). Moreover, *in practice*, there may be more overlap between interpretive and positivist research than our heuristic dichotomy (see Table 6.1) and our discussions here portray.[14] Our purpose is to help those from diverse research communities *recognize* interpretive research as a distinctive logic of inquiry and to *develop* what this means at the design stage. All too often, interpretive research projects are acknowledged upon completion to be significant contributions to knowledge and/or practice, but the positivist language of design tends to foreclose that appreciation at the proposal stage, with a deleterious effect on funding.

And just as the positivist label elides huge differences in scientific practices, so, too, does the interpretive label. Interpretive schools and methods have family resemblances, in Wittgenstein's sense—but they also have specific differences. This variety limits the extent to which we can spell out specific designs or design principles. For this reason, the book rests at a certain level of generality, emphasizing concepts and processes of interpretive research design—albeit with concrete illustrations from published research—to achieve utility across a wide range of interpretive practices.

"Science" is not, and has never been, a single practice. Even within the natural and physical sciences, scientific processes and procedures are done differently by botanists and chemists, astronomers and zoologists. Moreover, what it has meant to do science and to be scientific has been changing over time, ever since natural philosophy developed and eventually turned into "science."[15] Interpretive social science takes its place within this panoply of meanings and practices. Our mission in this volume is to provide interpretive researchers, as well as those who review or teach such research, with the rationale to understand and argue for the logic of inquiry underlying this kind of science in ways that are consistent with interpretive methodological presuppositions and the methods that enact them. The "new" engagement with or (re)turn to interpretive methodologies and methods does not eschew design, rigorous systematicity or explanatory (constitutive) causality. None of these need be sacrificed in doing science that stays true to interpretive presuppositions.

1

WHEREFORE RESEARCH DESIGNS?

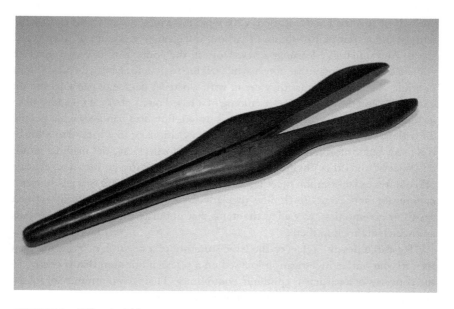

FIGURE 1.1   What is this?

Photo credit: Merlijn van Hulst.

What is this? How does it work? And how will you figure that out?

Whatever it is—we will get to that later—it is represented here through a photograph. That means that you are restricted to observing it with your eyes (assuming you are sighted, another issue to take up later, in Chapter 7) as you seek to make sense of it. It is analogous, in this sense, to a word, a phrase or a visual image you might encounter during field research, whether in historical documents you have accessed in an archive or in contemporary research-relevant documents made available to you in the organization or other setting in which you are talking to people (including formal interviewing) and/or observing. If you have only the document(s) or painting, say, to go on, as in historical research, you will have to figure out the meaning of the unknown term(s) or image on your own, using the judgment that you have been developing in an "intertextual" fashion as you have been studying other materials, perhaps from other sources, that come from the same time period and the same or similar context. (More on this in Chapter 5.)

But if you encounter an unfamiliar word or phrase in contemporary documentary research or in the course of an interview or more casual conversation, you can ask for clarification—what it means, when it is used, how it is different from some other term or concept. We do this all the time in learning new languages, on entering new workplaces or on moving to new locations. Whether it is an unfamiliar concept that you have encountered or an object, you will want to know how it is used and not used, with what meanings and referents or in what settings and activities, by whom, for whom it has other meanings or usages, and so on. And much like learning a new word in the context of its verbal usage, if you encounter an unfamiliar object while talking to people (who tell you about it) or while observing them (as they use it, with whatever degree of participation on your part), you develop an understanding of it based on its physical (in addition to its linguistic) usage—where it resides or is stored, how it is handled, what people do with it, what it feels like to use it, on what occasions or in what circumstances it is used, who is forbidden from using it, and so forth. Here, the material world of "objects" and other physical artifacts can include built spaces, such as executive office suites or labor union meeting halls or street corners where strikers or youth congregate, and events (including regularly recurring ones, analytically termed rituals or ceremonies), as well as the items that populate these spaces and events and which are used in them.

"Research design" refers to the basic structure of a research project, the plan for carrying out an investigation focused on a research question that is central to the concerns of a particular epistemic community. That is a community of scholars who share a way of seeing and defining research problems and questions and a way of generating knowledge about these, as articulated in its theoretical or other research literature (see further discussion at the end of Chapter 2). The research design is where the kinds of questions spoken to in the previous two paragraphs, concerning objects, acts, language, actors, settings, and so forth, are articulated and where the researcher indicates how she plans to engage these. The conduct of research entails making choices about all of these matters, including both research questions and sources of evidence that will bear on them, as well as about particular data-generating and -analyzing processes. These choices are worked through in designing the research, and the design document itself provides the rationales for those elements and processes chosen as well as, where appropriate, those not chosen.

Crafting research designs also provides an opportunity to think through the two central hallmarks of scientific practice (as distinct, say, from a religious one): its systematic character, conducted with an attitude of doubt. When researchers (typically, those doing positivist-informed work) talk about "rigorous" research, it is its systematicity they are pointing to—a systematicity of procedure, of argumentation, which is how that hallmark would be discussed in interpretivist work. When those same researchers talk about "testability" (the requirement that propositions be subjected to testing of various sorts), they are pointing to the same concern carried out by interpretive researchers in their own constant, reflexive questioning enacted in various ways to check on sense-making with respect to knowledge claims advanced, subjecting their research processes and analyses to doubt. The design of a research project, whether positivist or interpretive, demonstrates these two central characteristics of science, showing that the researcher has thought about them and how they will be engaged and enacted in the research process.

Research designs are commonly found in research proposals; the two terms are even, at times, used interchangeably. Novice researchers might first encounter a full-blown research design in crafting a proposal for thesis and/or dissertation research to be submitted to departmental committees for approval, although they might also encounter it, in whole or in part, in introductory coursework, especially in research methods courses. Research designs are also the backbone of research proposals submitted for funding by researchers at all levels of research seniority, in all disciplines and across all institutional arenas of research practice. Even when conducting a research project that does not require funding or other approval, crafting a research design can help the researcher prepare more systematically for the research, thinking through the sorts of issues engaged in this book. This kind of preparation is conducted by interpretive researchers as much as it is by positivist ones.

The thought experiment with which this chapter begins allows us to introduce what is perhaps the key difference between interpretive research and other ways of knowing, one that has central implications for designing research projects which enact an interpretive methodology. Note that in all of the circumstances discussed there, the meaning of the term or object—it could equally as well have been an event, interaction, situation, image, document, and so on—which the researcher seeks is its situated, contextual meaning: that specific to those who are its everyday creators and/or users. Other approaches to research typically begin by stipulating definitions of the concepts that researchers want to study ahead of time, then operationalizing those concepts in ways that are intended to render them "testable" when the researcher gets to the research setting (whether in the archives or in an interactive "field" that draws on interviews, surveys, field experiments, focus groups, and the like).[1] This requires turning the concepts into variables abstracted from the lived experience they represent. Some of these variables are understood to "depend on" other variables, and researchers conducting such research generate formal hypotheses about the relationships among these independent and dependent variables. They then conduct those "tests" to see how good—how accurate—the hypothesized relationships were as explanations or representations of the social phenomena of interest.

Interpretive research designs, by contrast, do not set out to test key concepts defined before the research has begun. If they are interested in studying a particular concept (e.g., work practices, violence) or role (school principal, mid-level manager), they will have developed a sense of how those concepts or roles are discussed in the established, research-relevant literature. This is what Geertz termed an "experience-distant" concept: "one that specialists of one sort or another . . . employ to forward their scientific, philosophical, or practical aims" (Geertz 1983: 57). It is parallel to what Pike (1990) called an *etic* perspective on the concepts, categories, and rules of behavior that characterize the social group being studied, which is rooted in formulations meaningful to the scientific community studying that group. But interpretive researchers working with such concepts and perspectives are not bringing their own scientific definitions with them to field settings in order to *test the accuracy* of those understandings.[2] Researchers want, instead, to understand how those concepts, roles, and so forth are used in the field. They want to let their understandings and, indeed, the very existence of concepts that are key to a particular setting or situation "emerge from the field"—as they often say, although that language is not unproblematic, as we discuss further in Chapter 2. What the phrase is meant to capture is the distinction between definitions that are shaped by interactions between the researcher and the theoretical literature, determined a priori before the field or archival research begins, and definitions of concepts that are shaped by their situational use and by the lived experience of those "naturally" working, playing, etc., in the study setting. These include those long gone whose lived experiences have been captured in the written word and stored in archives of various sorts or in oral histories, stories, narratives, and the like.

This difference is of central significance for the design of a research project. We will pick up this discussion and add other points of distinction in later chapters; but first, we engage the importance of research designs and then look at a typical outline of one.

Research Design: Why Is It Necessary?

In the process of designing their research projects, researchers make choices. These can be of a theoretical, ontological, and/or epistemological character; researchers also choose specific methods of data generation and analysis to use in their studies. Researchers want their "findings"—the insights into the focus of their investigations, which emerge through systematic analyses of research-related evidence that has also been generated systematically—to be persuasive. They want the members of their epistemic, scientific communities, along with other readers, to accept their results. For research to be persuasive, the choices of method need to be consistent, logically, with the methodology—the presuppositions about the "reality status" (ontology) of what is being studied and its "know-ability" (epistemology). A research design presents these choices, along with the argumentation that explains and justifies their selection (at times, discussing alternatives not chosen), in light of the intended purposes of the research project.

A research design can usefully be seen as a signaling device (an observation brought out in analyses of scientific work from a practice perspective, which includes seeing its persuasive, political character): it communicates certain things to the reader of the research proposal, often without naming them explicitly. To begin with, a well-crafted research design signals to a reader, such as a reviewer of a grant or dissertation proposal, that the researcher has the *ability to plan* a research project, especially one of significant scope and ambition. It also signals that the researcher has mounted a *serious engagement with the established literature* particular to that research topic. The design itself indicates the extent to which it is feasible for this plan to be implemented, in general and with respect to the length of time designated in it. More indirectly, the text of the research design indicates that *this* researcher is qualified to carry out *this* research (in addition to whatever explicit arguments the researcher also makes, e.g., via an attached CV, references, and/or some other text).

But importantly, a research design implicitly signals which epistemic community the researcher is a member of or is positioning her- or himself to join. This is done through many subtle ways. One of these is in the framing of the research question, including through the selection of literature. The research literature on most topics these days is quite large, such that a "literature review" does not, and cannot, encompass it all. In selecting those works that are key to a particular way of thinking about the topic, researchers position themselves in a particular epistemic community with respect to the subject of the research (discussed further in Chapter 2). Moreover, in the choice of methods and citations to methods sources, researchers also signal membership—this time, in a methodological epistemic community. Reading a reference list often provides a quick indication of the ways in which a researcher is positioning her- or himself with respect to both theoretical and methodological concerns.

An Outline of a Research Proposal, Including the Research Design

An ideal-typical outline of a proposal to conduct an interpretive research project might look like that presented in Table 1.1.

TABLE 1.1 An ideal-typical outline of a proposal for funding, IRB or doctoral committee approval of a research project

---

Project Title
Abstract

1. **Research question**
2. **Methods**

    a.   For generating data (for privacy issues, see 4a)
    b.   For analyzing data

3. **Anticipated learning**

    The purpose of the research in light of broader theorizing

4. **Anticipated dissemination of research manuscript**

    a.   Confidentiality of organizational, participants' or other identities, and other privacy issues

5. **Timetable**
6. **Budget** [if applicable]

References
Appendices [e.g., applicant qualifications]

Sources: In addition to our general familiarity with such outlines from years of teaching, advising, writing proposals, etc., we have drawn on several specific sources in compiling this outline, among them the Haverland-Yanow Netherlands Institute for Governance "General Methodology" research design course syllabus and the Graduate Research Fellowship Application, Eccles Graduate Fellowship Application, and Institutional Review Board project template, all at the University of Utah.

Individual departments, faculties, universities, or funders are likely to have their own specific requirements for proposals, leading to differences in terminology and/or in the order in which they expect these items to appear. Some will want other, fewer, or additional sections. The subsection under item 4 is intended to indicate that placement of some information is variable: privacy concerns could equally as well be discussed in the methods section, as noted.

Within this general proposal outline, it is item 2—the planned methods for generating and analyzing data—that constitutes the research design in its purest form. However, as a methods plan would make little sense without the research question (item 1) that motivates it, the research question is also considered part of the design. And it is the connection between research question and methods that reviewers evaluate. They are likely to ask: Do the research methods (item 2) connect logically to the focus of the research (the research question, item 1)? They might frame their evaluation in terms of whether the research methods (item 2) "address" the research question (item 1) in ways that are likely to lead, logically, to the anticipated learning from the research that would potentially make a contribution or be of value or significance to the research community or some other audience (item 3). And they are also likely to be asking: Is the research question (item 1) worth investigating? That is, what is its significance, addressed to some extent in item 1 in terms of debates in the relevant theoretical literature, as well as, in one form or another, in item 3 in terms of the likely value of its projected learning for the academic or other community? As research is carried out with some eye toward the future—toward its contribution to a scientific undertaking or its potential utility in addressing some policy or practice—and as the dissemination of that learning is key to enacting that contribution, item 4 (dissemination) is also at times considered part of a research design.

You might be thinking that this outline does not look all that different from any other you've seen before. In part, that is because we have written it as an ideal type, reflecting the broadest understanding of the items that are often called for, whether by funding agencies, IRBs, doctoral committees, or some other evaluating body, regardless of methodology. When we look at the contents of several of these sections when fleshed out from an interpretive methodological perspective, however, as we do in the next chapters—especially the treatment of a research question and the issues that arise in generating data—the differences between interpretive and positivist content become clear. For instance (and to anticipate the later discussion), the distinction drawn in item 2 between *methods for generating data* (2a) and *methods for analyzing those data* (2b) points to a difference between interpretive and some qualitative research designs, on the one hand, in which the generation and analysis of data are often intertwined, and quantitative and some other forms of qualitative research designs, on the other hand, in which data generation and analysis are completely separate. The distinction is useful in showing how interpretive–qualitative and positivist–qualitative research part company: as noted in the book's introduction, both use the same methods for generating data—some combination of observing, talking, and close reading—but their orientations toward those processes are quite different and they often use very different methods in analyzing those data. In addition, this section (usually called "Methods") is where the methodological orientation of the research might be discussed. We note that this is not common for positivist research, although interpretive researchers might be expected to make their presuppositions explicit.

Some of the language commonly used in talking about the parts of a research proposal—in particular, "projected results," "impact," "outcomes," "findings"—derives from experimental research and its design, a point we take up more fully in Chapter 4. For this reason, we have not used those terms in Table 1.1, relying instead on language that is a better fit with interpretive research.

Chapters 3–6 explore the contents of item 2 (research methods) at length, as seen from an interpretive perspective. Before then, Chapter 2 takes up in greater detail what it means to do research from the perspective of interpretive logics of inquiry or ways of knowing.

There is one item missing from the outline in Table 1.1 that we think merits attention, thought, and discussion but that, typically, has not been part of a research proposal: research ethics. Meskell and Pels (2005: 1) argue that the "dominant tendency [is] to disembed, exteriorize, and alienate ethics from everyday scientific practice," an observation consistent with the general silence on ethics in this ideal-typical research proposal outline (see also Lincoln and Denzin 2003: 4–5). Silence on this topic has been mitigated to some extent by requiring researchers working with "human subjects" to indicate whether they have already obtained or will obtain Institutional Review Board approval (IRB) for their designs. But ethics boards' approval is not the same as engaging with ethical issues. In fact, the addition to research proposals of inquiries about IRB approval seems largely to have sidelined discussions of research ethics, as IRB procedures bureaucratize the topic. We see this in perusing the two dozen methods textbooks on our shelves: about half of them have no discussions of ethics, and those that do primarily engage questions of informed consent.[3]

In interpretive social science, ethical concerns are not a separate subject, but instead emerge throughout the project, "reembedded in the practices, politics, and presentation of research results" (Lincoln and Denzin 2003: 5). The interpretive emphasis on the agency of those studied along with its understanding of field interactions as relational (both discussed in Chapter 4) means that consideration and contemplation of research ethics needs to be integrated into designs. Unfortunately, as we take up in Chapter 7, the contemporary ethics review environment (at least in the US) means that interpretive researchers' energies are often absorbed in trying to show why ethics issues are different for these forms of research and how IRB policies are, at times, ill-suited and may even be harmful to its stated goals. We look forward to a time when research proposal outlines include ethics discussions rather than marginalizing them.[4]

But wait! What *was* that object with which we began? It is commonly known, in English, in the UK, US, Canada, Australia, and New Zealand (and perhaps elsewhere), as a glove stretcher. This one, made of mahogany, was purchased at a flea market in Amsterdam in 2009; non-wooden ones can be found in ivory or bone. But now that you know its name—albeit in one language and several national settings—what do you know about it? Or, to put the point more bluntly, as physicist Richard Feynman learned from his father on a walk in the Catskill mountains:

> "See that bird?" he says. "It's a Spencer's warbler." (I knew he didn't know the real name.) "Well, in Italian, it's a *Chutto Lapittida*. In Portuguese, it's a *Bom de Peida*. In Chinese, it's a *Chung-long-tah*, and in Japanese, it's a *Katano Tekeda*. You can know the name of that bird in all the languages of the world, but when you're finished, you'll know absolutely nothing about the bird. You'll only know about humans in different places, and what they

call the bird. So let's look at the bird and see what it's doing—that's what counts."

(Feynman 1988: 13–14)

And Feynman adds, parenthetically: "I learned very early the difference between knowing the name of something and knowing something" (1988: 14).

In interpretive research, we seek to understand what a thing "is" by learning what it does, how particular people use it, in particular contexts. That is, interpretive research focuses on context-specific meanings, rather than seeking generalized meaning abstracted from particular contexts. Glove stretchers were used in Victorian times—late nineteenth–early twentieth centuries—to stretch the fingers of cotton, lace, or kid gloves when new or after they had been washed and dried, to make it easier to get the glove on, especially given the custom of wearing gloves a size smaller than the hand, because of contemporaneous notions of fashion and beauty. But more than that: understanding how a word or an object, a ritual, ceremony or other act is used, in context, potentially reveals (or raises questions about) assumed, unspoken or taken-for-granted ideas about a range of values, beliefs, and/or feelings. In this example, knowing more about this wooden object and its intended uses at the time of its creation raises questions about contemporaneous ideas concerning such values as modesty, dignity, and respectability, or about beliefs concerning what constitutes "proper" dress and what it means to cover the hands and to cover them *properly*, or about feelings concerning going out in public with bare hands, rather than covered ones, in terms of status, social class, femininity, and so on. That is, understanding what an object is can tell us a lot about the world of which it is a part.[5] And the point holds for words, phrases, images, and other human artifacts, as well as for acts.

Could that object depicted at the beginning of the chapter "be" something else? Of course—but by that statement, an interpretive researcher does not mean to suggest that the object (or word, or act, etc.) has an essential, timeless, universal meaning. Its identity—its meaning-in-use, as it were—is seen as context-specific (to both time and place). To know the answer to that question, we would need to observe its use in situ, by users "native" to that setting, to talk to them about that usage and perhaps to use it ourselves, or to find a primary text that details such adaptive reuse (or a secondary one that rests on primary sources). That purchased glove stretcher in the photo, for instance, serves one of the authors very well as a book mark, at some times, and at others as a large paper clip. These are the sorts of issues that interpretive research designs engage.

2

WAYS OF KNOWING

Research Questions and Logics of Inquiry

> Interesting work begins not just with a problem . . . but with a puzzle. . . . Great leaps forward . . . often take place when someone sees puzzles, where others have only seen facts.
>
> —*Robert O. Keohane (2009: 360)*

Research designs answer the question: How are you going to conduct the research that will address your research question? Before one can even begin to design a research project, then, one needs not only a topic of research but a research question—and, although sometimes used interchangeably, the two are not the same![1] Articulating that research question itself can reveal the approach or logic of inquiry it contains and rests on; and that logic of inquiry—that way of knowing—itself presupposes the answer to the question: Where does this research question come from? Let's get at this matter through a research story.

Armed with theories and concepts from his doctoral studies at the University of California at Berkeley, Cyrus Ernesto Zirakzadeh set out to survey 50–100 political activists, first in Pamplona, then in Bilbao, for his dissertation on the sociological origins of nationalist movements, looking at the case of Basque separatists. In his words:

> By the end of my stay in Pamplona, I realized that ETA [Euskadi Ta Askatasuna, a Basque nationalist liberation organization] was much more multidimensional and programmatically eclectic than U.S. academic literature had suggested. I also realized that [the concept of] "modernization" did not capture the economic issues that concerned local residents. . . . The

voices and views of Basque politics were more numerous and diverse than I had expected.

By the time I reached the Bilbao metropolitan area, . . . I had decided to jettison my survey. I had discovered that whenever I used it . . ., my battery of questions (for example: How intensely do you feel about independence? How would you classify yourself in terms of class status?) bored the respondents. The survey had little to do with how nationalists (and local residents in general) saw themselves, understood their political disagreements, and defined their political options. I concluded that if I were to write a dissertation that would be meaningful for everyday people (a legacy of my New Left background that I could not shake), I had to find a way to represent the world that captured participants' understandings, feelings, and choices.

(Zirakzadeh 2009: 104)

How did Zirakzadeh get from his research design to his field research? Or more precisely, how might he have gotten to his research question, even before he came up with the formal design, and what happened to that design as he became ever more immersed in field realities?

   We do not know how he himself would answer these questions—he doesn't say, nor have we interviewed him; but these passages enable us to illustrate how an interpretive researcher might proceed. Rather than start out with a philosophical discussion of ontological and epistemological priors, we will use these illustrations to derive the key methodological elements that characterize interpretive research, outlining them in brief at the end of the chapter. We begin with a series of answers to the question: Where do research questions come from?

Where Do Research Questions Come From? The Role of Prior Knowledge

The germ of an idea for research may come from the formal scholarly literature, but it need not do so. Sometimes it comes from scholars' everyday, human experiences—from their own histories and lives: particular gender, race-ethnic, or other perspectives, prior professions or occupations, volunteer positions, and activities that span the possibilities from religion to sports. It is not uncommon, for instance, for interpretive researchers to conduct research that returns them to places familiar from prior activities, in which they draw on previously acquired cultural knowledge (such as places where they previously worked, lived, or studied for other purposes or where they have family or ancestral roots). Moreover, interpretive research can at times begin without the researcher quite knowing it—for instance, while talking with people with whom the researcher regularly interacts or while visiting a particular site, in either case without the intention of doing research on that topic or in that setting.

Examples of such beginnings might include Goffman's (1963) research on public behavior (see Homan 1991: 117–118), Becker's (1963) on jazz musicians' drug use, Liebow's (1993) on homeless women, Venkatesh (2008) on his Chicago slum research, or Wacquant's (2004) research on boxing, which he describes as "opportunistic" (p. 9). Sociologist Beate Littig reports that her study of the "sequential use" aspects of a neighborhood sauna emerged from her 20-year membership in a group that met weekly "to sweat," and her analysis of the meaning of high heels worn by women in tango dance sessions (milongas) developed after she had been dancing for ten years (personal communication, 11 January 2011). In both cases, she could not have developed a research question without intimate, "local" knowledge of the settings and their modes of action and interaction, something she acquired over extended periods of weekly activity.[2] Prior setting-related knowledge can include places where the spoken language(s) is (are) something the researcher learned previously, including in his family or the surrounding community. Such prior knowledge of cultures and languages is also one of the advantages of what in anthropology and other disciplines is known as "native ethnography" (Narayan 1993) or "at-home ethnography" (Alvesson 2009, Leap 1996).

This and other kinds of a priori knowledge—drawing on a classic Kantian and then phenomenological (neo-Kantian) point about new understanding emerging from prior knowledge, including experiential knowledge—is seen as an integral part of interpretive methodologies. Although positivist researchers may also be motivated to pursue particular questions or research topics as a function of personal experience (e.g., a US Congressional scholar may have been motivated to pursue that topic as the result of an undergraduate internship there or a job as a legislative aide), textbook discussions rarely acknowledge such experience and may even present it as something to be contained and avoided (as it would be in positivist research approaches; see Chapter 6). From an interpretive perspective, in contrast, not only is the role of a priori knowledge in subsequent research explicitly acknowledged. It is seen not only in shaping the development of research interest, but also as potentially playing a key role in the conduct of that research. Indeed, sometimes such experiential or other background knowledge can later be key to such conduct—e.g., to obtaining access to a community or to interviewing in a given language. But how does such prior knowledge translate into a research question?

Where Do Research Questions Come From? Abductive Ways of Knowing

Examining the passage from Zirakzadeh's research experience and the essay from which it is excerpted, we can find at least two different logics of inquiry at work. Methods textbooks typically note that quantitative research follows a deductive logic of inquiry—reasoning that begins with theories, which lead to hypoth-eses, from which testable concepts are generated and then tested against a set of observations (i.e., deducing the particular from the universal). The initial research design implied in Zirakzadeh's narrative—to administer a survey questionnaire and then, presumably, to analyze the resulting answers in statistical terms, in order to test one or more hypotheses—is an example. His concepts and his survey ques-tions derived from the theories in the academic literature he had been reading. They were the source of his research question; and his design—which would have been submitted to his Ph.D. supervisor (but not, at that time, to an IRB, which came into being subsequently)—would have plotted out both the procedures for administering his survey questionnaire to "collect" his data and the techniques he planned to use in analyzing them.

By contrast, as methods textbooks would point out, qualitative research fol-lows an inductive logic of inquiry—reasoning that begins with observations of particular instances from which general laws are developed (i.e., inducing the universal from the particular). One might understand Zirakzadeh's statement that he wanted to "represent the world that captured participants' understandings, feelings, and choices" in this light. These two logics and the contrast between them have been widely discussed until very recently, and still are presented in methods textbooks, as if they exhausted the possible logics of inquiry in research.[3] But there is a third logic of inquiry at play in social scientific ways of knowing, one that methodologists are increasingly suggesting informs interpretive research: abduction. Given what Zirakzadeh says about his unfolding thinking as he con-fronted the field-based social realities that did not fit the hypotheses of his deduc-tive research design, we can find this logic, too, as we reflect on his *ex post facto* account of his research process.

Articulated first, and at length, by US pragmatist Charles Peirce,[4] abductive reasoning begins with a puzzle, a surprise, or a tension, and then seeks to expli-cate it by identifying the conditions that would make that puzzle less perplexing and more of a "normal" or "natural" event. One asks oneself, in other words, what circumstances would render an event, a word, a relationship, or whatever else one is seeking to explain more "commonsensical"—less surprising, less puz-zling (see, e.g., Agar 2010, Locke *et al.* 2008, Van Maanen *et al.* 2007).[5] In this puzzling-out process, the researcher tacks continually, constantly, back and forth in an iterative–recursive fashion between what is puzzling and possible expla-nations for it, whether in other field situations (e.g., other observations, other documents or visual representations, other participations, other interviews) or in research-relevant literature. The back and forth takes place less as a series of discrete steps than it does in the same moment: in some sense, the researcher is simultaneously puzzling over empirical materials and theoretical literatures.

For those accustomed to thinking in terms of deduction and induction, "abduc-tion" may be a difficult concept to grasp initially: its prefix does not endear it as a word. Considering its uses in other contexts and its meanings there might help:

from Latin roots meaning to lead away, an abduction is the "leading away" of one individual by another (typically through the use of force, without the former's intention or volition); one person abducts another.[6] In abductive reasoning, the researcher's thinking is led, or, more actively, directed, in an inferential process, from the surprise toward its possible explanation(s).[7] The researcher may feel caught up in the puzzle, and if there is an ensuing "struggle," it is the researcher grappling with the process of sense-making: of coming up with an interpretation that makes sense of the surprise, the tension, the anomaly. Their shared inferential process is what may make abduction and induction appear to be similar, if not identical; but abduction's point of departure—a puzzle or surprise—marks its distinctiveness, as does its search for possible explanations that would render the surprise less surprising. Unlike inductive (and deductive) reasoning, it is not immediately after general principles or propositions induced from specific events (or general laws deduced from testing hypotheses against data): the explanation(s) it generates is (are) as situated as the puzzle with which it begins. A second contrast lies in their respective senses of movement: both deduction and induction are described as following a step-wise, linear, "first this, then that" logic; whereas abduction follows a much more circular-spiral pattern, in which the puzzling requires an engagement with multiple pieces at once.[8] Whether one's favorite analogy is a jigsaw puzzle, Rubik's cube, or Sudoku, the non-linear, iterative–recursive play with different possible resolutions that these suggest are useful in thinking about abductive inquiry.

But where do puzzles or surprises come from? Although qualitative and interpretive researchers often say that their puzzles emerge from the field, a more precise articulation of this process would be to say that they commonly derive from a tension between the expectations researchers bring to the field (based on their prior knowledge, discussed in the previous section) and what they observe and/or experience there. As Friedrichs and Kratochwil (2009: 714) put it, rather more formally, an abductive logic of inquiry is typically brought into play "when we become interested in a class of phenomena for which we lack applicable theories." The search for explanation presumes that the occurrence of this surprise is not random—that whatever it is entails patterned action and is therefore subject to explanation. So, when Lichterman (2002: 123), quoting Michael Burawoy, talks about researchers making discoveries "when repeated observation reveals an 'anomaly'," he is pointing to the kind of surprise that sets the researcher off in search of an explanation.

What makes a surprise or a puzzle "anomalous" is a misfit between experience and expectations, the latter often informed by theory relevant to the research question. A research design that seeks to test pre-developed concepts rooted in the theoretical literature may falter on the shoals of lived experience. The experience surprises, in light of the theory the researcher has brought to the field, which may be an inadequate explainer of that experience, misapprehending it, if not missing it altogether (Lichterman 2002: 124). (We note here briefly, and then return to the idea below and in Chapter 4, that positivist research designs, drawing on an experimental prototype, would require the researcher to hold fast to the initial design; but from an interpretive perspective, changing a design in light of field realities would be par for the course.) A research design might also, however, be inspired by expectations deriving from experience itself, with the puzzle emerging from the contrast between two events or conversations or other experiences (one version of the "intertextuality" we take up in Chapter 5). The researcher might then turn to theoretical literature in search of an explanation. In either case, the effort to resolve the puzzle and make the theory-event or event-event contrast less anomalous is what "abducts" the researcher's reasoning, capturing her thinking and leading or directing her explanatory efforts to a new bit of theorizing (often revising or extending an existing theory in some fashion). Where one begins one's theorizing depends on what sorts of concepts and/or categories one is interested in—another aspect of prior knowledge, and the place where theoretical literature clearly plays a role, as discussed in the next section.

We might speculate (on the basis of further analysis of his chapter and the discussion at the conference panel at which it was originally presented) that the first of these scenarios is precisely what happened to Zirakzadeh: his theoretical preparations led him to certain expectations of what he would find in the field; but specific events and experiences once he got there led him to be surprised—and perhaps also to some bewilderment at that surprise—and then, further, to experience a certain tension between expectations and lived experiences. In an effort to resolve this puzzle, he began to theorize, drawing on his prior theoretical knowledge and on other sources, in ways that rendered these events explainable.

This is one of the reasons that "stranger-ness" is so important in generating interpretive knowledge, a point that is clearest in ethnographic or other participant observer research but also operational, in its own way, in interview and archival or documentary research (Agar 1996/1980, P. Jackson 2006, Riles 2006). Being a stranger to one's physical setting or topic (in the case of archival research)—and trying to hold on to that quality for as long as one can—is desirable in order to see as explicitly as possible what for situated knowers is taken-for-granted, common sense, and tacitly known. Strangers are constantly violating norms, often meeting strong reactions from those who know the unwritten rules. The surprises that emerge out of such encounters are often the sources of puzzles that spark an abductive reasoning process. Yet at the same time, approximating ever more closely the "familiarity" with which situated knowers navigate their physical and cognitive settings is important for generating understanding of what is puzzling only to a stranger. Striking and maintaining a balance between being a stranger and being a familiar, as difficult as it is to achieve, lies at the heart of generating research-relevant knowledge.

In crafting research designs (and advising those undertaking them), as Agar (2010) notes, the key question to ask and answer should be not "What is your research plan?" but "Where are you going to start looking for answers to your

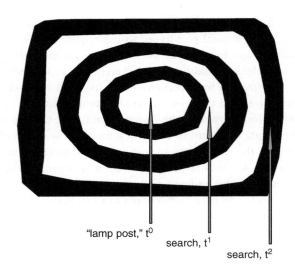

"lamp post," t^0

search, t^1

search, t^2

FIGURE 2.1 Beginning "where the light is" and expanding the research in ever-widening circles.

puzzle?" and "Now where are you going to look?" This brings to mind an old joke about a passerby who sees a drunk looking for his lost keys under a street lamp. Wanting to be helpful, the passerby asks the man where he dropped his keys. When he points to a place at some distance from where they are standing, the passerby asks him, with some surprise and consternation, why, then, he is looking over here. "Here is where the light is," the drunk explains, pointing to the overhanging lamp. Although the joke is told at his expense, there is some experiential, and even pedagogical, truth to it. As good teachers know, learning departs from what one already knows, from where the light is, so to speak (see, e.g., Freire 1970). Interpretive researchers look both "here" and "there," in an ever-widening set of concentric circles (see Figure 2.1): in seeking to puzzle out our perplexed expectations, we might well start looking "here" where the light—familiar literature or setting—is; and we move our way, gradually, over "there," in an effort to bring light to an ever-expanding realm.

This depiction enacts an idea inscribed in the hermeneutic circle, a way of articulating the sense-making that goes on in interpretive processes. A concept developed in the nineteenth century work of Wilhelm Dilthey (1976) and further extended by his student Hans Georg Gadamer (1976), among others, a hermeneutic, sense-making circle expresses the idea that there is no fixed starting point for inquiry: the process of sense-making begins wherever the individual "is" in her understanding at that moment, with whatever grasp of things she has at that time. It also suggests that there are no "conclusions" in the sense-making research cycle: there are only momentary stopping points, to collect one's thoughts, perhaps to publish or otherwise disseminate what one understands at that point in time, before one continues on the interpretive path. As the interpretive dance "moves forward in time in a continual process toward deeper and richer understanding" (Bentz and Shapiro 1998: 170), the resulting research style is better conceived of as a spiral than as a circle.[9] It was Gadamer who observed that as a description of sense-making, the hermeneutic circle characterizes learning processes in general. By this logic, a researcher begins a project, whether in the field or in a text, with some degree of prior knowledge—that is where the metaphoric light is shining; and his sense-making develops both as he confronts particular elements and as he gains a sense of the wider context. The circle-spiral describes the intimate relationship between part and whole: how the meaning of a phrase or act depends on its relationship to the whole, but, as well, that the meaning of the whole cannot be grasped independent of its constituent parts.

Another analogy, also illustrated by Figure 2.1, captures a different facet of abductive ways of knowing. Skipping a stone over a pond's surface creates ripples in the water; the stone sinks below the surface, but we continue to track those ripples, the impression the stone leaves on the water (at least for a while longer). Interpretive research tracks the residual "ripples" encountered when events—stone-surprises—impact people, places, acts: those things we wish to understand. The stone-surprise may no longer be visible, but we can surmise that a stone had been there when we see the ripples, and we can "look" to clarify aspects of the impact it had as it passed.[10] The "looking" is the talking, observing (and perhaps doing), and reading that comprise interpretive research as we search to clarify and explain the puzzle of the surprising ripples. To mix a metaphor, in the mathematical sense in which a bouncing ball that keeps halving the height of its bounce never ceases motion, human actions and events may continue to ripple even after the stone and its impact can no longer be seen. The intersubjective sense that various people make of a stone-surprise—their agreements (tacit and otherwise), certainly, but especially their contested interpretations—reverberate through time, manifested in diverse ways, from memorials and museums to debates over national identity and origins.

To take an extended example from the field research of one of us (Yanow 1996): Why would a national government community center corporation in poor city neighborhoods and rurally-located towns use cutting-edge architectural designs and comparatively opulent construction materials for its buildings? Why would an organizational founder compare the as yet undesigned and unplanned community center entity to a "functional supermarket"? Why, ten years after beginning operations, would the CEO of the organization still be asking, in the public forum of the annual meeting, what the organization's goals are? And why did the existing implementation literature not provide a satisfactory explanation of the public policy dynamics within which these and other organizational puzzles were playing out? Each of these surprised, and at times confounded, the researcher's expectations. An example each from the realms of physical materiality, language, acts, and theory: each, the first two in particular, left ripples in its wake that reverberated long after the initial stone was thrown, so to speak. Each could be studied only by starting when its surprising aspect was recognized: when it became clear, for instance, that there was nothing "natural" in seeing a community center as a supermarket (functional or otherwise). And research and analysis could proceed only by starting where the "light" was: reading correspondence, annual reports, and other documentary materials in organizational archives and newspaper morgues; visiting multiple centers across the country to see and study their designs; talking, in formal interviews and informal conversations, with retired and still active founders, national and local government officials, agency and department heads, center directors, community organizers and other center staff, neighborhood residents, and so on.

Here is the iterative–recursiveness so characteristic of abductive reasoning. It is iterative in that the same logic of inquiry is repeated over and over again. It is recursive in that we perform abduction within abduction within abduction, as one "discovery" leads to another—much as a hermeneutic circle-spiral might suggest. The different kinds of engagements in the research setting took place "at the same time"—some of them within a single day, others within a single week or, at times, month. It is only in retrospect that the learning process can be described in what sounds like a very patterned way. At the time, all of the strands of puzzlement felt intertwined, much more like a tangled ball of yarn than like a neat circle-spiral. A sequence of surprises, especially on related topics, can elicit the feeling, as Kathy Ferguson (2011) put it with respect to research in archives, of "Oh, look, there's another one!" Although exhilarating, it can also at times be overwhelming. Still, what was learned from one source contributed to understanding other sources; one bread crumb led to another, as the rings of "light" fanned out; until gradually, what had seemed anomalous was no longer so: the puzzles could be explained, rendered more "normal," in various ways. This iterative–recursive strategy that characterizes abduction builds on both human learning and the joy of curiosity. As Agar (2010: 289) says, "Surprises never stop; just the time and money do."

Abductive reasoning on its own does not require that one search for meaning, or that that meaning be context-specific, as Agar (2010: 290) notes. But interpretive research does! Since in research settings there are likely to be impediments that make the original, clear pattern of ripples difficult to discern in all but unusual circumstances, that explanatory search in interpretive research requires not just external, objective "looking" but "interpretive looking" from a position among the ripples, so to speak. It requires both the iterative–recursive processes characteristic of an abductive logic of reasoning *and* a focus on contextual meaning: *this* lamp post, not all lamp posts, not even *that* one over there—although after the researcher knows more about both lamp posts, she might find that the same meanings that characterize events "here" hold for those "over there," or some other researcher might extend the first study to a second site, and so on. This focus on meaning and insistence on its contextuality or situatedness, as well as on the situatedness of those claiming knowledge of it, whether researchers or researched, are central characteristics of interpretive research, ones that distinguish it from positivist-inflected research. The methodological sources of this distinctiveness rest in different treatments of the "reality status" of what is being studied and its "know-ability"—that is, on ontological and epistemological presuppositions, to which we return at the end of this chapter.

The notion of abductive reasoning makes available a number of ideas that enable us to speak more clearly about several features of interpretive research in ways that the language of induction does not permit. We list them here, pointing to the chapter or section in which they are taken up at greater length. For one, the researcher needs to attend to and register the presence of a surprise or a puzzle: as things, acts, words, concepts, etc., that surprise do not arrive pre-labeled as such, attention must be paid. And, as Agar (1986) makes clear, in the process of becoming more familiar with the research topic, including its settings, actors, and so forth, without careful fieldnote practices (discussed in Chapter 5) or other sense-making methods the researcher may forget what was initially surprising. Second, marking something as surprising requires attending to the expectations and other prior knowledge one brings to the field. We see this in Zirakzadeh's reflections on his research process: he makes explicit in his narrative the ways in which the theoretical literature led him to expect certain things, but field realities did not follow suit, leading to a tension between expectations and experience that he sought to resolve by theorizing in different ways. Moreover, interpretive researchers try to retain an openness to the possibility of surprises, as well as to resist the "rush to diagnosis" that prematurely closes down analytic possibilities (discussed further in Chapter 6).

A third feature highlighted by attending to abductive reasoning is that new concepts, relationships, explanations or accounts are created in the process of theorizing these surprises or puzzles. This point draws attention to the iterative–recursive relationship between theory and data in interpretive research and to the researcher's dual role as both participant-familiar (even in a metaphoric sense, when working with documents) and theorist-stranger: the abducting surprise comes from encounters in the field and/or the archive, informed by but not necessarily beholden to prior encounters in the literature. The explanations of that surprise may come through juxtaposition with other field or theoretical encounters. We extend this line of thinking in the next section.

Fourth, the requisite attending to expectations and giving accounts provides a methodological rationale for reflexivity, including on one's own positionality, another hallmark of interpretive methodologies and a subject treated at length in Chapter 6.

In departing from that which puzzles, abductive reasoning is a far cry from beginning with formal hypotheses. This explains something else about interpretive research design: why it is so challenging to write research proposals that stipulate ahead of time, before immersion in the field, what the researcher expects to find in that research, such as the concepts meaningful to actors (i.e., in non-interpretive language, the concepts to "measure" or "test"). Interpretive research puzzles draw on field engagements that the researcher cannot fully anticipate or know ahead of time—including those puzzles that tell the researcher that the existing literature is missing something, in that it does not provide an adequate explanation of what the researcher has encountered in field experiences or in archival documentation of events, thoughts, experiences, and so forth. For this reason, the conduct of interpretive research is, perforce, dynamic and flexible, and that flexibility is echoed in research designs that, for all their detailed forethought and planning, must remain open.

Indeed, the abductive logic of inquiry that characterizes interpretive research rests on the idea that researchers will learn more about their research question in the process of conducting their research. From the perspective of researcher learning, the circle-spiral's unfolding process contrasts with the "front-loading" of the hypothesis-testing model. A tremendous amount of preparation goes into the initial phases of that research design, and once hypotheses are formulated, variables designated, and tests designed, researchers are expected "simply" to apply these to the test site(s).[11] Whatever learning takes place in the context of applying the design to the site(s) is bracketed and put on hold until the analysis of the data during deskwork and their presentation during textwork phases of the project. Moreover, that learning cannot be treated as part of the knowledge claims of the study. It is treated, instead, as speculative, perhaps being mentioned in the concluding section of the research manuscript as a direction for further study, precisely because it has not been tested with independent evidence (see, e.g., the discussions in King *et al.* 1994: 20–23 and Lamont and White 2009: 85–86). We take up these points in discussion of design flexibility in Chapter 4.

By contrast, the circle-spiral model denotes a process that has just as much advanced preparation, but in which learning transpires across the "life-span" of the research project, including during the fieldwork phase. Aspects of the design are very carefully worked out beforehand, to the extent possible. But such ongoing learning is expected to, and typically does, revise the research design while its implementation is in progress. This also helps explain the requisite flexibility of interpretive research and its design, as the researcher needs to respond to field conditions, considered further in Chapter 4.

Where Do Research Questions Come From? The Role of Theory and the "Literature Review"

For interpretive research, then, both empirical material and theoretical literature are necessary, but neither is sufficient on its own:[12] there is a recursive and reiterative process not only across data sources in the field, but also between theoretical and field encounters. The initial part of a research proposal (item 1 in Table 1.1), which is also usually considered part of the research design, typically begins with a "review" of those portions of a field's literature that are significant in the formulation and discussion of the research question in the project being designed. In addition to framing the domain of the research project, this review demonstrates the researcher's scholarly competence in the field of study to those evaluating the proposal, at the same time that it signals the researcher's aspiring or actual membership in a particular theoretical and epistemic community.

The phrase itself, "literature *review*," may seem daunting: the literatures relevant these days to a research topic are often extensive. How can one possibly "review" all that has been written on that topic? Here is where the distinction between a research topic and a research question becomes useful: as noted earlier, a research "question," however formulated, is not the same as a research "topic." The former is far more focused, and the thinking underlying it more developed, than the latter, and that focus can be a way of narrowing the range of literature considered. The implementation of welfare policy, for instance, might be considered a general research topic; how clients and street-level bureaucrats differently experienced the 1996 US welfare policy reforms (Soss 2000) articulates a possible research question—and it points to the underlying existence of researcher expectations about what these experiences might have entailed, based on prior knowledge that derives from experience and/or theoretical literature, as well as to methods appropriate to studying that question, both of which would be elaborated in a research design.

Having narrowed a research topic to a question, a researcher might consider what the ongoing academic or research conversation is that he wishes to join: in which epistemic community is it being carried out, and who are the main parties to this conversation? It might help novice researchers to envision this piece of writing as the record of a dinner party conversation to which the leading thinkers who have something to say about the research question have been invited. The researcher greets his guests at the door, hands each a glass of wine or prosecco, leads them into the living room, and introduces each to the others. After the requisite weather chat, a conversation then develops among them—focusing on the researcher's question! What does each of them have to contribute to its discussion? Where do they agree, and where do they disagree? The record of this conversation, written up by the researcher, constitutes the major part of that "literature review." (Understanding which scholars constitute this epistemic community and in which conferences and journals its conversation is being carried out suggests likely outlets for later dissemination of the research.)

But, from the researcher's perspective, this conversation can also leave or create "holes" (missing pieces or problems) in its account of the issue—pointing toward the puzzle that the researcher wishes to resolve. Here is where the researcher's voice joins the ongoing conversation—which continues in seminar debates and on the printed page long after the guests have finished their coffee and parted company. How will the researcher's thinking and theorizing and the research that is being designed (as described in subsequent sections of the proposal) contribute to filling this hole, resolving these problems, expanding the epistemic community's understanding of the identified puzzle by providing missing pieces (which later makes a contribution to that wider understanding through the dissemination of the research, items 3 and 4 in Table 1.1), and so forth?[13]

Ah, but you ask: if the puzzle or anomaly emerges only from an encounter between expectations and field realities, how can it be articulated in the literature review, whose development is understood to precede the formal research design, which in turn precedes field or archival research? It is worth remembering that although books and articles may be read from page 1 to their end, they are not always written that way. The hermeneutic circle again appears: one has to start somewhere, with whatever (prior) knowledge is at hand. In the iterative–recursive abductive engagement between theory and lived experience, the puzzle that the research seeks to explain grows from lesser to greater specificity (and, hence, clarity) as sense-making proceeds along the circle-spiral. Here, too, is that other characteristic of interpretive research—that in research designs, not only are there not formalized hypotheses; the expectations that drive the research and which will be confronted with field realities can be only partially spelled out prior to the commencement of data generation (unlike what would be the case were the research subject to the strictures of positivist approaches, experimental design in particular), precisely because of the dynamism of the social world researchers expect to find. These constitute provisional "hunches" about what might make the initial puzzle less puzzling. They will be subjected to confirmation or refutation in an iterative fashion in the field, and revised as necessary.

Interpretive research designs may therefore appear, to those familiar with hypothesis-testing ones, less programmatic and more dynamic and open-ended by contrast. This greater openness and flexibility to respond to local circumstances reflects their underlying logic of inquiry, not the (in)adequacy of the researcher or of the proposed project. It is a response to researchers' expectations of finding the social world they study to be dynamic (and nuanced), rather than stable and fixed. But this doesn't mean that interpretive researchers are always on "shaky" or "loose" ground. Rather, it means that, like captains of a ship, they are more attuned to changing weather conditions and riding the resulting waves, instead of strictly following the initial course that they might have laid out on dry ground.[14]

In developing the literature review section of a research design—which sows the seeds for what is commonly the first main section of a research manuscript (see Chapter 7)—the researcher articulates the research question. Some disciplines and their journals, some universities or departments, some individual dissertation advisors understand this to mean literally a formally constructed question, and some places or advisors further expect it to be written with a nested series of sub-questions and even sub-sub-questions, in numbered sequence (1, 1.1, 1.1.1, 1.1.2, 1.2, etc.). In other cases, disciplines or advisors expect a more narrative identification of the focus of research and its entailments, although even here this is commonly spoken of as a research "question," even when it does not take that form. Joe Soss (personal communication, 1 March 2010) suggests that the formulation of formal questions and nested sub-questions "too often assumes a hypothesis-testing model. Committee members push students to state *the* question they will answer and then show how their design will guarantee an answer that, in principle, could go 'either way'," i.e., either confirm or refute the hypothesis.

We agree with Soss's suggestion that although for pedagogical purposes it can be useful to ask students to formulate formal questions, "we . . . should view these questions as starting points that will give [researchers] a foundation for developing better questions in the field." His explication of this strategy itself enacts the iterative–recursive thinking and field-based learning that characterizes an abductive logic of inquiry:

> The point is not to ask the question so that you can go out and find the answer. The point is to ask *a* question so that you can clarify your thinking now and raise the odds that you'll discover what's wrong with your thinking when you get into the field. . . . The initial question sets you on a path, and, while it may get disrupted in the field, it's likely to get disrupted in ways that reflect your original formulation.
>
> *(Joe Soss, personal communication, 1 March 2010, original emphasis)*

And he adds, in a thought consistent with the flexibility that characterizes interpretive research, "We need to promote the assumption that questions should change during research *and also* fight the idea that this means we should care less about the initial formulation of the question" (personal communication, 1 March 2010, original emphasis). This formulation of the matter provides the basis for engaging the character of "hypotheses" in interpretive research, discussed further in Chapter 3.

So far, so good. But what constitutes an "adequate" literature review can vary according to the epistemological presuppositions endorsed by a scholarly community. Interpretive and positivist research can be equally theoretical, but the purpose, value, and character of theory are conceived of quite differently. Interpretive and positivist approaches differ in how the literature is handled in the research writing and what work it is expected, and made, to do in the logic of inquiry enmeshed in the research design. In positivist research the literature review and the generation of hypotheses are intimately connected—the literature is assessed in order to generate precise hypotheses that are or can be related to specific theoretical propositions. In interpretive research, the research literature is typically used to develop the researcher's prior knowledge about the issues that inform a research question, as well as about the setting in which the research will be carried out. Theorizing remains connected to lived experience, understood in all of its messy contextuality, rather than following more "formal" expostulations in language and logic, often in mathematical forms.[15]

And then there is the "peculiar" status of concepts in interpretive research, at least from the perspective of other, more objectivist approaches.

Do Concepts "Emerge from the Field"?
More on Theory and Theorizing

In arguing that they want to allow the relevant concepts to "emerge from the field," interpretive methodologists have obscured the status of theory and theorizing in their work for those in other epistemic communities, in ways that are not helpful for mutual understanding. As noted in Chapter 1, the phrase is intended to signal an orientation toward concepts as they are encountered and used in the lived experience of those who are "native" to the context that the researcher is studying (by contrast with concepts defined a priori by the researcher, privileging theoretical literature over lived experience). Understood among members of interpretive epistemic communities as a kind of shorthand for a broader set of methodological concerns, this articulation is not the most precise description of research processes to use in discussing interpretive knowledge generation with members of other epistemic communities, implying as it does that researchers enter the research arena as blank slates, with no prior knowledge, whether theoretical–conceptual or experiential.

Phenomenologically, this is not possible—one always brings one's prior knowledge, based on experience and on personal, educational, and other background, to a setting (whether research or other). Researchers do not enter the field or the archives as *tabulae rasae*, but they do seek to ascertain and explore concepts as these are used by the human agents they are studying—the everyday, "ordinary language" (the concept comes from Austin and Wittgenstein; see Schaffer 2006) that characterizes the setting being studied, in its time and in its place. Given their focus on meaning-making and the production of contextual knowledge, interpretive research projects are designed to foster context-specific, situated ("bottom-up") concept development. This approach contrasts with the considerable attention to a priori concept formation and the associated operationalization of concepts into variables and indices that characterize positivist research, whether quantitative or qualitative (Adcock and Collier 2001).

The statement about concepts emerging from the field also minimizes the role played by the theoretical literature that informs the research question, focusing and shaping the researcher's attention in particular ways, discussed above. Misunderstandings or even misuse of Glaser and Strauss's "grounded theory"—one of the methods commonly cited by qualitative and interpretive researchers (Glaser and Strauss 1967; see also Locke 1996)—have contributed to this confusion. As clarified by Strauss and Corbin (1990), this method posits a particular, iterative relationship between theory and data, the former both emerging from and framing the latter. Although the concepts-from-the-field shorthand resonates with members of interpretive epistemic communities, because its literal sense can be methodologically misleading for both newer interpretive researchers and those in other epistemic communities, it needs to be used with care. Depending on the context within which it is used, its meanings may need to be spelled out.

Even though interpretive researchers seek to understand the concepts and meaning-making of those who are "native" to the context they are studying, it does not follow that they are simple conduits of research participants' concepts; researchers are also, perforce, sense-makers. In other words, the ontological character of the *representations* of the worlds they study, as assembled and published in research texts, is also of concern. An interpretive methodological approach understands researchers' texts as "ways of world-making" (Goodman 1978)—not merely describing the social and political worlds they present, but actually creating them for the reader through the judicious selection of words and phrases (see also Clifford and Marcus 1986, Golden-Biddle and Locke 1993, 1997, Gusfield 1976, Polkinghorne 1988, Van Maanen 1988). As Kevin Bruyneel (2011) writes, with reference to postcolonial analysis and citing Giyatri Spivak, this understanding translates into a refusal of "the notion that there are objective or benign ways to write and to read . . . ." Such issues of representation have been extensively theorized in interpretive, feminist, and other methodological literatures (e.g., Becker 1967, Nader 1972, Harding 1993) in terms of researcher identity and power. The latter are manifest in choice and articulation of an initial research topic and question, in the ways in which evidence is generated (rather than discovered), and in deskwork and textwork treatments—all issues considered initially in a design. "Writing up the results," then, is not an afterthought of interpretive research, a secondary task of "mere communication" in which author-speakers direct a "signal" through a communications channel to a reader-receiver. It is understood, instead, as fundamentally a scholarly, political act of persuasion that requires careful attention to the many elements it can (or should) contain which produce a trustworthy research study (Schwartz-Shea 2006, Yanow 2009, Schwartz-Shea and Yanow 2009). One element in particular, reflexivity (taken up in Chapter 6), provides one way these complex issues are recognized and made transparent for readers.

Where do concepts come from? Concepts emerging from the field in a bottom-up fashion—concept development, rather than a priori concept formation—clearly demarcates interpretive from positivist research designs. At a more philosophical level, this discussion points to the interrelationships among "facts," "concepts," and "theories." Whereas "theory" is often understood as conjectural, "fact" is taken to have the opposite meaning—as certain, real, truthful, proven. But "facts" can be understood as crystallized concepts—areas of lived experience that have produced widespread intersubjective agreement such that only a historical excavation can reveal their constructedness. The facticity of "time" as understood now, for example, only formally emerged with the establishment of Greenwich Mean Time in 1884 at the International Meridian Conference. "Concepts" stand between "facts" and "theories"—and this position, which encompasses some slippage between the other two, depending on the research approach, explains their distinctive treatments in interpretive and positivist logics of inquiry.

In the last several sections, we have been chasing the puzzle, abductively, of where research questions come from. What this discussion should bring into high relief is the notion that interpretive research does not begin with formal hypotheses, nor does it have a single, uniform, universal first step. Instead, it begins with something puzzling. And that may originate with some personal experience (sometimes in a work setting, but not always) that the researcher is puzzling about and wishes to understand more fully; or it may have its origins in some aspect of a discussion in the theoretical literature that the researcher likewise finds puzzling and wishes further to understand. The research idea develops out of an iterative engagement between the two—lived experience and theory—and becomes more fully articulated in the process of thinking back and forth between and across them.[16]

With this clarification of the place of concepts in interpretive research and the roles of prior knowledge, expectations, puzzles, and theoretical literature in generating research questions, we turn in the final section of this chapter to a more explicitly philosophical–methodological rendering of the ontological and epistemological presuppositions that underpin interpretive methodologies and methods.

Where Do Research Questions Come From? Ontological and Epistemological Presuppositions in Interpretive Research

Underlying the preceding discussion is a set of methodological presuppositions concerning the ontological and epistemological standpoints that inform a particular piece of research. Much has been written on this topic, and as our purpose in this volume is to engage at greater length with research designs than with the philosophy of (social) science—to the extent that these can be separated—we will give only enough of a background to show how the foregoing discussions and the subsequent chapters relate methodologically to these philosophical tenets. We point the reader to the brief bibliography at the end of the chapter and to the reference sections of other cited works for treatments of these topics at greater length.

In brief, the differences between research approaches that are informed by positivist philosophical presuppositions and those informed by interpretivist ones hinge on whether the scientist treats research and the theories it "tests" or generates and supports as an exact replication mirroring the social-political world, which the researcher studies from a position external to that world, or sees research findings as resulting from intersubjective, meaning-focused processes that themselves interact with and potentially shape the worlds we study. Even though, within the philosophy of science, neopositivists have accepted the idea that observation is theory-laden—which would mean that the researcher is always positioned within a way of seeing and knowing characteristic of an epistemic community (one meaning of Kuhn's use of "paradigm"; Kuhn 1996: 176–91), rather than capable of purely external observation and exact replication—this view has largely not made it into textbook and other discussions of empirical research and, in particular, into the evaluative standards used to assess empirical work.

To return to the example of interviewing, from the perspective of a methodology informed by positivist presuppositions, which hold that social realities exist independently of the researcher or the researched, interviews would be conducted to ascertain what "really" happened in a particular situation; and if different interview "subjects" provide different versions of what should be, in this view, a singular truth, the data are suspect. In this approach, an interviewer is, or should be, concerned with whether subjects are lying; and if they are, the material they narrate is not considered good data and cannot be used (on this and the counterargument, see Fujii 2010).

By contrast, from the perspective of a methodology informed by interpretivist presuppositions, which hold that we live in a world of potentially multiple, intersubjective social realities in which the researcher (as well as the researched) is also an interpreter of events that transpire and sometimes an actor in them, an interview might be conducted to ascertain how the particular person interviewed experienced the event in question; and if different interview participants provide different versions of the event, that is normal and to be expected. Indeed, it is precisely those differences that are of analytic interest to the researcher, as they suggest what is significant—what is *meaning*-ful—about the event to each person speaking. What the researcher is after, in fact, are the several interpretations, in order to understand wherein the differences of experience and interpretation lie. This is what Gusfield (1963), for instance, did in analyzing changing intersubjective attitudes toward drinking that led to the US temperance movement, the 18th Amendment to the Constitution, and its eventual repeal. Luker (1984) follows a similar path in analyzing the "pro-choice" and "pro-life" groups in the US abortion debates, noting that what divided their members is a set of values concerning the meaning of woman and motherhood. In public policy studies, such analyses can help explain difficulties in policy implementation (in environmental policy, e.g., see Linder, 1995, on electro-magnetic frequency emissions or Swaffield, 1998, on the meanings of "landscape" in New Zealand policy debates).

The discussion throughout the chapter and, indeed, the book as a whole rests on key ideas that derive from hermeneutics and phenomenology. Focusing on the fact that human meanings are not expressed directly, but instead are embedded by their creators in (or projected onto) the physical, linguistic, and enacted artifacts they create, hermeneutic thinkers articulated a set of guidelines that could be agreed upon within an interpretive or epistemic community for making meaning of those artifacts. Initially, this meant interpreting the written word: given its origins in sets of contending rules for interpreting Biblical texts, hermeneutics' initial concern in its application to the social world more broadly was with written artifacts (including, e.g., fiction, poetry, non-fiction; here is where inter-pretive methods' linkage to mid- to late-twentieth-century literary theories and the focus on language come from). This conceptualization was later extended to analyses of spoken language, acts, and physical artifacts and their meanings. The older hermeneutic idea of formal sets of accepted rules to guide interpretation is carried forward in some types of social science, such as conversation analysis in some of its forms. In other modes of analysis, what is carried over from hermeneutics is primarily the idea that "text analogues" (Taylor 1971; see also Ricoeur 1971) are susceptible of interpretation in order to learn their intersubjectively shared, and different, meanings. Ethnographic, participant observation, ethnomethodo-logical, and other modes of analysis are infused with this understanding of their meaning-focused, semiotic character: they seek to elicit meaning by rendering spoken words and/or acts, and the objects referred to or used in these, as written texts and applying to them a hermeneutic analytic sensibility.

Phenomenology, from Edmund Husserl's late-nineteenth-century writ-ings to Alfred Schütz's mid-twentieth-century ones, focuses on the meaning-making that takes place in the "lifeworld" (*Lebenswelt*) of the individual and in social, political, cultural, and other groups. Everyday life is understood to consist of common sense, taken for granted, unspoken, yet widely shared and tacitly known "rules" for acting and interacting, the articulation of which constitutes one of the central concerns of phenomenological analysis (including ethnomethodology, its and other forms of conversation analysis, symbolic interaction, ethnography, and participant observation). The social scientist, himself embedded in that social real-ity, must estrange himself sufficiently from that unspoken, intersubjective com-mon sense to render it "uncommon," reflect on it, and make sense of it.

The key ideas generated by these philosophies which together form the back-drop for interpretive methods are:

- that the artifacts humans create, whether in the form of language, objects, or acts, embody what is meaningful to their creators at the time of their creation;
- that those artifacts may, however, have other meanings to other (groups of) people who encounter and/or use them: knowledge is situated and contex-tual (or "local"), as are "knowers" (including researchers);
- that what is meaningful at the time of an artifact's creation might change over time or in a different location of usage;
- that meaning-making—the interpretation and understanding of those arti-facts and their meaning—has no one, single starting point; instead, meaning-making begins wherever it begins, with whatever the interpreter (including researchers) knows or understands at that point in time, in that place (his or her prior knowledge);
- that meaning-making draws on "lived experience"—a term that has come in some treatments to include the holistic, embodied ways in which humans move through the world;

- that meaning-making is a social practice, as well as an individual one (in many cases, the former providing the interpretive repertoire for the latter);
- that language is not a transparent referent for what it designates nor does it merely "mirror" or "reflect" an external world but, instead, plays a role in shaping or "constituting" understandings of that world, and is itself, in this sense, one of the "ways of worldmaking" (Goodman 1978).

One additional point: phenomenologists have been criticized, largely by critical theorists, for being too preoccupied with individual meaning-making, at the expense of a consideration of more institutional phenomena, including power. Whereas this criticism may well hold at the level of philosophy, when phenomenology is brought into the context of political and other social sciences, its concerns tend to shift, or expand, to include collectives such as organizations, communities, governments, and the like. What might be called an "applied" hermeneutic phenomenology, then, perforce engages power dynamics—although the extent of this engagement varies among scholars and across disciplines and analytic approaches, with discourse analysts perhaps more inclined than ethnomethodologists to focus on power and related dimensions. Further explication of these and other ideas in interpretive thinking can be found in the list of sources that follows on the next page.

A Short Bibliography of Key Sources in Interpretive Social Science

Berger, Peter L. and Luckmann, Thomas. 1966. *The Social Construction of Reality*. New York: Anchor Books.

Brown, Richard Harvey. 1976. "Social Theory as Metaphor." *Theory and Society* 3: 169–97.

Bruner, Jerome S. 1990. *Acts of Meaning*. Cambridge, MA: Harvard University Press.

Burrell, Gibson and Morgan, Gareth. 1979. *Sociological Paradigms and Organisational Analysis*. London: Heinemann.

Dallmayr, Fred R. and McCarthy, Thomas A., eds. 1977. *Understanding and Social Inquiry*. Notre Dame, IN: University of Notre Dame Press.

Fay, Brian. 1996. *Contemporary Philosophy of Social Science: A Multicultural Approach*. Oxford: Blackwell.

Fish, Stanley. 1980. *Is There a Text in this Class? The Authority of Interpretive Communities*. Cambridge, MA: Harvard University Press.

Geertz, Clifford. 1973. "Thick Description: Toward an Interpretive Theory of Culture." In *The Interpretation of Cultures*, 3–32. New York: Basic Books.

Hawkesworth, M. E. 1988. *Theoretical Issues in Policy Analysis*. Albany: SUNY Press.

Hiley, David R., Bohman, James F., and Shusterman, Richard, eds. 1991. *The Interpretive Turn*. Ithaca, NY: Cornell University Press.

McCloskey, Donald N. 1985. *The Rhetoric of Economics*. Madison: University of Wisconsin Press.

Polkinghorne, Donald E. 1983. *Methodology for the Human Sciences*. Albany, NY: SUNY Press.

Rabinow, Paul and Sullivan, William M., eds. 1979, 1985. *Interpretive Social Science*, 1st and 2nd eds. Berkeley: University of California Press.

Rorty, Richard. 1979. *Philosophy and the Mirror of Nature*. Princeton, NJ: Princeton University Press.

Taylor, Charles. 1971. "Interpretation and the Sciences of Man." *Review of Metaphysics* 25: 3–51. Reprinted in Dallmayr and McCarthy, 1977, 101–31 and in Rabinow and Sullivan, 1979, 25–71 (both cited above).

3

STARTING FROM MEANING

Contextuality and Its Implications

> Kellogg's set up a branch in India and started producing corn flakes to give consumers the real thing. What they didn't realize was that Indians, rather like the Chinese, think that to start the day with something cold, like cold milk on your cereal, is a shock to the system. You start it with warm milk. But you pour warm milk on Mr. Kellogg's corn flakes and they turn to wet paper. You pour warm milk on the sturdier Indian corn flake, it holds up. Does it taste better than Mr. Kellogg's? No. If Mr. Kellogg's is eaten as Mr. Kellogg intended, it is somewhat better than Indian corn flakes. The point is that . . . you have to know something about . . . a place and its cultural rituals.
>
> —*Homi Bhabha, quoted in*
> *"A Humanist Who Knows Corn Flakes" (2005: 64–65)*

Having an initial sense of their research question, interpretive researchers begin designing their research project by thinking about the kinds and sources of evidence that would enable them to engage it. Most start off by thinking about the setting(s), archives, event(s), actors, and so forth among which and whom they will conduct their study. Although we would prefer to go directly to those matters, in keeping with the rhythms of an interpretive research project, we have decided to defer that to the next chapter in order to address, first, the reader who is accustomed to thinking from a different starting point. This is the reader who believes that the first step in a research design has to be the identification and definition of concepts, their operationalization in the form of variables, and the stipulation of hypotheses that establish the relationships among them. Underlying this starting point is a particular orientation toward knowledge and its sources. In order to be able to speak more clearly about where interpretive research begins, and why, we need to discuss its contrasting orientation toward knowledge, with its focus on meaning-making and on contextuality.

How does an orientation toward contextuality bear on these matters? Concepts and some form of hypothesizing and conceptions of causality are central to scholarly endeavors from both interpretive and positivist approaches. What is meant by these terms, however, and even the precise terminology used, varies across the two approaches and contributes to significant differences in thinking about designing a research project.

Contrasting Orientations toward Knowledge

All researchers seek to contribute to knowledge. Yet this common goal elides complex questions: Knowledge *about what*? Knowledge *for what purpose*? Knowledge *for whom*? The *sine qua non* of interpretive research—the sensibility that is its hallmark and which makes it distinctive in comparison with other research approaches—is its focus on meaning-making: it seeks knowledge about how human beings, scholars included, make individual and collective sense of their particular worlds.

In interpretive research, human beings are understood not as objects, but as agents. Such persons are seen as actively and collaboratively constructing (and deconstructing, meaning both critically assessing and changing) their polities, societies, and cultures—along with the institutions, organizations, practices, physical artifacts, and language and concepts that populate these. At the same time, those same political and cultural contexts frame these agents' possibilities for thought, discourse, and action. Interpretive research understands that the motivation that animates these several activities is meaning—both its expression and its communication to others. As language is at the nexus of meaning, context, and action, interpretive research "tak[es] language seriously" (J. White 1992). For this reason, the interpretive turn in theorizing about ways of knowing joined the linguistic turn (Rorty 1967, Fraser 1995), the metaphoric turn (Lorenz 1998), and other such "turns," including the practice turn (Schatzki *et al.* 2001) with its attention to acts and physical artifacts.[1]

In interpretive methodology, the ambiguity and plasticity of meaning-making and of the systems of symbols (e.g., language, visual images, etc.) used to express and communicate meaning to oneself and to others are understood as creating the possibility for multiple interpretations of acts, events, settings, and so forth. This is, ontologically, the reason for attending to humans' use of language in constructing their worlds and, epistemologically, in making sense of them. The possibility of the multiplicity of meanings is one of the things that makes connections to context critical for both the conduct of interpretive research and its design: the reasons things take *these* particular forms and not others has to do with their specific contexts of time and place. It matters that the corn flakes are being eaten in India rather than in the US, in Homi Bhabha's tale that serves as the epigraph to this chapter. Another point about multiple possibilities and the importance of context is the understanding that the artifacts humans create to express and convey meaning—not only language, but also acts and the physical objects engaged in doing and speaking—can take myriad forms, depending on time and/or place. For those studying humans in group form—as neighborhoods, communities, polities, organizations, and so on—a distinctive aspect of research concerns the artifactual meanings that members share and which separate one epistemic–interpretive group from another, perhaps provoking not only disunity but also conflict.

Researchers in positivist modes also seek to understand humans and their behaviors; but what language and other artifacts mean for these researchers, in terms of their uses in research, is quite different. In positivist methodology, ambiguity is the enemy of measurability, where each instance of a phenomenon must be classifiable in one and only one category. As concepts need to be operationalized to produce variables for measuring phenomena and for assembling data sets (on the same unit of analysis) for subsequent statistical assessments, initial attention to their specification is imperative. In this process, their definition is, and must be, both precise and abstracted from context. Short of a pilot study, conceptual definitions are "locked in" to the stipulated variables and their definitions at the point of measurement (e.g., when a survey is administered). If, in the course of the research, it is judged that the measure of a concept is poor, rendering it an inadequate indicator of subjects' meanings, the concept cannot be redefined and re-measured in that same study.[2]

Just as interpretive research is distinctive in its focus on meaning-making (knowledge *about what?*), it also has different sensibilities about the uses of knowledge: knowledge *for what purpose, for whom?* Interpretive methodologists dispute the usefulness (and desirability) of knowledge that claims to "rise above" its context. This does not mean that interpretive researchers do not theorize. Instead, they seek to theorize on the basis of knowledge that makes clear its connections to specific (kinds of) human beings in specific, historically and culturally understood settings.

This presents a strong contrast with positivist methodology, for which "generalizability" is a widespread concern. Researchers in that tradition are often asking, "Are the results generalizable?" This orientation implicitly places responsibility for the applicability of "findings" from one research setting to potential others *on the shoulders of the researchers*; i.e., it is they who must demonstrate that their results hold for all other settings or for those specified in the "scope" conditions of mid-level theorizing (which delimit that theorizing from a-historical, a-cultural theorizing). In this research approach, the overarching goal is building general theory for the purposes of prediction (and explanation).

By contrast, members of interpretive research communities ask: "Is the research sufficiently contextualized so that the interpretations are embedded in, rather than abstracted from, the settings of the actors studied?" Seen from an interpretive perspective, the positivist orientation toward the general obscures the intimacy (and inseparability) of the link between research purpose (anticipated learning, in light of broader theoretical concerns) and the context(s) that sparked or drove the research. Interpretive methodology shifts responsibility for the applicability of research learning to other research settings from the researchers to the readers of the research. As Lincoln and Guba (1985) long ago argued, scholars should describe their research contexts in sufficiently "thick" ways that *readers* of their work (including researchers engaged with other research questions) can assess the relevance of the research to their own settings.[3] Whereas positivist methodologists understand "findings" as useful for building general theory solely for the purposes of prediction and explanation, interpretive methodologists observe that research can also be useful for a variety of other purposes—not only explanatory ones, but emancipatory and critical ones, as well.[4] The quality or value of contextualized knowledge (theory) is to be assessed by users, whether academic or other, who decide themselves the extent to which that knowledge fits their circumstances and purposes, i.e., whether it works *in context* (Avenier 2010, Tsoukas 2009). The centrality of context to interpretive methods lends weight to treating *contextuality* as a more appropriate indicator of the achievements of interpretive research than "generalizability," its equivalent in positivist methodology: it is a better fit with interpretive methodological orientations to knowledge creation and use.[5]

The interpretive orientation toward knowledge, with its focus on meaning-making (instead of a priori model specification) and contextuality (rather than generalizability), ripples through the entire research design process.[6] Contextuality provides a direct methodological rationale for the "thick description" (Geertz 1973) that has been widely taken up by methodologists as a key characteristic of qualitative–interpretive writing, which embeds meaning in context. But this desideratum requires "thickly written" fieldnotes, themselves resting on "thickly crafted and experienced" observations, interviews, and documentary reading. To take as an example the field research narrative that Geertz uses in developing this concept, a "thin" description might be rendered this way: Cohen, a Jewish trader, stole some sheep from a Berber tribe, and so the French authorities imprisoned him (1973: 7–9).

A thicker description would add the "whys" and "hows" that underlie this statement's "whats," contributing all manner of historical, demographic, economic, geographic, and cultural nuances, as relevant to the research question and what the researcher is seeking to theorize, that contextualize the seemingly simple event. Such is, in fact, the research tale that Geertz narrates, over three pages of text. Neither the events nor their description need to be out of the ordinary: what matters is the detail, as this bit from Liebow's examination of Tally's corner's fathers shows:

> Together with Calvin, a frail and ailing forty-year-old alcoholic and homo-sexual who looked after the children in exchange for a place to live, Leroy

bathed the children, braided the girls' hair, washed their clothes at 'the Bendix' (laundromat), played with them, and on their birthdays went shoplifting to get them gifts.

(Liebow 1967: 52)

The information is presented without judgment; and what is significant is what it will enable Liebow to argue, later, with the support of additional evidence in terms of the data's implications for the theoretical issues that concern him in this study. In order to be able to produce a research text of such detail, a researcher has to have observed, talked, and/or read enough, and noted all of that, to generate material for those layers of contextualization.[7]

Good interpretive research designs think through the crafting of situations—the selection of research-relevant settings, actors, events, documents, and so on—that can lead to those sorts of "thick experience," as well as of ways to "thicken" encounters in the field (see discussion of mapping for exposure and intertextuality in Chapter 5). In thinking through the specifics of a research project, investigators seek to design research in ways that respect and preserve the meaning–context link such that readers are enabled to understand local preferences for warm milk over cold, even if it means breakfasting on less tasty corn flakes, as Bhabha puts it.

Contextuality and the Character of Concepts and Causality

Putting contextuality front and center in a logic of research bears significantly on how one thinks about concepts and on the understandings of causality that are ensconced in hypotheses. We further defer a discussion of where and how interpretive researchers begin to design research in order to discuss these two matters, as they are commonly ones on whose use interpretive researchers are challenged and on whose grounds interpretive research is seen as deficient. We seek here to show researchers not familiar with interpretive logics of inquiry why this is not the case, by contrasting interpretive understandings of "concepts" and "causality" with positivist ones.

Concepts: Bottom-up In Situ Development

All researchers use concepts. We conceptualize as we build theories from our empirical research, and we use the concepts developed in that process to communicate with one another. Following Geertz (1983), we characterize these sorts of concepts as "experience-distant"—part of the scholarly world, but not commonly part of the worlds studied by social scientists (unless they are studying researchers, as science studies scholars do). Interpretive researchers seek to understand the worlds of those they study from the latter's perspectives. They seek, to complete Geertz' taxonomy, the concepts that are "experience-near" (1983: 57)—used by those on the kill-floor of a slaughterhouse (Pachirat 2009a), in government discussions of national security (Cohn 2006), or on the receiving end of US government welfare processing requirements (Soss 2000), to take but three examples. In part, this practice of searching for experience-near concepts derives from the conviction that participants possess valuable "local knowledge," concepts and their situated definitions that have grown out of their own daily practices and interactions, reflecting their own lived experiences of the setting, events in it, interactions, and so forth: that is what researchers want to understand.[8] Learning experience-near concepts may provide entrée to such knowledge, which for those using the concepts in everyday ways is often tacit, in Polanyi's (1966: 4) sense that we "can know more than we can tell."

Interpretive research design plans for concept "development" to take place during fieldwork, not before it. In one sense, this might be considered development to the extent that a researcher needs to develop her own understanding of what for situational actors is common sense. Depending on the research question, design possibilities for acquiring local concepts range from the choice of quite formal methods (e.g., some versions of grounded theory, Charmaz 2006; ordinary language analysis, Schaffer 2006) to more open-ended attention to how participants talk, their use of special terms, jargon, vernacular, modes of reasoning, metaphors, etc. Hanging out with medical students, for instance, Becker (1998) was puzzled by their use of the word "crock." Finding out and exploring what this word meant to them—a patient who did not advance students' learning—and how they used it became central to his understanding and analysis of medical education. Looking at shop-floor workers' interactions on the job, Roy (1959) explored what they termed "banana time," jokingly named after the ritual "theft" of one colleague's mid-morning snack, to generate insights into job satisfaction in routinized work settings. Soss (2000) found that welfare recipients enrolled in two government programs, Social Security Disability Insurance (SSDI) and Assistance to Families with Dependent Children (ADFC), used the same phrase—being treated "like a number"—but with contrary meanings in each program due to their quite different contexts. SSDI recipients used the phrase to express their feeling that they were treated impersonally, but with respect, whereas AFDC recipients used the same words to convey their feeling of being dehumanized by their treatment. In all three examples, the concepts were already "developed" in the field by those who used them in everyday sorts of ways; what researchers needed to do was to develop their own knowledge of those concepts in their situated usages—to learn how to use them in the "local language" of each research setting.

By contrast, the a priori concept formation characteristic of positivist research design, essential to the operationalization of variables, fixes the meaning of experience-distant concepts in ways that preclude or make exceedingly difficult the interpretive research goal of understanding participants' views. Recognizing this limitation, some positivist pilot studies look for ways to ameliorate this difficulty for some topics and to some extent. For example, rather than relying solely on their own terminology and on questions they craft themselves, some survey researchers hold focus groups before finalizing their questionnaires to try to learn the language that is meaningful to potential respondents; they then use that knowledge to frame better survey questions. From an interpretive perspective, however, such preparatory work does not foreclose the possibility that participants responding to the reframed survey questions will interpret the same words or phrases in different ways, whether from one another or from the survey designer's intended meanings, due to their own distinctive contexts.

It bears mention that an interpretive research focus on bottom–up concept development does not assume blind acceptance by researchers of what they are told. We discuss in Chapter 5 how researchers check their sense-making across multiple sources, seeking a sort of thickness by "mapping" the research setting to gain exposure to multiple perspectives on the research focus, thereby achieving a kind of "intertextuality" across sources of evidence. For instance, a researcher might map participants across the neighborhoods that make up the community that is the study's setting, or departments or hierarchical levels across a bureaucratic organization, seeking out multiple possible views on the subject of analysis, which may include contradictory narratives. This means taking participants' views seriously—as authors of their own lives—even if the researcher, in analyzing them, also offers critical perspectives or insights into the tacit understandings and assumptions that underlie those views, including discussing conflicting views heard or read in various corners of the research terrain.

A focus on local knowledge and concepts, then, does not mean that interpretive researchers foreswear the use of experience-distant concepts. Researchers might coin their own experience-distant concepts, as called for by a specific analysis, or draw on those common within a particular research community in order to join the theoretical and analytic conversation taking place there. Still, bottom–up concept articulation and use is a key marker of interpretive research's commitment to embedding human participants' meaning-making in its social, political, cultural, and historical contexts. The research ideal is to be able to use local concepts in everyday, adult ways, rather than tripping over them as a child or neophyte would. This extends to the particularities of everyday speech, as when Liebow quotes one of his corner men as saying, ". . . he stone took care of her and her children" (1967: 84) and then explains in a note that "stone" is "An intensive, in this case meaning 'Really took care'" (1967: 84, n. 17).

But What of Hypothesizing? Constitutive Causality

Because of this commitment to meaning-making in context and the attendant engagement with participants' concepts *in situ*, many key positivist design concerns are not relevant to interpretive research design. These include three that figure there centrally: (1) the a priori definition of concepts (just discussed); (2) assessment of the validity and reliability of the variables that operationalize them;

and (3) construction of relationships among variables—whether in the form of null and research hypotheses (for simple bivariate relations) or as multivariate relationships (for a regression or other statistical or formal model).[9] But if these concerns are not engaged, what happens to causality, and to hypothesis-testing that seeks to establish causality?

Methodological positivists seek to predict phenomena, ideally on the basis of a causal law or mechanism connecting specified independent variable(s) to the phenomenon under investigation (the dependent variable). Positivist methodology treats causality mechanistically: in what might be called a "billiard ball" understanding, investigation looks to see how one thing—in the analogy, a moving cue stick—leads to another—a ball that then moves on impact. Positivist-informed research seeks to identify that first thing in order to be able to predict ensuing reaction and, thereby, to control its movement or development or, if that is not possible, to move other things out of its way or prepare for its effects. This orientation is especially clear in Campbell and Stanley's (1963) influential book that extends the logic of experimental design from the laboratory to field settings.

There is considerable debate about "causality" within interpretive research communities (see Bernstein 1978, Taylor 1985) and, perhaps, no consensus. P. Jackson (2011), for example, articulates three versions that are distinctive from what we have termed "billiard ball" causality. L. Hansen (2006), by contrast, eschews all discussion of "causality." In our view, methodological interpretivists seek understanding within specific settings: how the actors in them understand their contexts, explicitly and/or tacitly, and why they conduct themselves in particular ways. This "why" takes the form of "constitutive" causality,[10] which engages how humans conceive of their worlds, the language they use to describe them, and other elements constituting that social world, which make possible or impossible the interactions they pursue. It is an effort at explanation that does not insist on producing abstract accounts of events. What it is after is explanation that rests on "descriptions of the . . . interweaving of codes [of meaning] in particular situations," processes whose parts are contingent upon one another, rather than being "logically derivable from the codes themselves" (Hammersley 2008: 55).

Anderson's (2006) treatment of the power of nationalism, for instance, can be understood in this constitutive fashion—as the conception of an "imagined political community" for which millions have been willing to die. Or consider the rechristening of the estate or inheritance tax in recent US debates over tax policy as the "death tax" and the ways in which this reframed conceptualization has been a mobilizing idea for anti-tax activists (Luntz 2007; cf. Lakoff 2008). In an extended historical analysis, P. Jackson (2006) details how certain post–WWII German politicians drew on the rhetorical commonplace of the *Abendland*—the broad notion of Western civilization—to solidify their political position and alliances, while marginalizing their competitors. These are examples of a constitutive causality that seeks to explain events in terms of actors' understandings of their own contexts, rather than in terms of a more mechanistic causality.[11]

These contrasting aims and understandings of causality, themselves embedded in distinctive conceptions of human agency, mean that hypotheses and hypothesizing are also understood quite differently. Because interpretive methodologies rest on local knowledge, interpretive research designs commonly do not specify formal hypotheses that a study is expected to falsify or support in a single, definitive test. Instead, the researcher's understanding of the relationships that in positivist-informed research would be articulated in the form of hypotheses is allowed—and expected—to develop over the course of the research project, as it unfolds. Whereas many forms of positivist research, say a laboratory experiment, require a completed design prior to generating the data that will test the hypothesis, interpretive research requires an iterative process of researcher sense-making which cannot be fully specified a priori because of its unfolding, processual character. Initial research expectations are treated as educated provisional inferences that will be considered and explored, rather than as formal hypotheses that will be "tested" in the narrower sense implied by the standard usage of "hypothesis testing."

The Centrality of Context

Research logics and purposes matter. The logics of interpretive and positivist methodologies are distinctive, as are their intended purposes, and this means that their respective approaches to conceptualization, hypothesizing, and causality are, likewise, distinctive. As we have just discussed, the logic of interpretive inquiry— focused on meaning-making in context—requires researchers' central attention to the concepts used by the human beings they study. This logic also means, consistent with the iterative character of hermeneutic sense-making, that researchers' initial conjectures are assessed and reassessed in the field. Perhaps most striking, it entails a conceptualization of causality that is at odds with the conventional wisdom offered in the vast majority of methods textbooks.

Having laid this groundwork explaining why interpretive research does not begin with the same orientation toward knowledge as positivist research, we can now pick up the thread of interpretive research design and its own rhythms: establishing the setting(s), event(s), actors, and so forth among which and whom researchers will conduct their studies and, following that, the evidentiary character of that material.

4

THE RHYTHMS OF INTERPRETIVE RESEARCH I

Getting Going

> The observation of which I shall speak is, for lack of a better term, interactive observation. It is not like looking through a one-way glass at someone on the other side. You watch, you accompany, and you talk with the people you are studying.
>
> Much of what you see, therefore, is dictated by what they do, and say. If something is important to them, it becomes important to you. Their view of the world is as important as your view of that world. You impose some research questions on them; they impose some research questions on you.
>
> That interaction has its costs—most notably in a considerable loss of control over the research process. It also has benefits.
> It brings you especially close to your data.
> You watch it being generated and you collect it at the source.
> It is not received data.
>
> —*Richard Fenno (1986: 4; paragraph breaks added)*

With some sense of a research question in hand, along with the debates that inform it, a researcher is prepared to proceed to the more formal design elements of the research project: potential sources of data, and methods for generating those data. Note that opening: *with some sense* of a research question in hand. The extent to which this will be formalized depends on research communities, departments, specific advisors, funding agents, and one's own proclivities (including tolerance for ambiguity). We are in agreement with John Van Maanen (2011: 222) that "we should also allow our questions to determine our theories," meaning that "one need not stake out a theoretical claim on how the world is before beginning a research project." But at the same time, we recognize that this degree of openness and flexibility is likely to feel more comfortable among those who are old hands at interpretive (and in the case of Van Maanen's topic, qualitative ethnographic) research, whereas those more accustomed to the relative closure of experimental and quasi-experimental research designs are far more likely to desire more formalized research questions at the outset.

Due to the researcher's ongoing and evolving learning while in the field, as well as his or her limited control over settings and the persons in them, or over materials in an archive, interpretive research is, and has to be, much more flexible than other forms of research. This flexibility is a conscious, intentional strategy, and it applies not only to the need to respond in the moment to things said or done, but also to how the research process may be changing initial research designs and questions. Some research questions can lead the researcher to discover the most unexpected "answers," which in turn can lead to revised research questions, also potentially unanticipated, which could not have been posed without having stumbled on the unexpected answer to the initial question. In abductive fashion, puzzles grow on the backs of other puzzles.

A design appropriate for this sort of research needs to reflect and make space for its iterative, recursive, and adaptive character. The design process itself is not necessarily as linear as the chapter's opening sentence suggests. Often, in the course of working out the design, the research question comes into focus in new or different ways; and that focus can send the researcher off in search of other literatures, other settings or archives, or both. The design process is, in other words, itself quite "circular"—the hermeneutic circle once again. We might even say iterative and recursive, each of its parts informing and folding back on the others, enacting the same sense-making spiral that characterizes the conduct of interpretive inquiry.

Perhaps because the process, the rhythm, of interpretive research manifest in these aspects is so contrary to the emphasis on control and other specific characteristics of positivist research, this iterative and recursive strategy and its significance for research flexibility are not widely recognized or well understood across the social sciences, something noted also by Becker (2009) in his assessment of recent US National Science Foundation recommendations for the conduct of qualitative research. Moreover, its requisite open-endedness and flexibility often make interpretive research designs appear—from the perspective of the much more closed-ended and controlled positivist design—underdeveloped. This, too, reflects a lack of familiarity with the different rhythms of these two research modes.[1]

Much of the creative, intellectual work in positivist research projects (e.g., quantitative analysis, survey research, experiments) is "front-loaded" in particular ways: the choice of variables and how to operationalize them, the phrasing of survey questions and their ordering, the setup of experimental "manipulations"—all of these are established a priori in the research design or in the first stage of research, *before* the researcher engages with data sources.[2] Only when this prior "stage-setting" is completed does the researcher turn to the data themselves: measures are taken, survey questionnaires are administered, experiments are conducted. And only after that stage is completed does formal analysis begin: many of these approaches make a relatively clean distinction between data collection and data analysis. There may be some monitoring of results while the data collection phase of research is in progress (notably in double-blind health experiments, as required by human subjects protections monitoring); but most often, analysis begins when the data collecting phase has been completed, to avoid what in this view would be considered an error of *ex post facto* reasoning (which undermines the logic of tests of statistical significance).[3]

The rhythms of interpretive research are quite different. Its design revolves around front-loading of a different sort: the development of the researcher's a priori knowledge, so to speak, in the kind of clarification of expectations explored in Chapter 2, including, perhaps, preparations of body and emotions as well.[4] These initial understandings—the researcher's provisional sense-making—will be "tested" in the field or archives, not literally, as in the case of significance tests in statistics, but by bringing them together with field realities, even to the point where those realities might take analytic primacy. Initial understandings are likely to be reformulated in light of new insights, new understandings, new knowledge acquired, and those reformulations will be subjected again to further inquiry, in that iterative, spiral-circular recursiveness of abductive reasoning described in Chapter 2. It is this continuous juxtaposition of conceptual formulations with field realities and the requisite flexibility that accompanies it that comprise the foundational rhythm of interpretive research.

In this dance of inquiry, data generation and analysis are ongoing and intertwined. Initial sense-making (analysis) commonly begins in the field or even beforehand, in the process of designing a research project, with the recognition that it will continue after fieldwork is completed, during the deskwork phase of research (formal analysis, working with fieldnotes and other materials, including the theoretical literature). And this iterative sense-making process continues on into the textwork phase, too (more argument-construction and word-smithing than analytic note-making and roughing out a draft), in which text-making takes on its "worldmaking" character (Goodman 1978). This means that writing is more than a "mere" description ("writing up") of research "findings" (see also Clifford and Marcus 1986, Geertz 1983, Van Maanen 1988). These iterative–recursive processes take place within particular understandings of causality, hypothesizing, and analysis (taken up in Chapter 3)—which means, in turn, a different shape and sense to the research design.

In what follows, we engage the sorts of issues that interpretive researchers commonly consider in the first phases of research design: the selection of settings, actors, events, and/or texts, or archives, in which or among whom they are most likely to be able to address their research question or puzzle. This requires examining two features of the envisioned study: how the researcher expects and will arrange to gain access to the setting, actors, events, and/or texts; and in what role the researcher will do so. The question of access to archives takes on a different sense, and we touch on it in a separate section. We note those design elements and concepts that are shared by positivist and interpretive approaches, and we also mark the differences in ordering or "flow" between these approaches: the more step-wise process of positivist approaches compared to the distinctive rhythm of an iterative, recursive interpretive research process. In the chapter's final section we return to the matter of requisite flexibility in a research design, which we now elaborate on in terms of the agency of research participants: rather than a matter of lack of thought or planning, or even simple convenience, flexibility is essential to intelligent maneuvering in the field so as to pursue the situated, contextualized meaning-making of those whose lives, interactions, situations, written records and visual images, and so on are being studied.

In order to make the issues raised by these features as evident as possible, we draw on examples that provide the sharpest contrast to interpretive research practices, such as experiments and surveys, both of which entail a priori speci-fication of cases based on an assumption of case homogeneity. We do so in recognition of the ways in which the positivist/interpretive dichotomy can, as noted previously, be an oversimplification when it comes to demarcating forms of research. Positivist ethnographic or case study research, the latter typically entailing heterogeneous cases, may share some research practices with interpre-tive researchers using related methods (but informed by different methodologi-cal presuppositions).[5] For lack of space, we do not fully engage these similarities and differences.

Access: Choices of Settings, Actors, Events, Archives, and Materials

In many interpretive research projects, the research question is intimately con-nected with a particular setting, a particular time period, a particular set of actors, and so forth—or with some combination of these. This would be the case with a research question developed out of a setting the researcher became involved with initially without any intention of doing research there, as discussed in Chapter 2. In that case, the necessary choices with respect to further particulars of set-ting, events, actors, and so forth develop reiteratively with the elaboration of the research question. The same holds for archival research, as inquiry follows what is found in the materials. In other cases, the researcher may have an idea about a topic and then go in search of appropriate settings and so forth in which to explore it: where the research will be carried out, with or among what actors or in which archives, investigating which events, and so on. Merlijn van Hulst (2008a), for instance, knew that he wanted to study an aspect of local governance, and he went in search of municipalities in which he could develop and then delve into his research question. Timothy Pachirat (2011) wanted to explore what he saw as the routinization of violence in the US, and thinking along those lines led him to consider carrying out his field research in a slaughterhouse.

All researchers focus on identifying settings, actors, archives, events, eras, and/ or texts that will enhance the likelihood of being able to explore the questions that interest them. This can include clock and calendar features that might affect research-relevant evidence. In all approaches, the rationale for choices made is a key part of the research design: the logic that links research question, setting(s), actors, documents, etc., and data-generating and -analyzing methods needs to be elaborated. For example, Kevin Walby (2010: 643) provides such a rationale when he writes that he chose to conduct his interviews against the background noise of coffee shops or outdoors at bus stops and park benches, settings that afforded anonymity and confidentiality. And Fujii (2009: 37) writes about her interview-based study that she "avoided market days because people were usually not at home" then. We underscore a central trait of interpretive research designs and their implementation already mentioned, to which we will return: these design specifications are initial formulations of the research question and choices of settings and so forth and of methods. Any of these may change once the researcher gets to the field and begins the encounters that comprise the research—something completely normal and legitimate in interpretive research (as discussed in Chapter 2 and the last section of this chapter).

But identifying settings and actors is only the first step. It does not automatically grant the researcher "access," a permission-acquisition process—something researchers need to obtain at times from governmental and/or organizational entities at various levels, but also from individuals in a less formal, more interpersonal fashion. Researchers seek access to people in various kinds of settings: their homes (Soss 2000), a neighborhood corner, bar, or coffee shop (Liebow 1967, Zirakzadeh 2009, Walsh 2004), a community center organization (Yanow 1996) or gym (Wacquant 2004), a police department (Van Maanen 1978), government office (Rhodes *et al.* 2007), hospital (Barley 1986, Iedema *et al.* 2011, Katz and Shotter 1996), or factory, business, or corporation (Barley 1983, Dalton 1959, Kunda 1992, Roy 1959, Shehata 2009). The question for researchers is how to arrange this and what is entailed in doing so.

Initially, as the concept of "access" emphasizes, researcher bodies need to move through gates of various sorts. The term has customarily referred to securing formal permissions, a holdover from its methodological origins in archaeological and social-anthropological field research, especially in colonial settings. There, it was necessary to secure a traveler's visa to enter the field site to reside for an extended period of time, commonly requiring an administrator's permission. For interpretive researchers as well as for many working in a qualitative vein, however, "access" is not simply a matter of knocking on a door, literally or figuratively, in order to get in. As social anthropologists learned, this did not automatically gain them entrée into a village's social network. For that, the approval of the local "chief" was also needed, and this entailed more than just a piece of paper.

Participant observer sociologists and others doing interview-based studies also came to understand "access" in a less literal sense, linked to the more interpersonal notions of establishing rapport with their interlocutors.[6]

Today, access is increasingly being understood in the context of the relational character of engagements with research participants in the field. In experimental, survey, or focus group research, the character of relationships is largely defined in terms of a "professional-expert researcher" who explains the conditions for participation to potential "research subjects." The interaction is likely time-bound; and the implicit expectation is that the researcher remains in the proper, distant role of professional-expert throughout. The parameters of any relationality between researcher and researched are clear, even if not governed by explicitly stated codes of ethics. Moreover, the relationship has the texture of a contract, something made more formal in consent procedures developed in many human research participant protections policies (such as ethics review committees), whose signed documents, formal language, and potential oversight of researcher conduct mimic legal contracts and procedures.

By contrast, field relationships are less time-bound and more complex. Recurring interactions between researcher and researched mean the possibility of developing relationships that go beyond those in the model of researcher-to-"research subject" relationship characteristic of the contractual model of consent (see the discussion, below, of participants' agency). This is a feature especially of projects in which the researcher dwells among the participants—participant observer or ethnographic research, in particular, but holding as well for interview research that involves repeated encounters with the same participants. In archival research, important relationships can develop between researchers and archivists (Bellhouse 2011). Relationship complications can arise when the researcher is acting in a consultant role or has the possibility of turning the research contract into a consulting one at its end (e.g., in school, hospital, or other organizational settings). The relational character of these interactions requires researchers to attend to the humanity of those who give of their time, and perhaps other resources, in helping the researcher gain greater understanding of her research topic—to treat them in their full human-ness and not just as means to an end (e.g., "my informants," "my data").[7]

Focusing on the humanity of research participants is part and parcel of treating them as agents in and of their own settings. More than that: just as "normal" relationships require ongoing maintenance, so do research relationships. This means understanding access as an ongoing process (Feldman *et al.* 2003), not a one-time-only unlatching of a door. It requires researchers to think about how "research friendships" are, or might be, different from non-research friendships. Walby (2010: 652), for instance, writes about trying to balance a degree of friendliness with self-presentation as a research sociologist "conducting a rigorous study." It also means that researchers need to think about and plan for their leave-taking.

If this is a research friendship, does the researcher say goodbye forever when exiting the field? Or does he maintain contact and, if so, what kind? As Librett and Perrone (2010: 745) note, quoting Milne, "'[C]aring interactions are established and maintained over time rather than a contract that once signed is forgotten'" (see also Henderson 2009: 292). Such engagements also bear on some aspects of research ethics, as well as the emotional side of field research (taken up in Chapter 7) and choices about what Burkhart (1996: 40) calls "the privileged grounds of ethnographic knowledge and appropriate ways to write about information gained through friendship." The lines between researcher and friend (and perhaps even family member; Jacobs 1996: 296) may at times blur, and fieldwork relationships may also include elements of secrecy (Leap 1996). What, for instance, might a researcher have done to prompt a participant to exclaim, with whatever mixture of confusion, sadness, and even anger, "But I thought we were friends?" (Beech *et al.* 2009; see also Ellis 1995). D. Mosse's (2005, 2006) post-research troubles—in which colleagues with whom he had had professional relationships prior to the publication of his field research accused him of betrayal—illustrate this point.

Both institutional access-related negotiations and interpersonal ones can be or become political contexts that enable entrée for some bodies but not for others. Prior knowledge, including language skills and personal contacts (perhaps developed through previous non-academic field experiences), may make some projects doable for only some researchers, enabling them to gain access where others cannot.[8] And formal permissions do not guarantee interpersonal access: the classic complete "stranger" of anthropological lore may not be welcomed, perceived with indifference, if not suspicion (and left without local family or friends to fall back on for emotional support; see Ortbals and Rincker 2009). These and other dimensions of researcher–researched relationships put the researcher in the position of supplicant in which he may be less powerful than those in the position of granting or denying access: the knowledge, institutional, economic, social, and/or cultural bases of the laboratory researcher's customary sources of power may not be operative in these circumstances.

Power and Research Relationships

At the design stage, researchers need to anticipate and consider the potential forms research relationships might take, as these may vary not only with the research question but also with respect to the relative power of the different individuals and groups studied. Within a research setting, power is relational, and the power of the researcher, the researched individuals, and the types of research relationships they may develop can vary considerably. In a single site, such as a school, hospital, or other form of bureaucratic organization, for instance, agency executives have different power resources than front-line workers and clients. Middle managers can enact different sorts of power relative to their employees than they do vis-à-vis their own bosses. In addition, researchers may have the initial power to set agendas, but participants may refuse to proceed with those agendas, reshaping them to their own purposes and meaning-making (see, e.g., Walby 2010: 654). How these situational variations will affect interactions and negotiations with the researcher cannot always be predicted, but need to be considered.

Interpretive researchers often study individuals with considerable social power—bankers (Abolafia 2010), lawyers (Pierce 1995), national security analysts (Cohn 2006), and other members of elite sociopolitical strata and areas of expertise. Although in such cases, those studied may expect the researcher to fulfill a "professional-expert" role—one who has mastered the substantive issues (e.g., regulations, executive orders, acronyms, and other situational jargon), with the status and power attendant on such expertise—experts and elites have considerable status and power themselves, and it is not clear that researchers will always have the upper hand in such situations. When scientists study other scientists, there is a complex interplay of power and knowledge dimensions. Drori and Landau (2011: 25) noted with respect to the nuclear scientists they studied that their own "role as researchers at Gamma resembled that of an equal participant in a conversation in which, regardless of the subject under discussion, the researcher and informant found themselves equally at ease." But several of the authors in Bogner *et al.* (2009) remark on less equal dynamics in the political dimensions of interviewing experts. Indeed, Xymena Kurowska (personal communication, 4 April 2011) remarks on the "blurring between private and professional life" characteristic of the interactions among researchers, think-tank analysts, and practitioners within the landscape of European security research, who depend upon one another "for the reproduction of the setting," at the same time as they occasionally envy one another's lifestyle.

Interpretive researchers also study individuals and groups with less ascribed social power, such as cocktail waitresses (Bayard de Volo 2003), secretaries (Kanter 1977), gang members (Venkatesh 2008), labor union members (Warren 2005), Native American women activists (Prindeville 2004), political campaign volunteers (Super 2010), neighborhood gangs (Whyte 1955/1947, Liebow 1967), homeless women (Liebow 1993), or professionals operating at the limits of the law (Cramer 2008). In such cases, the researcher may have considerably more social power than those with whom she interacts. But power, and powerlessness (Kanter 1977), are also situational, something that research settings may also reflect and determine. In one interview project, some "very old and frail people . . . were seen to have exercised considerable power over the course of the research and to have participated very much on their own terms" (Russell *et al.* 2002: 15, citing an earlier project of Russell's). As Fujii notes:

> When American or European researchers, who are often white, educated, and highly privileged by local standards, enter the [non-American, non-European] world of the researched, they *still* enjoy structural forms of power. People with high social status vis-à-vis potential study participants

cannot entirely control the world they enter, but they can certainly shape it to their liking in various ways.

(Personal communication, 29 August 2009, original emphasis)

These ways include getting instant appointments because of their ascribed status, having computers, cars, and other technologies at their disposal, and the option of paying participants (see Note 7, this chapter).

Interpretive research designs, then, need to anticipate the ways in which these potential relationships might affect the generation of evidence (and one's decisions to write about these encounters). Considering whether research relationships are likely to be neutral, friendly, professional, or possibly even hostile and combative can also be part of preparing oneself emotionally for the research project. As Drori and Landau (2011: 25) observe concerning their interactions with the nuclear scientists:

> [W]e were attributed multiple roles, with distinctive characteristics, such as advocates, consultants, and researchers. The scientists related easily to our role as researchers, even offering their own suggestions regarding methodology and other questions of research. Our role as advocates, the most appealing to the scientists, served as an effective trigger for full-fledged research cooperation. It also provided them an outlet for expressing their own ideas regarding various organizational issues.

They quote one of the scientists who shared with them, extensively, his vision of the desired organizational structure: "'Maybe many of us are frustrated social scientists, you ask me a question and I'll give you an analysis, you want information and I'll give you an interpretation.'" And they remark on the continual awareness of the responsibility demanded by this multiplicity of roles, requiring them constantly to monitor the data they were generating, clearly distinguishing between data for research and data for consulting purposes.

All of this means a requisite attention also to the "presentation of self" (Goffman 1959) in the field. Participants of all status and power levels will size up a researcher quickly, making initial assessments interpreting bodily characteristics (e.g., sex, stature, age, etc.), dress, tone of voice, and manner: all those elements that comprise nonverbal communication. Walby (2010: 651) writes about "policing [his] own gestures and speech acts to hinder respondents' sexualization of [him]," and Lin (2000: 187–8) describes her concern not to convey nervousness to prison staff or inmates: "Both the staff and prisoners usually picked that up [the lack of nervousness] and responded with relief: a visitor who treads each step fearfully reminds everyone, uncomfortably, that the prison is abnormal and that their lives are on display."[9]

Ascribed identity is not directly under the researcher's control: ". . . respondents can read different identities onto us before and during interviews, subverting our attempts to position [ourselves] as researcher[s]" (Walby 2010: 652), a point that holds for other forms of field research. And yet, identities, along with understandings of the research matter at hand, are both produced and contested (as Walby 2010 extensively notes), and researchers can sometimes use the identities participants ascribe to them to their advantage. Cohn (2006), for instance, turned some of her interlocutor's condescension toward her—a more senior, experienced, male professional facing a younger, less professionally experienced woman—in a more productive direction for her interviewing purposes, making herself his student on security issues. Fujii (2010: 233) recounts how the rumor that she was a local woman's long lost daughter led people to identify her as part Rwandan, "not as 'Black', 'Asian', or 'Hispanic' as I would be typed in the USA." That understanding "provided a useful entry point for talking about ethnicity"—key to her research on the genocide in Rwanda. As these examples illustrate, a researcher's "presentation of self" is neither simple nor static, but an ongoing process that rests on self- and other-awareness, learning, and adaptation to the field. Others' constructions of the researcher's identity may also shift over time, as the researcher becomes better known in the field setting.

Interpretive designs cannot be expected to predict and detail all of these intricacies, but those that articulate an awareness of the potential issues (and associated literatures) demonstrate the researcher's readiness to head into the field and negotiate the varieties of relationships that may develop therein. Because they enter others' worlds seeking to understand from the perspective of those studied (rather than as journalists seeking facts, for instance), researchers need to be aware of the ethics entailed in field relationships (see, e.g., Blee 2002, Burgess 1989, Huggins 2002, Humphreys and others 1976, A. Kelly 1989, and Riddell 1989).[10]

Researcher Roles: Six Degrees of Participation

To speak of research in relational terms has implications for the ways in which researchers think about their roles in field settings. In the case of participant observation, the researcher needs to decide the extent to which observation will be coupled with some degree of participation and, if so, the degree and kind of participation in the activities and events taking place in a given site. In short, participation comes in different forms.

The degree and kind of participation may vary, ranging from a role in which the researcher participates as researcher alone, to one in which the researcher is present as both researcher and situational participant, but subordinates the researcher role to the situational one. Participation of the latter sort positions the researcher in dual roles: at the same time that he is participating in his situation-specific role, he is also always observing as researcher (Gans 1976). This includes observing himself as well as others. In the researcher-only role, when responding to something said or done, it is in the capacity as researcher. In the dual role, responses come out of the situation-specific role, rather than the researcher role.

In between these two poles lies a repertoire of role combinations. Some studies may combine several different points along this continuum, linked together like the six degrees of relationship that reportedly separate any two individuals. The researcher studying community development, for instance, may be a "local resident" (*de novo*) participating in community meetings in one set of activities, whereas he is a researcher when interviewing city planning officials in a different set of activities. Autoethnography, which turns the researcher's membership in a class of actors into the object of study, is at the far end of that continuum, coming close to collapsing the distinction between the two roles.

A research design that includes a situation-specific role needs to assess what is feasible in that situation. Depending on the setting, aspects of the role may need to be negotiated with its members, including possible legal and/or ethical dimensions. Situation-specific roles often draw on researchers' a priori knowledge and experiences, including prior membership, abilities, and inclinations. In turning a present or former member situation into a research project, a researcher would want to consider the impact this might have on fellow members, including colleagues and friends. Various factors may limit participatory roles, from physical ability and ablebodiedness (see Chapter 7) to culturally defined gender roles, from a lack of expertise in a project's central activities, where that cannot be learned on the job (e.g., Cramer's, 2008, study of midwifery), to not wishing to risk improper or illegal activity (such as drug-dealing; Venkatesh 2008). The legal and/or ethical implications of the latter need to be anticipated and considered, to the extent possible. Stuffing envelopes as a staff worker in a non-profit organization portends little risk of either legal or ethical problems (at least on the face of it); but a volunteer in, say, a rehab clinic might find herself asked for medical or other advice which, if she gave it, could raise both legal and ethical questions should she lack therapeutic training and a license to practice and put her in violation of written or verbal agreements as a researcher and of the access terms she negotiated. A researcher who has thought through these issues and incorporates them in a research design will be better prepared if faced with their actualization, and the research design itself is likely to be judged more favorably because the issues are considered there explicitly, transparently, and reflexively.

Although for most field researchers, the advantages of being on location are self-evident, in order to explain this to others who are less familiar with them, a research design might well make explicit what is to be gained by the participation being proposed, especially as participating can make research more complex. The primary justification for participation is that it enables researchers to learn more about participants and their relationships to the subject matter of the project, including their activities and ways of thinking about all of these, than they would know without it. Whether sitting with mothers whose children have disappeared (Bayard de Volo 2009), running the winding machine on the shop floor (Shehata 2006), or using an electric shocker to hurry the cattle through a chute to the kill location in a slaughterhouse (Pachirat 2009a: 152), the researcher is potentially able, physically, emotionally, and verbally, to access participants' experiences—of grief and fear, monotony and exhaustion, or solidarity and laughter—and the local knowledge that is embedded and carried in these, including the tacit knowledge underlying embodied practices. As Fenno indicates, in the chapter's epigraph, you are there—in the midst of data generation, "at the source," rather than being the more passive recipient of "given" data (the Latin origin of the term: data are things handed over, given). Reflecting on these participatory experiences may bring initial expectations or assessments into sharp relief, suggesting other ways of understanding than what the researcher initially anticipated.

Another justification is instrumental: depending on the situation, some degree of participation may engender greater trust in the researcher on the part of participants, and this may facilitate interactions important to the co-generation of evidence. Allina-Pisano (2009: 57–9), for instance, recounts how her silence in a day-long meeting in post-Soviet Ukraine unnerved those in attendance: it reminded them of secret police surveillance in earlier times. Her participation as a "normal" member would not have raised eyebrows; it was her silence, in fulfillment of her perceptions of an appropriate researcher role, which generated participants' discomfort and distrust. (This example also shows that it cannot be automatically assumed that observation without participation is either "unobtrusive" or less "intrusive.")

Despite the possibility of extensive degrees of participation in some kinds of settings, contemporary researchers understand that they are not, and usually will not become, full members of that setting. Even "native anthropologists" (Narayan 1993) or "at-home" ethnographers (see Alvesson 2009, Leap 1996)—researchers studying settings of which they are or were at one time members—are commonly only temporary members of the research venue, usually intending at some point to leave to return to their research base.

That said, what is the researcher to observe, and how? In some disciplines and research projects, it is sufficient in designing the study to identify settings, actors, events, texts, archives. It is assumed (and at times, is treated as self-evident) that once on site, the researcher will situate himself in some vantage point that will enable general observation of a range of persons and/or activities and events. This would be the classic case of a participant observer, interview, or ethnographic study of a neighborhood or community or of a school, hospital, or other bureaucracy. Consider Zirakzadeh, for instance, finding a bar stool where he could eat *pintxos* (the Basque version of tapas) and strike up conversations with ETA activists. Increasingly, however, researchers are thinking of such projects in more dynamic ways, in terms of "following" something. One form of research, "shadowing," entails following a lead actor (or more than one) around through her day. This, for example, was Wolcott's (2003/1973) approach in studying a school principal. In more spatially-oriented disciplines, such as planning and human or social geography, following key actors through their own physical terrains, such as homeless men and their places of congregation, is developing into a distinctive method useful in other research inquiries: "footwork" (Hall 2009) or the walking interview (P. I. Jones *et al.* 2008; see also Kusenbach 2003, Pink 2008, Stavrides 2001). In some cases, researchers are using map-making activities as ways of concretizing such movement (Wood 2009). Other researchers, often influenced by science studies and the sociology of knowledge, think of following "facts" (an idea borrowed from Latour and Woolgar's, 1988, study of a scientific laboratory; see also Brandwein 2006), ideas, policy issues, and the like. Following in this way might also entail asking what *work* the entity being followed is doing in its context(s). This is another way of asking about the meanings underlying or embedded in the item(s) in question.

The shift from a seemingly more static study to a more fluid one appears to be linked to changes in research topics (or perceptions of them) from relatively more bounded settings (villages, neighborhoods, departments) to less apparently bounded ones (multi-national corporations, multi-level governmental entities, networks). This has itself given rise to a new term: "multi-sited" studies. "Rhizomatic" studies are another version of this, in which the researcher moves among linked sites, following actors, concepts, issues, objects, or other entities central to the research question (see, e.g., Nicolini 2009).[11] We anticipate that earlier "island anthropologies" and "village sociologies" were themselves not fully bounded, although they may have seemed that way from an outside point of view; researchers certainly moved from one "site" to another within them.

Still, considering a researcher's location in the field setting (discussed further in the next section) in relation to what is "flowing" or otherwise moving through it, and how and where she is going to move about with respect to that position can provide a useful perspective on the research question. We suspect that, given its links to researcher positionality and the anticipation of multiple interpretations (see discussion of intertextuality, Chapter 5), this attention to flow and to following things may catch on as a key characteristic of interpretive research design.

Access, Researcher Roles, and Positionality

Ranchers are notorious about sizing someone up within the first five minutes of meeting them. I've seen it happen over and over, growing up with them. I also knew from growing up around ranchers that as a group, they are notoriously reserved. . . . Oil representatives don't trust anyone. . . . And elected and non-elected officials are guarded when questioned by outsiders.

. . . [A] life lived in Wyoming [US] among ranchers and roughnecks told me that ranchers and oil-men viewed academics as having "agendas." Particularly, environmental agendas. If either of these groups suspected that I meant to do anything other than relate to them and their story or seek their expertise to help inform my research, . . . they . . . would have never opened up to me as much as they did. . . . I needed them to "size me up" from the start as "one of them"—as someone who could be trusted with their story and tell/analyze/interpret it from their perspective, not mine.

Preparing for the interviews, it became clear to me that government officials and oil association executives had become targets of serious criticism from ranchers (their untraditional nemesis) and environmental organizations (their traditional nemesis). This same preparation also told me that ranchers had become wary, even skeptical, of anyone seeking information from them concerning the political conflict I was examining. Once in the room [with the ranchers, oil association directors, or politicians], I made small talk . . . about being a "born and bred" Wyoming boy, or about my first job out of high school as a "roustabout in the oil patch," or that "my dad was a former city administrator in a very small town in Wyoming . . .". As the interviewees found out about me, they saw me as something other than a Ph.D. candidate. . . .

As you might suspect, from my perspective the "presentation of self" is a process that begins first with getting to know whom you are interviewing and then having the wherewithal to step outside of the researcher role long enough to relate to the person being interviewed. It is then that the interview begins. And even then, it's really just a continuation of the conversation you began when you introduced yourself to the interviewee.

—*Robert Forbis*
(Personal communication, 16 December 2010)

For interpretive researchers, matters of access and researcher role raise an additional methodologically relevant issue, related to interpretive research's goal of building contextually grounded knowledge and to its acknowledgment that scholars are human beings with specific histories, capacities, and characteristics. Known as positionality, it has two aspects, one of which might be called demographic, the other, locational or geographic. Forbis's research narrative, above, includes both, as they relate to his desired access to particular field settings and the persons who inhabit them and to his researcher roles.

First, researchers' demographic characteristics and personal backgrounds may be critical to accessing research settings and/or actors. Sex, age, education, physical agility and (dis)ability, class, religion, race-ethnicity, language mastery and accent, birthplace, possessing a driver's license, and other elements in a growing list of intersectional factors comprising individual "identity" can all contribute to generating access to research situations—or to having it blocked. As Schwedler (2006), Ortbals and Rincker (2009), and the essays in "Field Research Methods in the Middle East" (2006) show, none of these factors is an automatic, universal key to open all doors: each one can play either or both ways, sometimes opening doors, sometimes shutting them. Samer Shehata (2006), for instance, notes the extent to which being male enabled entrée to some circumstances in his Egyptian factory studies while shutting off access to other potentially research-related settings. For Walby (2010: 649), it was addressing or avoiding questions concerning his sexuality that either opened up or closed off the conversations he was trying to have.

Second, as field relationships develop and unfold, the types and degrees of access achieved position the researcher geographically in the field setting, which itself can shape access to other circumstances and groups; and this, in turn, can profoundly affect what the researcher sees or does not see, learns and does not learn. This process can take place as one is drawn more deeply into one network rather than another, opening some doors while simultaneously closing down other avenues. Zirakzadeh's (2009) happenstantial refuge with one group of ETA activists rather than another is one example. Alternatively, it may unfold due to organizational or community rhythms or rituals that create various opportunities: the holiday party that enables rubbing shoulders with certain people—a boss, for instance—who might not normally be encountered (Rosen 1988); the ending of a contract or a promotion (Pachirat 2009a). These cases illustrate the extent to which field realities cannot always be anticipated and planned for, requiring flexibility in the field. Despite such limits on planning, researchers need to proactively reflect on the ways in which demographic and locational positionalities might affect their access to research settings, persons, texts, and so forth and—as discussed further in Chapters 5 and 6—on the possible effects of such positionalities on data generation and analysis and ensuing knowledge claims.

Access and Archives

The language of access has been most prominent in ethnographic or other field research, whether within domestic locations or in a country other than the researcher's institutional base. Access issues are also critical for archival research (regardless of the methodological approach). Archives may be restricted; researchers may need an institutional affiliation, letters, or security clearances (the latter, e.g., for classified government documents) to secure entrée. Even here, however, both prior knowledge and flexibility often play a role. As feasible, researchers try to develop some sense ahead of time concerning which archives, and which documents in those archives, are relevant to their research question. At the same time, they need to be open to surprises as they encounter new and previously unknown information, including material that points them to other archives, elsewhere, which had not been part of their initial design plans. In addition, their research may depend on special skills to make sense of—to "access"—the meanings in those documents, such as knowledge of legal terminology, specialists' jargon, or languages other than their mother tongue (see, e.g., Bellhouse 2011, Ferguson 2011, Wingrove 2011).

With respect to sources of artifactual materials (documents, paintings, photographs), difficulties of access can vary, and it is not always useful to equate accessing action settings (neighborhoods, organizations, governmental offices) and actors (experts, officials, town residents) with accessing materials in archives, newspaper morgues, or other locations. In "Western" countries in particular, where archiving and public access are commonplaces, broad public availability of documentary materials may render matters of access to archival materials methodologically insignificant compared to the need to decide *which* among these many texts or images to analyze. The language of "selection" is a better fit for this particular situation (see, e.g., Oren and Kaufman 2006 and the discussion in the next section). For other locations, especially in developing countries, restrictions on the public availability of documentary materials can subordinate selection challenges to the need to identify and locate materials to begin with.

Access versus Case Selection

In thinking through the selection of places and persons in which and with whom the research question might reasonably be explored, interpretive researchers might appear to be enacting the same task as their research colleagues who are engaged in "case selection" for theory testing; but interpretive sensibility and research purposes render the two activities quite different. For positivist researchers, selection and access are typically understood as separate and separable. Consider three examples:

- In experimental research design, the gold standard is the random assignment of cases (individuals) to control and experimental groups in order to render the groups statistically equivalent such that differences arising from the experimental treatment can be assessed. Individuals who are not "accessed" because they decline participation are replaced by others who do agree to participate.
- In survey research design, the bias associated with respondents' self-selection (the bane of the call-in polling so popular in entertainment venues, among other settings) is prevented through random selection from a "sampling frame," as complete a list as possible of the population under study from which the sample is to be drawn. Randomized selection of research participants achieves a sample that is representative of the population being studied, such that inference from the sample to the population is unbiased, in statistical terms. Here, too, those who decline to participate are replaced with others, again chosen randomly from within the sampling frame (although high refusal rates raise the further question of how those who do choose to answer surveys differ from those who opt out).[12]
- In positivist "small n" case study research, selection of cases is complicated by their potential non-equivalence (evident in comparative studies of countries, schools, hospitals, and the like) and, depending on the research question, by the subsequent lack of guaranteed entrée to the places, archives, or individuals (often, elites) that constitute the cases. But the methodological literature is silent on the work involved in *accessing* such cases once selected.[13] Instead, drawing on an experimental template, that literature (e.g., King *et al.* 1994, Gerring 2007) focuses on proper selection to ensure that descriptive and causal inferences are unbiased.[14]

In all three of these, access, if treated at all, appears relatively unproblematic, conceptually. It is as if such selection were entirely within the researcher's power and control, without access difficulties interfering; and one case is treated as if it were as good as another for the purposes of causal inference (which would not be so for constitutive causality). In these three positivist approaches, the concern with case selection is driven by the goal of building general theory: cases do not have value in and of themselves. As Gerring put it with respect to case study research, its purpose "is—at least in part—to shed light on a larger class of cases (a population)" (2007: 20).

For interpretive researchers, by contrast, choices of cases and access are often intertwined—reasonably so, given the research purpose of understanding meaning-making in particular sites. In addition, for interpretive research, both randomized selection and substitutability of one case for another are problematic, for related reasons. We illustrate the point with the example of documentary research, in which the notion of the random selection of texts ("cases") is rarely appropriate or feasible. For one, as mentioned above, random selection requires a sampling frame. Depending on the research question, compiling a complete list of documents from which to sample assumes the availability of and unfettered access to collections that are open and whose materials are organized and catalogued, prior knowledge of what these contain, as well as a priori judgment about which documents are likely relevant—all of which are problematic in various ways from the perspective of interpretive research, as well as the realities of archives and other repositories, especially in the "non-Western" world.[15]

Even more importantly, the possibility of substitution is material: one text, one photograph or painting, or one person is not as good as any other, in all situations. Rather than seeking texts or other cases for purposes of generalization, the interpretive documentary researcher wants not just any text but *those that matter (or mattered) to the agents under study*—another way in which context is significant. An interpretive documentary research strategy follows the "intertextual" trail from initial documents to related ones—Ferguson's "Oh, look, there's another one . . ." experience (quoted in Chapter 1)—as the researcher's knowledge deepens and his or her research question(s) become(s) more nuanced (L. Hansen 2006, C. Lynch 2006; see Chapter 5).[16] The same holds for following ideas and persons in an interview- or observation-based study.

Furthermore, the language of "case selection" implies considerable researcher control—warranted in the case of experimental and much survey research, but potentially problematic in field research where denial of access to particular archives, persons or other sorts of "cases" cannot always be solved by simple selection of an equivalent, replacement document, individual, or case. For these reasons, the language of "case selection" is not appropriate to interpretive research design: it fails to recognize the significant ways in which access may be contingent on the identity of the researcher, as if *any* researcher, in *any* circumstance, possesses the ability to select *any* case at will.[17] Interpretive design needs to be concerned with the choices of settings, actors, archives, and so forth and with a focus on access and its relational dimensions. By contrast with the language of selection, the language of access recognizes the embodied and inescapably social aspects of the research process.

Regardless of methodological approach, denial of access to field or archival settings is possible no matter how assiduously contacts have been cultivated. For instance, a researcher studying public hearings on impending urban renewal might find those hearings delayed by months or even years. Or increased press scrutiny of an agency the researcher had planned to study could mean that previously supportive gatekeepers withdraw their approval. The promulgation of the Common Rule in the US in the context of Institutional Review Board policies and practices, by making consent more bureaucratic and legalistic, has also complicated researcher negotiations for access. Still, there remains a key distinction between positivist and interpretive approaches to the relationship between access and knowledge claims, and it hinges on the centrality of *contextuality* to the research. Because the meaning-making of those studied is intimately linked with context, the complex issues of researcher access—including the relative power of individuals and groups, the possible kinds and degrees of participation, and positionality—need attention from the very beginning in designing an interpretive research project. These issues are understood as methodologically relevant to the research project, and they therefore need to be considered and taken into account in its design.

Design Flexibility: Control and Requisite Researcher Skills

Assuming that access can be achieved to one extent or another, together with a research-appropriate role, an interpretive design needs to consider the implications of contextuality for the execution of the research. Specifically, a researcher's expectation (or that of evaluators, such as thesis or dissertation supervisors or grant reviewers) that the project will be implemented *as designed* is likely to be frustrated. Interpretive research designs *must* be flexible due to field realities, stemming from participants' agency. The researcher lacks control over research participants as well as over unfolding events, as Fenno notes (in the epigraph). But that is a principal reason that the researcher himself goes to these settings: he is interested in how meaning-making occurs *there*—without the kinds of controls on participants that characterize positivist approaches.[18] Three aspects of this matter are worth elaborating: the relationship between control and positivist approaches; the logics of control and interpretive research processes; and the resulting skills and competences needed for interpretive field research.

Control and Positivist Research Design

The general expectation of positivist research designs as presented in methods textbooks, at least, is that they by and large can, should be, and are implemented as initially designed. In a laboratory setting this is a feasible expectation. Hinging only on human subjects protections, the researcher utilizing a laboratory has complete control over the research setup, participants' recruitment, the tasks they will be asked to perform or will be subjected to, and so on. It is because of these controls—and the typically time-limited tasks requested of experimental "subjects" (a term originating in medical and psychological research; Danziger 1990: 53–4)—that the Principal Investigator (PI) can hand over data "collection" work to trained assistants. The PI's role in all of this is to design the study, analyze the data, write the research report, and train and manage lab assistants, relieved of the responsibility of having herself to interact with every research participant.

All of the processes that the PI has detailed in the design—recruitment strategies, scripts for research assistants to read to participants, protocols for debriefing participants, etc.—are expected to be executed without significant variation. If variations in these processes do occur, it may mean that research results will have to be discarded: according to the logic of this research approach, such variations, rather than the treatment variable of interest, may have produced the experimental effects observed. This idea is extended to non-laboratory-based research, such as surveys, focus groups, and positivist case study research. In research designs for those kinds of projects, the underlying logic of inquiry remains the same in that variations in execution of the design are understood as liable to produce "flawed" results.[19] For example, Yin (1989: 50) tells case study researchers that "if the relevant research questions really do change, the investigator should simply start over again, with a new research design," noting that shifting research questions produce "the largest criticism of case studies." Likewise, Gerring (2007: 149) recommends redesigning a study "after the new (or revised) hypothesis has been formulated" and then collecting additional evidence. Otherwise, in his view, the study should be termed "exploratory" or the evidence produced based on the initial design should be "jettison[ed], or deemphasize[d]."

Underpinning the expectations for invariant implementation of a research *design* may be its metaphoric source in architecture: a poorly designed building or bridge may crumble or collapse due to mistakes in the architect's blueprint; the designer's failure to understand the physical world—with whose constraints engineers have to contend—signals professional incompetence. So, it seems, is the positivist understanding of experimental research design: any need to vary from it in the execution of that blueprint is deemed a design flaw and a professional failure. This is part of what colors the negative and erroneous understanding of interpretive research design's flexibility.

The Logics of Control and Interpretive Research

Howard Becker (1998: 193) contests the kind of logic that requires researchers to "gather new data from a new sample" before they can take advantage of new insights:

Such an unrealistic requirement would, of course, put an end to qualitative historical research, because there is no gathering a new sample, and would make studies like Lindesmith's, based on interviews with hard-to-find addicts, impossible in any practical sense. More to the point, it treats as a sin what is actually a major scientific virtue: the willingness to revise your thinking in light of experience, the dialogue of evidence and ideas Ragin [citation] puts such emphasis on.[20]

Yet it is not just openness to revisions that is at play in interpretive research. For one, the interpretive goal of understanding the meaning-making of those studied (as contrasted with the positivist goal of mirroring the world with degrees of certainty) eliminates the concerns associated with positivist forms of causality. Changes in design cannot, therefore, be understood as threats to the trustworthiness of a research endeavor that does not understand causality in this way (as discussed in Chapter 3).

But more than that, positivist expectations for inflexible design implementation—as well as associated judgments that variations from the initial design threaten its trustworthiness—do not fit the logic of interpretive research. Flexible design is central to interpretive research for two reasons.

First, the abductive and hermeneutic reasoning that undergird interpretive research processes are both built on successive phases of learning: the researcher starts with what he knows, as encapsulated in the initial design, but his investigation builds on itself in a reiterative, recursive fashion. Although he begins with insights from existing literature and/or prior knowledge of the field setting, if these insights prove unhelpful, it follows from this logic of inquiry that they must be modified, including being discarded, if necessary. Interpretive logics and processes see researcher sense-making and learning as deepening with ongoing experiences in the field. As Drori and Landau (2011: 25) write, their research relationships with the nuclear scientists in the organization they studied were "based on ongoing reciprocity and mutual learning," a relationship that gained them "access to almost all divisions, branches, and laboratories," which itself allowed them "to observe a wide range of organizational activities and situations, within certain limits." Expanding and elaborating on the initial research question in its redesign is, in light of such ongoing learning, normal.

Second, a researcher entering the settings of research participants (rather than inviting them to the researcher's laboratory or controlling them through invariant survey questions or interaction scripts) lacks control over those settings and their individual and organizational inhabitants. Rather than being research "subjects" who participate in (positivist) research on the researcher's terms, in interpretive research it is the researcher who participates in the locals' activities, in their settings, on their turf. Participants are recognized as having their own agency over their own movements, meaning-making, will to participate, and so forth. This means that they are understood as having the power to affect initial research designs actively in various ways, such as refusing to accede to requests for entry, for interviews, for reading permissions in archives, and so on. Even if they do not decline altogether, participants may still desire and choose to participate in ways other than those the researcher has designed for them. On the other hand, they may also be enthusiastic partners in the (co-)generation of evidence (as discussed in Chapter 5), assisting the researcher in learning about their settings, of which they have local knowledge.

But the researcher cannot know which of these (or what combination) she will meet in the field; and so the design—as well as the researcher!—needs to be flexible. As Walby (2010: 647, 645) observes,

> Introduction of a speech act or gesture into the conversation between researcher and respondent can have unanticipated consequences for the rest of the dialogue. . . . However much scripts and roles guide our interactions with others, there is always an open tendency, such that the meanings which will be achieved from an encounter cannot be fully anticipated.

Interpretive Researcher Competence and Skill

That research participants are considered (and treated) as having their own agency is not problematic for interpretive researchers in the ways it would be for experimental and other positivist researchers, who depend on a level of compliance, and even submissiveness, from "subjects" in order to execute their designs invariably. The interpretive focus on participants' worlds, their local knowledge, means that the researcher cedes control to them as the experts in their own lives. However, this very lack of control means that interpretive researchers need to cultivate particular competencies and skills to maneuver effectively in the field(s) inhabited by agential research participants, skills not required of those following a positivist methodology.

Accepting the limitations of researcher control in field settings—recognizing that participants are active protagonists in their own worlds—means conceiving of research as fundamentally and dynamically relational in form and character (rather than contractual)—with all the attendant rewards, uncertainties, and risks life in "natural" research settings entails. Whether conducting conversational interviews or observing (with whatever degrees of participation), recognizing the agency of research participants means *the researcher* has to adapt to the field setting (rather than the *research participant* adapting to the experimental setting or the categorical choices available in a survey questionnaire). Instead of the skill set needed for executing a research design as invariably as humanly possible (and, later, for choosing and running appropriate statistical tests), the researcher needs an openness to learning and change, the willingness to revise thinking in light of experience (noted above), and a high tolerance for ambiguity, together with improvisational skills and an understanding of research design that makes room for their use (and, later, the ability to manage the myriad details of observations, interviews, and documents encoded in words and to choose and apply the most data-appropriate method[s] from among the many available interpretive analytical techniques).

Let us turn, once again, to the research of Zirakzadeh (2009; discussed initially in Chapter 2) to illustrate these several points. When he set out to conduct research on ETA separatists in Basque country, Zirakzadeh arrived with a research design that was strongly informed by the literature that characterized his theoretical approach. He learned, however, that that literature was a poor guide to the lay of the land. Instead of starting over *de novo* (as some positivist methodologists, such as Yin, 1989, and others would have had him do), he improvised with respect to his existing plan, revising his research design in the field.

One story from that research, alluded to previously, clearly illustrates the kind of "on the fly" revisions that are commonplace *and considered not only normal but legitimate* in such research. When, by happenstance, he ducked for cover from police shooting at members of one ETA group and found himself—"in sheer desperation" (2009: 105)—sharing the doorway with some of them, he was taken for a sympathizer by group members. That evening, he found himself the center of attention at the bar they frequented, where he had hitherto been ignored. But now, he also found himself *persona non grata* among other ETA groups from whose perspective he was no longer "neutral." A particular self-protective impulse, a particular doorway, made a world of difference to his research.

We see in this example an illustration of a researcher's willingness to revise his thinking, as Becker put it. This means being open to new experiences and insights and being open to learning new things as the research unfolds. Stacia Zabusky, in her ethnography of the European Space Agency (1995: 129), described the need for "being poised for movement, sensitive to flows and trajectories, . . . to disruptions and re-orientations. I had to be prepared to ride the ongoing currents of capital, people, and services . . . ." The inability to know ahead of time what will happen and to be able to plan for it—constraints that inhere in this openness and flexibility—requires a high tolerance for ambiguity. On a practical level, a rigid design that includes an invariable protocol for interactions in the field or in an interview would likely lead participants to see interpretive researchers as incompetent—"socially stupid," lacking in social intelligence (see, e.g., Gardner 1983, Goleman 1995)—in their inability to respond in ways appropriate to the situation at hand (see also Burkhart 1996: 34). Or it may lead participants simply to be bored, as Zirakzadeh (2009) says his respondents were (see Chapter 2), because the pre-planned questions are out of touch with their own lived realities and the researcher is incapable—by virtue of the constraining research design, not intelligence—of translating them in ways that make more sense to those involved.

The need to interact effectively with dynamic human interlocutors in a dynamic field setting requires the ability to improvise. As musicians and other performance artists know, improvisation does not mean "making things up" *de novo*; rather, improvisation is a skill that is learned and perfected through practice (Yanow 2001, 2009). Improvisation's "yes, and" attitude, for example, requires a researcher to listen to her interlocutors and respond in ways that build on their ideas; a negative response—a "yes, but"—can block and even shut down the exchange. And improvisational skills cannot be applied invariably across all participants. Instead, the researcher needs to be attuned to various participants' styles of interaction and sensibilities (e.g., which topics are "off limits"; Fujii 2010) and adjust her responses accordingly. Observational and fieldnote practices also need to be adapted to the context of the field setting (discussed in Chapter 5).

Interpretive field researchers, then, need listening skills, improvisational skills, and the knowledge and confidence that being flexible in the face of field realities is an appropriate and legitimate response, befitting this logic of inquiry.[21] An orientation toward flexibility and even improvisation is also part of an interpretive sensibility in archival research. Moving from text to text in a sort of textual ethnography (see also Darnton 2003, P. Jackson 2006), the researcher looks for text-based clues that will lead in fruitful directions, and he wants and needs to be able to follow these.

Because this skill set is learned over time, through the doing of research in a kind of apprenticeship, guided by more experienced researchers (dissertation advisors, more senior colleagues), and because the researcher is herself the instrument of inquiry and sense-making, in interpretive research the PI interacts directly with research participants (perhaps with the aid of a translator, as needed). Even when research assistants are involved, they will more commonly work in such an apprentice-like fashion, closely supervised and learning their research craft alongside the lead researcher (see, e.g., Maynard-Moody and Musheno 2006).[22] This presents a strong contrast with the training of research assistants in conducting experiments or executing telephone or field surveys: like the research design, their training is also "front-loaded," with learning taking place prior to the "application" of the "instrument." After training, they are commonly left on their own to execute the research (and their training entails learning *not* to react to the personal characteristics or inquiries of the experimental "subjects" or survey respondents).

Why produce a research *design* if flexibility is the rule rather than the exception? Does such flexibility render designing inconceivable? As discussed in Chapter 2, knowing that designs change does not excuse the researcher from asking significant and well-developed questions at the starting point in the circle-spiral of learning and understanding. First, interpretive research takes place in a theoretical context, and a research design is useful for considering previous research and placing the proposed project in its context, even if—or, as often, when—theoretically-based expectations are dashed by field realities. Second, it is certainly possible that a researcher's best attempt to access sources of evidence will fail, perhaps by chance, e.g., the vacationing, transferred, or suddenly-deceased senior executive whom the researcher had anticipated interviewing. Or evidence may not be available due to the agency of research participants and non-participants in the field who refuse access. Such unavailability may be unfortunate; Zirakzadeh's desire to research all ETA groups, for example, was stymied. However, although his actions cost him access to some groups because they no longer perceived him as politically neutral, he gained fuller access to one group, and all of the unfolding events led him to a greater appreciation for the complexity of the social and political landscape he was researching. Thinking through his initial research design provided him a baseline against which to compare field realities; it was the starting point from which learning could proceed.

Flexible interpretive research designs are, then, not only possible; they are needed, because they focus a researcher's attention on possibilities and limitations that need to be anticipated, including the flexibility to revise them in the field. Although at odds with the positivist conception of design, flexibility is a mark of competence in interpretive research and of a good interpretive research design. Its absence will stymie researchers in their efforts to generate data, the topic to which we now turn.

5

THE RHYTHMS OF INTERPRETIVE RESEARCH II

Understanding and Generating Evidence

Having thought through the locations in which and the actors or texts among whom or which he will search for evidence to address his research question, what sort of evidence should an interpretive researcher look for? What is its ontological status, and how does he indicate in the research design what he will be seeking? We continue here with the rhythms of interpretive research, making a second pass at matters of accessing settings and actors, researcher role, degrees of participation, and positionality within the setting, but now engaging another level in our hermeneutic–phenomenological circle-spiral.

Much as "empirical" has at times been understood (and perhaps in many corners of academia still is) to mean "quantitative" research alone, "evidence" has in the last decade or so often been construed narrowly as that which results from experimental research designs—especially under the influence of the contemporary "evidence-based" movement, such as in medicine, policy, and management (for critical assessments, see, e.g., Black 2001, Clements 2004, Parsons 2002, "The Evidence-Based Policy Movement" 2002, Trinder with Reynolds 2000). But "evidence" has broader meanings than that (as does "empirical"). For interpretive researchers, empirical evidence is understood as coming in a variety of forms, with no single form pre-judged as superior to another (e.g., privileging "hard" data over "soft" ones). Data occur in various shapes because they emerge from the varieties of human activity, from physical artifacts (trophies, paintings, built spaces) to acts (performance evaluation, company picnics, caring for others) by different actors (workers, scholars, organizations, governments, societies) to language use (in politicians' speeches, magazine articles, political cartoons).

In this chapter, we discuss the character of evidence from an interpretive ontological and epistemological position. We engage not only the variety of its forms, but also the ways in which it is "generated" (rather than "collected") and, in many circumstances, co-generated between researcher and research participants, as well as by researchers as they work with research-related documents and other materials. Field practices for generating evidence should be discussed in a research design, including how the researcher intends to map the study terrain (literally and/or figuratively) for exposure and intertextuality.

The Character of Evidence: (Co-)Generated Data and "Truth"

Positivist research designs appear to assume that the data for a project are in some sense lying around in a field, just waiting for a researcher to collect them. This ontological status of the material that constitutes evidence for a project hinges on an understanding of "evidence" that rests on the etymology of "data." Meaning things that are "given" (as noted in Chapter 4), it suggests that evidence exists independently from the research project that searches for it. The challenge for the researcher is to locate the data and collect them. This makes sense from a perspective that sees the research world and the researcher as completely separate, and separable. Moreover, analysis of those collected data means assessing findings' proximity to "real world" situations—with what degree of certainty can they be said to provide an accurate reflection of the world studied?—leading to the expectation that all research designs should begin with hypotheses that are falsifiable (through whatever means of testing is appropriate to the methods being used).

But interpretive researchers see the research world and the researcher as entwined, with evidence being brought into existence through the framing of a research question and those actions in the research setting that act on that framing. In this view, data have no prior ontological existence as data outside of the framework of a research project: the research question is what renders objects, acts, and language as evidence—for that specific research question. Rather than being "given," in this view data are created, at the very least by the research focus, which distinguishes among acts, events, persons, language, etc., that are relevant to the research and those that are not. Complete, all-encompassing perception and description are humanly impossible, whether in everyday or in research contexts: the "frames" or "lenses" in one's mind's eye filter out those elements of the perceptual world that are not central to concern in a given moment, and they "filter in" those elements that are relevant. Research is conducted with different foci, and in each of these the researcher superimposes a frame—the research question—on actors' lived experiences of cultural, social, political, economic, and psychic realities, in the past, present, and/or over time.

Seeing, in other words, is always partial. That conceptual and perceptual act is a selective one, and the research question "tells" the researcher what the research-relevant data and their likely sources—places, events, persons, documents, other objects—are. Consider, for instance, the specks of dust on Martin Luther King's shoes as he delivered his "I have a dream" speech. Few scholars or commentators mention them because they are of no consequence for understanding what is deemed to matter about that event (Jacqueline Stevens, personal communication, 2 September 2010). Imagine, then, a forensic investigation in which such details might, in fact, be the very key to understanding![1]

In selecting things and people, events and acts to attend to, as relevant to the research question at hand, the researcher may be said to "generate" data through research processes.[2] But more, still, than that: from an epistemological perspective, the interpretive researcher is trying to understand things, events, and so on from the perspective of everyday actors in the situation or, in the case of archival research, the equivalent in the form of written or drawn representations of or reflections on contemporaneous activities. Admitting of the possibility (and legitimacy, from a scientific perspective) of local knowledge in the search for understanding contextualized concepts and actor meaning-making of events, etc., opens the door to knowledge generated by others than the scientist alone. Sense-making by the researcher depends, in this view, on sense-making by those actors, who are called upon to explain them to the researcher (whether literally, in interviews, or in the common conversations of everyday living, or less directly, in written or other records that constitute the material traces of acts, things, and words). We might then say that research project evidence is "co-generated" by actors and researcher together—a statement that could be extended to the interactions of a researcher with research-related texts, whether historical or contemporary. Texts' authors or paintings' artists—even those still living—may not be able to "talk back" to researchers directly, but interpretive scholars doing historical work have been innovative in developing intertextual and other techniques to check their own interpretations of those authors' intended meanings as understood in their own times and by subsequent interpreters (e.g., Brandwein 1999, 2006, 2011; see, also, Fay 1996, Chapters 8 and 9).[3]

Understanding data to be co-generated means that the character of evidence in an interpretive project cannot be understood as objectively mirroring or measuring the world. The researcher is not outside that which is under study. Moreover, in field and archival research focused on meaning-making, the "research instrument" is the researcher in his or her particularity, as Van Maanen (1996) has argued with respect to ethnography. A methodological starting point for interpretive research design, then, is that both the researcher's prior knowledge and the embodiment of that knowledge may affect the data, whether these are interactively co-produced (as in interviews and participatory interactions) or where co-production means the researcher interacting with documents and/or other physical materials. A different researcher, possessed of different characteristics and prior knowledge, conducting the "same" set of interviews or examining the same materials, may (co-)generate data that vary in content and form from those produced by another researcher. Whereas this is what inter-rater reliability measures in positivist research are seeking to control for and prevent, in interpretive research it is not perceived as a threat to knowledge claims or research trustworthiness. Instead, researchers seek to be as transparent as possible about how they generated their evidence and the knowledge claims based on that, including the ways in which their own personal characteristics and background have contributed to that data generation. This is part of the notion of positionality discussed in Chapter 4 (see Chapter 6 for further discussion of how researchers check their sense-making).

Moreover, the potential existence of such differences among researchers says nothing about greater or lesser "accuracy" or "truth" of the data because it is expected that research participants respond to the particularity of researchers. For example, if a research participant is female, and male and female researchers interviewing her co-generate different interview evidence, it does not follow that one set of interview materials is "false" and the other "true." Instead, differences may reflect gender power differentials (among many possible explanations), and the interpretive researcher would be expected to make these transparent, reflect on them, and consider their contribution to the knowledge claims advanced (discussed further in Chapter 6). Watson (2011: 210) pointedly observes that "[a]mong most academic researchers there is surely some awareness that philosophers like Austin (1962) long ago established that speech is action (and never just 'saying'), and social scientists like Goffman (1959) showed that all communication has a 'presentation of self' dimension."[4]

The scientific import of participants' responses lies in the significance of what they and/or other situational materials narrate relative to the researcher's overall developing understanding—the parts having meaning in relation to the whole (as described in Chapter 2 relative to the hermeneutic circle). This requires a heightened transparency about analytic processes, achieved through reflexivity. Walby (2010: 645) comments on the "reflexivity [that] is part of the relationality of the encounter," with respondents exercising reflexivity in the interview every bit as much as the researcher is. As Fujii (2010) shows, it is not that researchers (as with others) cannot detect lies, but that lies, rumors, inventions, denials, evasions, and silences are themselves potentially data that are relevant to the unfolding analysis.[5] To put it somewhat differently, interpretive researchers are as interested in the frontstage as they are in the backstage, in Goffman's (1959) terms, or in what is made publicly legible, on view in the open square, as much as in what is hidden behind the façade or masked in the blind spot—to draw in the "Johari window" (Luft and Ingham 1955)—without attributing a "realer" ontological status to what is "behind" the presentation of self than to that very presentation. Although such situations are difficult to foresee, researchers might anticipate their possibility in the research design, depending on the research question, and discuss their potential implications for knowledge claims.

Positivist–qualitative researchers, by contrast, hold out for the possibility of objectivity in their interviews (and other data "collecting")—that is, for their ability to generate knowledge from a point external, conceptually, to the research setting. This is what explains the treatment of researchers' personal characteristics (including their prior knowledge) as irrelevant to knowledge creation (see Note 8, Chapter 4); and it is what, in that view, makes the replicability of interview and observational data by another researcher conceptually possible (discussed further in Chapter 6 and in connection with data archiving in Chapter 7). From this perspective, unless lies are being treated as a form of data, they are seen as errors that undermine accurate representation of what really occurred or beliefs or feelings truly held.

In interpretive research practice, researchers' prior knowledge and personal characteristics are actively theorized in considering the trustworthiness of knowledge claims (see discussion in Chapter 6).[6] At the design stage, researchers can try to anticipate concrete possibilities, e.g., how their persona may affect access to, and interaction with, various kinds of people or situations in particular research settings. Still, as Shehata (2006) details, researcher identity, too, is co-constructed: research participants are always "reading" the researcher's presentation of self, looking for signs (e.g., of equality or condescension, sympathy, fear, hostility) and interpreting and acting on them, much as we all do in ordinary, non-research, everyday life. This means that at the design stage, such anticipation can only be preparatory and conjectural, rather than predictive.

Understanding data to be co-generated also clarifies why use of criteria appropriate to positivist research designs, such as replicability (further discussed in Chapter 6), can mislead designers (and evaluators) of interpretive research. For example, if evidence is not understood as objectively mirroring or measuring the research world, the positivist standard of falsifiability, which rests on data findings' close approximation of reality, needs to be replaced with other approaches to the assessment of interpretive researchers' knowledge claims. The inadequacy of this standard for application to interpretive research is clearest in its statistical incarnation in the form of Type I and Type II errors, concepts that posit a "true" world (a "population") that can be misrepresented by a randomly drawn sample in two possible ways (either the false acceptance of a hypothesis that is contrary to that "true" world or its false rejection when it is a "true," accurate conjecture). This statistical device requires researchers to assign probabilities to these types of errors (i.e., levels of statistical significance that indicate confidence in the accuracy of the sample data: "confidence intervals")—which further testifies to the positivist epistemological presupposition that researchers are capable of getting closer and closer to that singular truth. In interpretive research, to the contrary, the goal is not to ascertain the singular truth of the "research world" but its multiple "truths" as understood by the human actors under study (or as expressed through their various artifacts)—including the potential for conflicting and contradictory "truths." The expectation, then, that all research designs should contain "falsifiable hypotheses" reveals a misunderstanding of the character and purposes of interpretive research.

Forms of Evidence: Word-Data and Beyond

In a key departure from positivist researchers, who approach data generation in the expectation that the evidence created by research processes will, ideally, be capable of being turned into the quantitative indicators constituting a "data set,"[7] interpretive researchers do not privilege quantitative forms of data over other forms. Instead, they engage data-generating tasks in the expectation that the evidence created by their research processes will typically retain in analysis the form it had in its origins. This is most often the form of word-data, but interpretive research also encompasses numerical data, such as accounting reports or accident statistics, when that is their situated form (e.g., Czarniawska-Joerges 1992, Gusfield 1981, Munro 2001).

Interpretive researchers might also generate quantitative indicators that "stick close to the ground," so to speak, in the sense that the logic behind the indicator is transparent (as in a relative frequency measure, by contrast with a regression coefficient). For example, to compare pre- and post-"9/11" US media representations of Saudi Arabia, Azerbaijan, and Kazakhstan, Oren and Kauffman (2006: 119) used relative frequencies of words' appearances, a statistic that adjusts the absolute number of references to thematic representations of those states (e.g., "oil exporter," "political repression") in terms of the total number of all references to each state (for the media sources selected from a wide range of newspapers). These statistics enabled them to show, for example, that references to Saudi-born terrorists had increased as a proportion of the (increased) overall coverage of Saudi Arabia after 9/11 (2006: 141). They go on, then, to more nuanced, interpretive readings of the changes in coverage of "terrorism" compared to other thematic representations ("oil exporter") within and between states. (These examples put the lie to the idea that it is the use of numbers that marks the difference between quantitative and qualitative or interpretive methods!)

This expansive and inclusive view of evidence-types has considerable importance for research design. A researcher needs to think in depth about how the forms of the evidence to be generated might relate to the initial research question. Does the research question point to the significance of meaning in the form of stories that might be gleaned from particular documents, letters, or reports identified? Might situational meaning be conveyed through the design and materials of a building or the layout of a neighborhood (which might add spatial analysis to a research design)? Or is the research question best explored through persons' conduct, and if so, what does the researcher anticipate being able to observe, and why are such observations crucial to the project? As a brief example, a policy project could begin with government documents whose official, collective meanings might be contrasted with street-level workers' understandings of those policies, the latter generated through interviews or, as in Maynard-Moody and Musheno (2003), directed story-telling. In turn, observations of those workers' acts may reveal yet other ways to analyze both official policy and individual workers' or clients' articulated views. Because of the time-intensive character of these various modes of generating data in their several forms, a research design needs to demonstrate a sensitivity to the potential contribution that various data forms can and cannot make to the project.

A mismatch between research question and the choice of data-generating method(s) or of kinds of settings, actors, texts, etc.—or even of time of day or season—is the key failing of a research design. That mismatch does not arise due to necessary changes arising from field realities. Instead, it is a matter of design logic in preparing the research project, and it can—or should—be caught in reviewing the research design long before the researcher heads to the field. Mismatches are produced when the particular method chosen will not yield the kinds of data the researcher needs to address his question, or when the kinds of data the researcher anticipates generating are not appropriate sources for the sorts of evidence needed to explore the research question she is puzzling about. Research based on interviews with physicians or on medical records review, for example, cannot generate data useful for a research question concerning the mutually influencing interactions between patients and doctors; some form of observation of such interactions would be needed so that the design generates data relevant to the research focus. Or, for research that seeks to understand from their perspectives why impoverished citizens continually re-elect wealthy representatives, for instance, data from expert interviews with pollsters and political psychologists will not help. Experts' views, while important for certain research purposes, are still removed from the firsthand sense-makings of patients or citizens; and so if the research question focuses on the latter, there is a poor fit between it and the proposed data sources on which these two research designs rest.

Although there is no simple, general test in interpretive research for assessing ahead of time what evidence will be generated, the character of different kinds of data sources—documents, participant observation, interviews, material artifacts, audio-visual materials—suggests whether these will yield the "right" kinds of evidence: evidence that will be appropriate to and adequate for the question specified. Interpretive researchers need to think through the broad array of evidentiary possibilities that might be available to them in their chosen settings and determine which are appropriate to their research topic. In the design itself they might explain how their choices of data sources and forms, and the methods for generating these, connect logically to their research question.

Mapping for Exposure and Intertextuality

Once the specific field setting or archive or set of actors has been chosen and initial access granted, where within it is a researcher to begin? Interpretive "mapping" in research design means anticipating "the lay of the land" in a particular research site for the purposes of "exposure" and "intertextuality."

Interpretive researchers believe in the possibility of multiple interpretations of the social and political events and worlds they study. The concept of exposure rests on the notion that the researcher wants to encounter, or to be exposed to, the wide variety of meanings made by research-relevant participants of their experiences, whether in face to face encounters or through written records. It rests further on the idea that occupants of various positions within a research setting might be expected to have different views on the subject under study. Interpretive researchers anticipate that experiences and views will vary according to participants' locations, literally and metaphorically, in the field of study: a neighborhood within a community (especially where these reflect class, race-ethnic, or other demographic factors that might be of interest to the researcher because they impact on experience and shape sense-making); a hierarchical position within an organization (because what one sees of and knows about organizational activities changes with exposure to different aspects of its work practices); a status and/or power position within a political configuration (e.g., party, legislature; for similar reasons). Participants, in other words, have their own "positionalities" analogous to researchers'.

The goal of mapping is to maximize research-relevant variety in the researcher's exposure to different understandings of what is being studied—particular events, policies, organizations, ways of life, and so forth. Such exposure to ideas and interpretations can require meeting and engaging different actors, in different roles, at different levels of responsibility, in different locations in the field. These can be different departments, horizontally, across a corporate hierarchy or different levels of a bureaucracy (e.g., Pachirat's, 2009a, view of activities on the floor from the catwalk of the slaughterhouse); different neighborhoods within a community; different contending parties within a social movement (à la Zirakzadeh's intention to engage different groups of ETA activists); different members of a social group. Interpretive research can also entail shadowing a single actor (e.g., a public figure in a leadership position; a CEO) which gains exposure of a different sort—e.g., to that key actor's network, way of life, organizational or community "map." Analogously, in a document study, a researcher might select documents that reflect the many different viewpoints actors had expressed concerning historical events.

The interpretive researcher maps these positional differences across research participants in the research setting. Mapping in this metaphoric sense means identifying the different "kinds" of people or roles (e.g., shop floor workers, agency directors, community leaders, paraprofessionals), the various locations, and the different kinds and sources of documents and other artifacts that may be available in the community, polity, organization, or other setting under study. Activities and people may vary not only by location in the field but also by time of day, day of week, and season—in sync with customs, standard operating procedures, and other rhythms that characterize the lived experience of research participants. The differences of interpretation and meaning that can emerge from exposure of this sort provide, depending on the research question, precisely the type of material that is of interest to interpretive researchers. Exposure supports interpretation.

Mapping in this way also points to the diverse forms of evidence that might be available, from interviews to objects to written reports or speeches. These can be "read" across each other in intertextual fashion for what they reveal about different interpretations of particular events, persons, disputes, and so forth. Its place in social science credited to Julia Kristeva's mid-twentieth-century writings, drawing in this case on Mikhail Bakhtin, the concept of intertextuality has a long history in Biblical hermeneutics and literary analyses of poetry and fiction, referring to the ways in which one text invokes another through the repetition of a key phrase, thereby drawing the other text's meaning into the understanding of the focal one. To speak in English, for example, of a serious storm as "raining for forty days and forty nights" invokes the story of Noah told in Genesis. As L. Hansen (2006: 8) writes, "Texts build their arguments and authority through references to other texts: by making direct quotes or by adopting key concepts and catch phrases" (see also Weldes 2006).

We extend the term in metaphoric fashion beyond texts alone to the ways in which different types of data draw on ("cite") material from other kinds of data, such that the researcher can "read across" them in interpreting meaning. Here, it is not just the appearance in one text or text-analogue of another; it is the active sense-making of the researcher, seeing "intertextual" links across data sources in ways that contribute to the interpretation of those data. As Brandwein (2006: 243, n. 24) observes, "Terms gain their meaning from their place within an extensive network, and in order to understand these terms, [researchers] must fully trace the entire network." Interpretive researchers "read" evidence analytically from a variety of sources "across" the experienced reality of the situation under study (whether rendered in literal texts or, analogously, in acts and/or physical artifacts, historical or current), to assess meaning-making around a particular idea, concept, or controversy. Prior knowledge of terms and concepts and theories that may usefully inform that reading is key. A researcher analyzing the US National Aeronautic and Space Administration, for instance, would miss something of significance if he did not know that it named its Enterprise spaceships, at many Americans' requests, after the science fiction Star Trek's fleet (Weldes 2003). Intertextual readings of this sort look for the dimensionality, ambiguity, and possible contradictions that might arise from broad examination of evidence, the researcher remaining open to the possibility of consensus and agreement without presuming or privileging it. It is seeing this intertextuality, and drawing on it in analysis, that leads to the "thickness" of interpretation—hearing in the Jewish trader's story (in Geertz's field research example) echoes of the Berber tribesmen's logic, and so on, in ways that enable analytic sense-making.[8]

Mapping for exposure and intertextuality is closely tied, in other words, to epistemological presuppositions and knowledge claims: the wider the map, the more varied the exposure, and the more transparent the account of these, the clearer the researcher's knowledge base and the more trustworthy the claims. In discussing the construction of memory, Wood (2009: 126) notes her skepticism concerning respondents' memories of having heard a radio broadcast of a tape in which a pilot is heard asking headquarters if he should really bomb streets where he sees civilians. Finding the same report, later, in two written sources, one academic, the other journalistic—what we are here calling intertextuality—leads her to modify her skepticism. This transparency enables a reader to follow her thinking and enhances our trust in her analysis and knowledge claims.[9]

These three concepts—mapping, exposure, and intertextuality—hold for archival or other documentary research, as well as for interview and participant observational studies. Here, exposure represents the often circuitous process of locating documents that will enable the researcher to map different, perhaps contentious, views in the historical account. It also may point the researcher toward other documents or archives elsewhere than what were planned for in the research design (C. Lynch 2006). L. Hansen's use of the concept of intertextuality (2006; see, esp., Chapter 4) in reference to following citations from document to document likewise builds on a researcher's exposure to initial texts that lead to yet other texts in a hermeneutic spiral fashion.

The concept of exposure can be contrasted with the idea of "sampling" as used in qualitative methods—whether purposive (the intentional selection of persons, settings, or documents thought to have something to contribute to the study); snowball (in which one person, typically, or document leads to the next); or theoretical (the intentional selection of persons, settings, or documents based on analytic grounds, as suggested by the developing theoretical argument; Glaser and Strauss 1967). The language of sampling originates in the probability requirements of inferential statistical science: it is a technical term that refers to the scientific possibility of generalizing from a sample of a population to the population as a whole, within some degree of certainty. The term signals researcher control over the selection process, an implication that often does not hold for interpretive research settings.

We see problems of methodological logic in adopting the term into interpretive methods. Even if initial access to a research site is gained, multiple obstacles may preclude a researcher's control—e.g., the ability to examine particular documents or interview key actors, however these were initially chosen (based on purpose, theory, or snowballing in the field). Moreover, snowballing risks enmeshing the researcher in the network of the initial participant interviewed, something of which researchers are not always cognizant, leading to or reinforcing the silencing of other voices. Although many qualitative researchers now recognize that random sampling is not sensible for initial case or site selection (e.g., Gerring 2007: 87), these various forms of selection that use the "sampling" term seem to do so strategically: the language derives from the positivist paradigm and seeks to show or to argue, by rhetorical means, that a non-random selection of individuals to interview, documents to assess, sites to observe, or cases to explore can be, and is, as scientific as quantitative social science.

Given that the language of sampling still retains the sense of researcher control in ways that commonly do not fit field realities, in the spirit of recognizing the political character of science—that is, its use of rhetoric to persuade other researchers of the quality of a project's knowledge claims—we would like to see interpretive methodologists and researchers stop trying to force-fit their own research into that mold, give up the rhetoric of the sampling term (which can never mask the fact that these selections are non-randomized, albeit systematic in their own particular fashion), and accept the exposure rationale for selection as scientific in its own right. In our view, "exposure" is a useful replacement for non-random forms of "sampling" as it captures what we think the latter is striving to achieve, without trying to ground it in randomized actions, which qualitative forms of such choice-making do not, and cannot, enact. To speak of choosing cases, persons, settings, etc., focuses more on the dynamic, processual character of research, by contrast with the more stable character oriented toward pre-established criteria suggested by "sampling" (Lee Ann Fujii, personal communication, 3 July 2011).

In positivist–qualitative approaches, the practice of using multiple sources of evidence analogous to intertextuality is often termed "triangulation"—a word taken from the seafaring technique of locating a third, hitherto unknown point using two points of data already known to the sailor. When used by interpretive researchers, it does not convey the expectation that "convergence" across the multiple points of evidence will reveal what is "true" (Mathison 1988). Given the multiple ways in which humans can make sense of the same event, document, artifact, etc., convergence is in fact expected to occur less often than inconsistency or even contradiction (Hammersley and Atkinson 1983, Schwartz-Shea 2006). Here, too, we think it more appropriate in interpretive research to relinquish the language of triangulation, with its realist implications, for terminology that captures the intent of the idea but which is closer to its methodological presuppositions. Intertextuality is such a term. Analyzing intertextually across evidentiary sources is a long-standing interpretive practice; it is a marker of research quality in interpretive studies.

Initial "maps" for purposes of exposure and intertextuality are informed by the researcher's prior knowledge and are likely to be revised by encounters in the field. In addition, access to the varied data sources identified by mapping cannot be guaranteed. But in the research design, interpretive researchers should try to think broadly across these matters. Mapping across distinctive programs that serve the same general population (i.e., payments for disabilities or impoverished children) led Soss (2005) to understand differences in the approachability and responsiveness of government administrators. Mapping what Rwandan genocide perpetrators said in interviews by contrast with what was noted in the official letters of confession led Fujii (2008) to understand how the several spoken representations of the same events revealed coping mechanisms and rationalizations. Mapping a woman's claim to be a victim against testimony from others enabled Fujii (2010) further to understand how dominant, contemporary discourses of the genocide worked to occlude past governmental abuses. Mapping across news media enabled Oren and Kaufman (2006) to see how an event in Azerbaijan was reported differently.[10]

Mapping potential data sources for intertextual readings can also be a check on the extent to which research participants might be purposely "performing" for the investigator, presenting an intentionally partial or skewed version of events, motives, etc. Participants' narratives can be made to speak to each other, whether in analytic deskwork and textwork or in actual field-based engagements (e.g., in follow-up interviews, contrasting documentary records), as well as in comparisons with the researcher's own experiences of the same events (see, e.g., Agar 1986: 67–8, Allina-Pisano 2009: 66–70). This is the work that exposure seeks to achieve, mapping not only across persons but across their physical locations, as relevant to a research question, and the different experiences and interests that are assumed to derive from these. In addition, exposure across time, so to speak, also serves to contextualize what a researcher sees and hears: archival research, in particular, often draws on a time dimension in mapping across sources.

Fieldnote Practices

Fieldnotes are another longstanding field research practice (see, e.g., Sanjek 1990, Emerson *et al.* 1995), one which crosses methodological approaches. These practices have rarely been connected, however, to the concept of research design, despite the fact that they are a major way in which scientific systematicity is enacted in the field. Because interpretive researchers anticipate a voyage whose endpoint is not self-evident, documentation of the research process, including what transpires in the field, is essential.

The fieldnote record enables researchers to be transparent about how they conducted their research. In a diary-like fashion, fieldnotes record day-to-day activities, events, and interviews, plus researcher sense-making of these, especially in light of initial expectations. It is in fieldnotes that the "thick descriptions" of the research site, events, conversations, observed interactions, and so forth are recorded. There, the researcher also reflects on her positionality (see Chapter 4; we take up reflexivity in Chapter 6) and includes other contextualizing comments that will be a reminder later on, especially during deskwork analytic activities, of thoughts, feelings, the texture of interactions, seeds of analysis, and the like. Fieldnotes are also used to track changes made to the initial research plan as a result of field realities, such as unrealizable access to particular documents, field locations, or interviewees.[11]

The combination of fieldnotes, researcher memory, and embodied experience (and other types of evidence) together provide the material for researcher sense-making. These materials provide the empirical grounding for claims about tacit assumptions, patterns of interaction, and language usage in the field site. But those claims do not rest on the notes alone: as Van Maanen (1988: 117) cautions, the "working out of understandings may be symbolized by fieldnotes, but the intellectual activities that support such understandings are unlikely to be found in the daily records." Analytic sense-making, done during fieldwork and later in deskwork and textwork, is not, in other words, contained solely in the fieldnotes themselves. And fieldnote practices do not necessarily, and cannot feasibly, entail making those notes intelligible to outsiders.[12]

Attending to fieldnote practices at the design stage means anticipating issues that might arise in a particular site. For example, extensive on-site note-taking might be infeasible for one reason or another—no time between "job" obligations, no place to sit quietly and concentrate—such that fieldnotes need to be completed in the evenings (Pachirat 2009a), and then one struggles with exhaustion or the desire to let one's hair down and escape fieldwork's strains and burdens for a while, or one is caught up in research-related activities and defers note-taking to the morning or the weekend. Also, note-taking during a research conversation or interview might be disruptive of interpersonal exchanges, leading a researcher to opt for less conspicuous practices. On the other hand, note-taking might be expected by research participants as a commonplace part of research practice, such that it is ignored (Fujii 2010). Participants might even feel slighted if the researcher does not take out a recording device—a notebook or a tape—and even doubt the authenticity of the researcher and the scientific character of the research. Planning for such circumstances is important because of the centrality of fieldnotes to research practices: they record the meaning-making and contexts that enable claims of constitutive causality, why humans act as they do due to their own understandings of their worlds.

6

DESIGNING FOR TRUSTWORTHINESS

Knowledge Claims and Evaluations of Interpretive Research

Doubt concerning the trustworthiness of research claims is fundamental to under-standings of science. Plans for subjecting these claims to doubt or to "testing," a hallmark of science, are commonly built into research designs. But these practices are enacted in dramatically different ways in interpretive and positivist approaches. Much of the extant literature on research design assumes a front-loaded, standard-ized research process based on positivist conceptions of knowledge and positivist standards of evaluating knowledge claims and the research process that has pro-duced them. These are at odds with the iterative, phenomenological–hermeneutic sense-making process at the heart of interpretive science, thereby producing a conundrum: How is one to assess an a priori design for a research process that is situated and iterative—that is, one that is inherently resistant to planning that fixes its details before the research commences? And in a more practical (or even politi-cal) vein, what design elements consistent with this logic will persuade proposal reviewers—many of whom are likely to believe that research designs *should be* fixed a priori in their concept development, hypothesis-based in their formula-tion, and unchangeable in their execution—of the trustworthiness of the project design, particularly given the upfront admission that it is expected to change?

This chapter aims to show that commonly accepted positivist standards for assessing research are limited in their applicability when it comes to interpretive research. These standards (also called criteria in the methods literature) are most appropriate and their logic especially clear for research conducted in a laboratory, with its focus on a particular understanding of causality, itself based on specific understandings about what is real and how reality can be known. These are the standards that have been extended to other venues. For interpretive research that is conducted with the goal of understanding contextualized meaning-making and which is based on another set of "philosophical wagers" (P. Jackson 2011) about reality and its know–ability, other standards, already in use, are more appropriate and need to be brought into play.

The commonly accepted positivist standards include "validity," "reliability," "replicability," "objectivity," and "falsifiability." The first part of this chapter engages at some length their grounding in positivist research practices in order to show how they do not fit with the presuppositions of interpretive science and why, therefore, these indicators are not useful for assessing its trustworthiness. We next engage two issues that are often presented as particular problems for field researchers: "bias" and the "contamination" of field realities due to researcher presence. The conceptualization of the latter as problematic makes sense from a positivist perspective, as we discuss, but both issues have been understood as afflicting all field research without regard to the distinctive goals and underlying philosophies of interpretive field research. Interpretive researchers have developed their own criteria for assessing researcher sense-making, which we then take up. Finally, we return to the critiques of "bias" and "contamination," engaging them this time in light of the preceding discussions.

Two items before we continue. One, as noted in the introduction, we engage here positivist standards as they are treated in textbooks, rather than in discussions in the more sophisticated methodological literature or as implemented in experienced researchers' practices. Second, precisely because these terms are so widely known and so familiar,[1] some of them, such as validity, have been taken up in research that is methodologically interpretive (e.g., Klotz and C. Lynch 2007: 20–2). But there, the terms convey meanings broader than the methods-textbook focus that we take here. Our discussions treat positivist usage, rather than the terms' adaptations in some interpretive research projects.

Understanding the Limitations of Positivist Standards for Interpretive Research: Validity, Reliability, and Replicability

In positivist research, the trustworthiness of researcher claims is discussed in two general ways that reflect positivist presuppositions about and goals for knowledge. The first focuses on the "validity" and "reliability" of operationalized variables and the general "replicability" of a study; the second focuses on "threats" to the goal of causal inference, which we mention here but take up in greater depth in the next section in the context of field research.

The general logic underlying the *validity* of a given variable (known as construct validity) concerns whether the particular indicator used by the researcher measures what it is supposed to measure. For example, is the learning of individuals in an organization, as measured by some before and after test, an adequate measure of "organizational learning"? Or, to take another example, are elections the best indicator of "democracy"? In either case, might other indicators, such as "collective practice" or a "universal franchise," be better for articulating what is at stake in these key concepts? The congruence between a theoretical concept and its operational measure—that is, the validity of the construct—is essential to positivist research design, because if the measure is not valid, then the results of the empirical tests using that measure will not provide an assessment that is germane to the concept (and its attendant theory). When experimentalists add "gender" to their analyses, for instance, perhaps hoping to increase the variation that their research can explain, but operationalize it as "sex-of-subject," the study's results speak to biological theories of sex differences but not to theories of gender, which construe that concept differently (Schwartz-Shea 2002). The operationalized measure (sex), in other words, is not germane to theorizing about the concept "gender." Hence, the considerable care given in positivist designs to clarifying concepts and to their operationalization.[2] This approach to validity assumes the kind of front-loaded research process discussed in Chapter 4, divorced from the meaning-making of research participants.

The *reliability* of a given variable, from the perspective of positivist presuppositions, rests on the idea that the same measurement procedure, carried out by two or more researchers working on a project (or even by the same researcher at another time within the same project or repeating it), can produce the same result (assuming the phenomenon under study has not changed). Reliability measures assess the extent of "measurement error" for a given variable. For example, "intercoder (or inter-rater) reliability" assesses the degree to which two or more researchers or research assistants assess observational, interview, or other data in the same way, as they code them using the categories established by the project's PI (Principle Investigator). The greater the extent of agreement between coders (or "raters"), the greater the reliability of the coding scheme for the variable in question. This reliability measure assumes that coder disagreement (i.e., coding the same observation differently) can be explained by human error in measuring the phenomenon being studied (and that explanation provides the rationale that legitimates the discrepancy—in this case, "normal" human error).

Replicability is a standard for assessing an entire research study (whereas reliability is applied to particular measures). It concerns the question of whether the same research project, from data "collection" to analysis, would, if carried out by another researcher, produce the same results. It is a practice taken from the laboratory sciences, where researchers might be seen rushing to their labs to try to replicate the results of newly published findings, as was the case with the reported discovery of cold fusion at the University of Utah. Replicability was central there and led to a scientific scandal: Utah scientists made public claims about the success of the research prior to peer review of the experiments (and even received money for it in a special allocation from the state legislature), but other laboratories were never able to replicate their results (Browne 1989). In the social sciences, replicability means, for example, that two different researchers should be able to apply the same statistical technique to a given quantitative data set and obtain the same results. For field research, the assumption would be that in the data "collection" process *and* in the analysis, different researchers with the same research question in hand should reach similar conclusions about which evidence matters and about the meaning of that evidence.[3] Researcher characteristics are assumed to be irrelevant in both of these research processes.

These three standards—validity, reliability, and replicability—make sense in the context of positivist assumptions about the stability of the social world and its know-ability by human researchers. They have been developed and applied in laboratory settings. Training of laboratory assistants, for example, is meant to control for any effect their physical presence in the lab might have on the conduct of the research; their personal characteristics are deemed irrelevant, making them interchangeable. The white lab coat, which serves to anonymize researchers and their bodies (Livingstone 2003), symbolizes (and to a great extent enacts) this ideal of researcher interchangeabilty. These and other practices, understood as providing the best assessments of positivist causality, have been extended and, as necessary, adapted to non-experimental settings, including field and archival research. In working with qualitative data, the researchers working on a project are also trained to code words in identical ways: one coder is (or can be trained to be) as good as any other. This interchangeability is precisely what survey researchers are trying to achieve in training assistants not to vary from the questionnaire they are administering, including not replying to requests for further explanation.

The utility of both reliability and replicability rests on the degree to which the social world is understood in terms of a relatively stable (and singular) truth that can be mirrored with ever greater accuracy in terms of general, a-historical, a-cultural laws.[4] Some positivist social scientists retreat from this assumption by limiting the "scope" of their theories to specified time frames or cultural locations (as mentioned in Chapter 3). They also adjust reliability and replicability to these narrowed claims in not expecting the theory and its concepts to be reliably replicated outside of the project's specified scope.[5] Even when they make these adjustments, however, the perspective on researcher characteristics (as irrelevant or contaminating unless controlled) remains intact.

These criteria and associated practices are ill-suited to interpretive research because it makes quite different assumptions about the stability of the social world and how researchers can know it. It has, therefore, developed quite different goals and a different logic of inquiry. With respect to (construct) validity, its "local knowledge" approach to concept development, its disinterest in measuring phenomena, and its constitutive understanding of causality, all focused on understanding meaning-making in context, put interpretive research at odds with that criterion's concerns, focused, as they are, on the adequacy of measures. Further, the standard of validity assumes there is a "real" meaning to data (whether in the form of words or of observations that are used to create numerical data sets) mirroring the world "out there" (see Rorty 1979), rather than seeing language as constituting meaning (the interpretive presupposition).

Furthermore, interpretive understandings of social phenomena as being dynamic and fluid, as well as historically constituted, are inconsistent with both concept reliability measures and requirements for replicability, resting as these do on a more stable, a-historical understanding of the social world.[6] Reliability and replicability are additionally suspect from an interpretive perspective because neither researchers nor research participants are assumed to be interchangeable. A data "collection" process repeated at another time and/or place would not be understood as capable of *guaranteeing* the production of the same data: both researchers and participants are seen as "embodied" or situated, and that situatedness, which can be person-specific, plays a role in the co-generation of data. (This bears on the matter of data archiving, taken up in Chapter 7.) At the same time, however, interpretive researchers work within an implicit understanding that interpretive processes are similar across humans, as well as that researchers and researched are acting as members of their respective communities (academic and "local"), such that continuity of interpretation, as much as differences, is what warrants explanation.[7]

Both positivist and interpretive researchers anticipate differences in interpretations between researchers, then, but the understanding of the source of these differences changes across these two epistemic communities. Therefore, whether different interpretations constitute a problem in need of fixing (and if so, how to fix it) is at issue. The contrasting views on this point hinge on perceptions of the necessity and possibility of the researcher's control over the conditions of research, as well as on the meaning and implications of difference itself. The one sees differences as problematic and control as necessary, and it seeks to control for different interpretations by limiting the flexibility of the research design and the flexibility and judgment of researchers and/or making the latter as interchangeable as possible. The other sees different interpretations as inevitable, rendering control impossible, and of research interest. It seeks to build flexibility into its designs, making potential sources of difference between researchers as transparent as possible and using those differences to account for the generation of knowledge claims—as taken up later in this chapter.

The Problems of "Bias" and "Researcher Presence": "Objectivity" and Contrasting Methodological Responses

Birthed in experimental and statistical research traditions, validity, reliability, and replicability rest on the removal of researcher "presence" from research processes, an idea central to positivist-informed methods. It is based on the assumption that the researcher can generate knowledge of the research setting, its actors and their acts, its events, language, objects, etc., *from a point external to it*. This is what it means for both researcher and research to be "objective": to stand outside the subject of study—meaning, to have both physical and emotional distance from it (Yanow 2006b). In laboratory research, this distance is enacted in a variety of research practices, including invariant scripts and protocols that strictly limit researcher interactions with their "subjects" while also requiring subjects' compliance with experimental procedures. In survey research, this distance is enacted in attempts to control for "interviewer effects," the influence of the survey-giver's demographic characteristics (e.g., age, race, other appearance factors) and demeanor (e.g., facial expressions, stance) on survey-takers' responses. Additional controls built into the survey design, such as Likert scales or close-ended questions, seek to limit the response options available to those being surveyed. In these and other forms of positivist research, distance is enacted in the practice of assembling indicators for concepts a priori—without opening them to possible "contamination" by situational social realities—and *then* assessing their validity and reliability.

Holding out the possibility that a researcher at a physical and emotional-cognitive remove from the people and issues being studied can gain objective knowledge controls for, if not eliminates, the potential for researcher bias. "Bias" implies that emotional and cognitive detachments have been breached. Since physical distance is seen as enabling, if not guaranteeing, emotional and cognitive "distance" (in a metaphorical sense), the lack of physical distance might be seen as engendering bias, which may materialize in research processes, from data "collection" to analysis.[8] These forms of distance—of objectivity—are expected to be engaged in a positivist research design.

The contemporary positivist understanding of researcher bias can be traced to a set of psychological experiments on subject bias that began in the 1960s (Wason 1960), a line of research that continues today (e.g., Hergovic *et al.* 2010). Subjecting laboratory participants to a variety of tasks at various levels of specificity—from Wason's (1960) assignment to infer a rule applying to triples of numbers, to Tabor and Lodge's (2006) asking subjects to read a series of research studies on gun control to assess their opinion change—researchers have found a form of bias in their reactions, termed "confirmation bias." The phrase refers both to subjects' intentional search for evidence that will confirm their prior convictions or beliefs (rather than disconfirm them) and to their evaluation of the character of that evidence. This form of bias may be seen as resulting from subjects' lack of *cognitive distance* from the study topic: both evidentiary search and evaluation are seen as slanted, rather than following the ideal of a value-neutral search and assessment (Devine *et al.* 1990, Klayman and Ha 1987, Trope and Bassok 1982).

Translated into the context of researcher bias, confirmation bias—which might well combine cognitive involvement with emotional attachment—might be suspected to induce the researcher to select only that evidence that will confirm a prejudice for or against an argument (whether in data collection and/or analysis stages). Alternatively, a researcher might become too close, emotionally, to particular ideas or individuals ("going native"; see Note 8, this chapter), losing the affective distance perceived as necessary for non-biased assessments of evidence. In archival research, the concern is less with the physical presence of the researcher interacting with research materials than with the potentially biased framing of the research project—its theoretical, historical, and other modes of contextualizing—which the researcher brings with him to his reading of the documents (much as "reader response theory" would lead us to expect; see, e.g., Iser 1989). In laboratory research, both random assignment of subjects to control groups and double-blind procedures (in which neither subjects nor experimenters know what the theoretical model predicts) are intended to prevent confirmation bias (Shadish 2007: 48–9). That such procedures are not (usually) feasible in field, let alone in archival, research renders the problem of confirmation bias additionally serious, from this perspective.[9]

The difficulty with researchers' *physical presence* in the research setting is tied not only to the potential biasing of research processes and analysis, but also to its potential to alter events in the field. This has been of empirical interest in the social sciences since the Hawthorne experiments of the 1920s–1930s, which demonstrated (among other things) the ways in which the workers studied responded more to the attention of managers and researchers than to the organizational climate factors researchers had set out to analyze (Mayo 1933; Roethlisberger 2001/1941). From a positivist, non-laboratory perspective, these results pose a challenge to the possibility that researcher presence can be neutralized. Non-neutrality threatens to undermine determinations of (positivist) causality: that is, whether the presence of the researcher herself, rather than the independent variable of interest, causes the effect perceived during the study. Campbell and Stanley (1963) called this type of problem "reactivity" (meaning, the ways humans react to the knowledge that they are being studied). It is deemed a threat to the "internal validity" of research findings—their trustworthiness as assessed in terms of whether the variable of interest (the independent variable) was the actual cause of observed change in the dependent variable (also understood as a problem in "causal inference"). It might be that human "reactivity" is what is actively causing different behaviors, instead. For these reasons, eliminating researcher presence is understood as desirable, for example through the use of "nonreactive measures" (Webb *et al.* 1981) or even disguised observation (where feasible; Allwood 2004).[10]

Methodological counsel such as this has led researcher presence to be widely understood not simply as irrelevant but as a *contaminant* in the research process (see Chapter 5 discussion). Inflexible survey instruments and experimental protocols are designed to produce physical and cognitive–emotional distance from research participants; researchers are expected not to adapt or adjust these in response to participants' questions or demands. Underlying such instruments and protocols is the concern that without the sorts of controls which seek to regulate researchers, the latter will respond, in very human ways, to their human interlocutors and in so doing bias the results of the survey or experiment.[11] Studies lacking such controls are, by this logic, at particular risk of bias.

From an interpretive methodological perspective, these conceptualizations of bias are problematic. First, the interpretive logic of inquiry has as its primary goal understanding research participants' meaning-making in their own settings, precisely *without* the kinds of artificial controls these treatments of bias recommend.

Second, researchers enter these field settings understanding that their embodied selves constitute the primary instrument for accessing and making sense of these individual and community meaning-making processes. Interpretive researchers and methodologists dispute the possibility of disembodied research, as if all researchers were interchangeable and as if they could conduct their research without interacting with situational participants and without having those interactions affect their interpretations and knowledge generation.[12] This problematic conception of objectivity has been theorized at length among feminist scholars and philosophers of (social) science (e.g., Harding 1986, Hawkesworth 1988, 2006b, Longino 1990, Polkinghorne 1983). Such a position has been called the "god trick" (Haraway 1988, in response to Nagel's endorsement of the "view from nowhere," the title of his 1986 book).

Without physical presence and absent an engagement—intellectual, surely, but at times also emotional—with members of the setting being studied, and even with its texts and other material objects, sense-making would hardly be possible. Controlling for researcher bias in such situations would seem to mean that researchers should aspire to be "blank slates" with no theoretical or other expectations, who can check their values, beliefs, and feelings—their own meaning-making—at the door. It also implies that they are incapable of monitoring and reflecting on their own learning, their own sense-making processes—that is, that they are trapped, unknowing, in their prejudices. The idea that researchers are incapable of recognizing bias and prejudice is logically inconsistent with the phenomenological and hermeneutic premises that underpin interpretive understandings of science. To presume that humans cannot be aware of their "biases" is to reject human consciousness—the possibility of self-awareness and reflexivity—and human capacity for learning.

Because of these methodological presuppositions, interpretive methodologists have long been involved in thinking through research practices that engage researcher meaning-making in relation to research trustworthiness, including the effects of researcher presence. These practices begin from the position that there is no place to stand outside of the social world that allows a view of truth unmediated by human language and embeddedness in circumstance. The search for knowledge, whether in the field or in the archive, begins wherever the scientist initially finds her- or himself (informed by research literatures and prior experience) and then proceeds toward new understandings of the research focus. This orientation toward processes of understanding privileges human consciousness as an inevitable and useful part of knowledge-making, and it accompanies the researcher's physical, cognitive, and emotional presence in and engagement with the persons and material being studied. The central feature of these methodological checks on sense-making is reflexivity, including analyzing how the researcher's identity—both as presented and claimed by the researcher herself and as perceived by others—may affect the research process (as the discussion in Chapter 4 attests). This is a key consideration at the design stage and continues as a methodological concern through the fieldwork, deskwork, and textwork phases of a project. Other checks on sense-making focus researchers' attention and analysis explicitly on the connections between their own meaning-making processes and the data they generate and analyze in the process of developing and advancing knowledge claims.

Researcher Sense-Making in an Abductive Logic of Inquiry: Reflexivity and Other Checks for Designing Trustworthy Research

Because of their focus on situated, contextualized meaning-making, interpretive researchers emphasize the following in their research, which is quite other than those bias-avoiding steps that characterize a positivist logic of inquiry:

- bottom-up, *in situ* concept development;
- constitutive understandings of causality;
- the relevance of researcher identity in accessing sites and archives;
- the need to improvise in response to field conditions; and
- data co-generated in field relationships (as discussed in previous chapters).

The character of these hallmarks explains why a meaning-focused logic of inquiry requires flexibility in its design. Instead of faulting interpretive research designs for being open-ended, dynamic, and flexible, evaluative criteria need to assess how researchers deal with these characteristics in accounting for the research processes on the basis of which they assert their knowledge claims.

Even though the research process is expected to be dynamic and flexible, a great deal of procedural planning goes into interpretive research. The discussion of these procedural details in (or absence from) the design becomes one of the ways in which interpretive projects are evaluated. We have already engaged several in Chapters 4 and 5:

- the relationship of researcher identity to choice of and access to field research sites;
- researcher role(s) and the degree of participation in research involving participant observation;
- mapping the site for exposure and intertextuality;
- anticipating forms of evidence and analysis of their relationship to the research question; and
- fieldnote practices.

Here, we take up three additional design elements, discussion of which reviewers of interpretive work increasingly expect to find in research manuscripts. The presence or absence of such discussion is often used as an evaluative criterion, suggesting the desirability of explicit, thorough, and thoughtful engagement:

- reflexivity, perhaps the most important of the three, an interpretive counter-point to positivist objectivity;
- data analysis strategies and techniques; and
- what is known in the qualitative methods literature as "member-checking."

Engaging in these practices and making one's engagement explicit and as transparent as possible in the research manuscript is understood within the interpretive epistemic research community as contributing to the quality of interpretive research. Anticipating them in the design becomes further grounds for evaluating it (as well as the later research manuscript).

All three are about practices that researchers engage in as *checks on their own sense-making*. They are part of the standards to which interpretive research aspires and the criteria according to which it is evaluated: their presence in a research project can directly contribute to assessments of the trustworthiness of researcher knowledge claims. From a design perspective, these are largely enacted after a proposal has been accepted and the research is under way, during fieldwork, deskwork, and textwork phases. But their possible later use can be considered in advance, even if their particulars will of necessity change to reflect research facts on the ground as the study progresses.

Checking Researcher Sense-Making through Reflexivity

"Reflexivity" refers to a researcher's active consideration of and engagement with the ways in which his own sense-making and the particular circumstances that might have affected it, throughout all phases of the research process, relate to the knowledge claims he ultimately advances in written form. Reflexivity includes consideration of how the researcher's own characteristics matter and, where feasible, assessments of the ways in which his particular scholarly community and even the wider social milieu impact the research endeavor. The concept and practice have a complex history to which we cannot do justice. (For a brief history of reflexivity as an interpretive criterion for evaluating research, see Schwartz-Shea 2006; for a fuller one, Alvesson and Skoldberg 2000.) In what follows, we emphasize the pragmatic side of this concept rather than its considerable philosophical complexities.[13]

The essential components of reflexivity vary at different stages of a research project. At the design stage, reflexivity is enacted in systematic consideration of the researcher's characteristics (in, e.g., "demographic," disciplinary, and other terms) and potential physical location in the field setting and what these might mean for access to persons and ideas and for researcher–participant interactions. Because the construction of researcher identity is interactive *and* dynamic, possibly changing over the course of the research project, reflexivity at the design stage is not predictive. But thinking ahead of time about possible identity issues, such as challenges of various sorts, can help a researcher later on in the field, if and when such challenges materialize.[14]

Once in the field, interactions begin (and analysis and sense-making continue), producing many possibilities for reflection. These include reflecting on:

- how the researcher's chosen role and/or physical location on site might be shaping the kinds of information being accessed or blocked;
- how the researcher and research participants are co-constructing the former's identity and what that appears to mean (at that point in time) for the co-generation of data;
- how the researcher's presence or personal characteristics may be affecting particular interactions;
- changes in degrees of participation along the observer-participant continuum;
- the adequacy of initial mapping for exposure and intertextuality;
- the development of the researcher's thinking as archival and/or other materials generate new understandings; and
- possible revisions, big or small, in research design in light of field realities.

Reflexivity may also serve as a check on researcher ethical misconduct, as Librett and Perrone (2010: 745) argue: in not distancing researchers from their research participants, reflexivity strengthens their personal responsibility for the research and its outcomes. Much of this can and should be recorded in fieldnotes contemporaneously with the descriptions of conversations, setting, events, interactions, and documents that provide the context for researcher sense-making. In all cases, reflective notes need to be self-consciously tagged as researcher sense-making (as opposed to description, even as interpretive presuppositions mean that "description" is never a mirror but itself a theoretically-informed interpretive act).

Reflexivity is essential to the field, but it cannot and should not stop upon exiting the field. At deskwork and textwork stages, reflexivity continues as the fieldnote records of researcher–participant and researcher–documentary interactions are woven into a publishable manuscript. What makes reflexivity interpretive—some call this critical reflexivity—is the link to epistemological matters. This includes the self-monitoring of the researcher's own "seeing" and "hearing" in relation to knowledge claims, including theoretical expectations, as articulated in presentations of the research setting, actors, and so on in the research manuscript, as well as of his or her own emotional reactions to events, people, sites, documents.

This seeing, hearing, and feeling produces researcher understandings.[15] The *practice* of reflexivity involves the self-conscious "testing" of these emerging explanations and patterns, including of what seems clear and what seems muddy at particular times in the field. Reflection may also reach both backwards in time—to contemplate initial theoretical expectations and past observations as understanding deepens—and forward as the researcher ponders emerging puzzles and/or silences and how field maneuvering might mean exposure to new people or documents that could shed light on these.

Reflexivity on the written page is methodologically significant for at least two reasons. First and foremost, reflexivity allows researchers to trace out the ways in which very specific instances of their positionality affect their research accounts and the knowledge they claim on the basis of those accounts. Pierce (1995), for example, explains that her greater degree of interaction with women than with men in the law offices where she conducted her research produced a generally flatter, less nuanced portrait of the men. Wood (2009: 130–1), by substantive contrast but equal reflective detail, notes that although women participated in the insurgent organizations she was studying, the men were far more active in her field interview settings, often interrupting the women's narratives despite Wood's best efforts to intervene, all in all leading her to rely more on men in her research. Shehata (2006) observes that some research participants related to him in terms of his birthplace; others emphasized their common religion; and still others worried that he was a spy for the company administration. Lin (2000) reflects on her standing as an Asian-American interviewing in US prisons with few Asian-Americans: "[N]either staff nor prisoners had any reference point for my racial allegiances," whereas "a white or black interviewer would have confronted more predictable problems, given the different racial mixes of white and black staff and prisoners at each prison" (2000: 189, 190). Black and white interviewees alike appealed to the similarities between their own racial groups and Asians, answering her questions in ways that were different from those a white or black researcher might have generated, given the "allegiances" implied by those racial identifications (2000: 189). In reflecting on the written page on processes shaping their knowledge claims, all four of these researchers enable their readers to assess how geographic and demographic positionalities shaped their knowledge generation and development. Reminding readers of the fluidity, open-endedness, and complexity of lived experience, critical reflexivity calls attention to the ambiguities and multi-facetedness of meaning-making.

Second, a critical reflexivity calls on researchers to think deeply about the ways in which their own research communities are historically constituted, such that particular socio-political contexts shape, in previously unarticulated or unrecognized ways, the research questions asked or the very concepts used to investigate phenomena.[16] Reflexivity may enable a researcher to grasp and explain how her initial assessment of the situation being studied was influenced by the socially-historically constructed understanding of the research community of which she is (seeking to become) a member. For example, C. Lynch's (2006) experiences in US social justice activities prior to graduate school gave her a basis for questioning the conventional academic wisdom that interwar peace movements were naïve, responsible for dangerous policies of appeasement and isolationism. Instead of privileging these experiences and assumptions in her analysis, she took a "strongly self-reflective stance" toward her own evidence and conclusions in order to "compare the logic of [peace movement] behavior against that of the 'lessons' taught me by the dominant narratives" (2006: 294, 292; see also C. Lynch 1999). Similarly, Oren (2006b: 220) reflects on the evidence-generating practices of the international relations (IR) scholarly community, himself included, to build an argument that data so produced are not neutral, despite widespread assumptions and/or claims among IR scholars to the contrary, because the "analytical concepts and coding rules [are] themselves historical subjects more than objective instruments without a history." This argument parallels that of sociologists and others concerning the ways in which metaphors shape theoretical reasoning (e.g., Brown 1976, Gusfield 1976; see also Ghorashi and Wels 2009, Sykes and Treleavan 2009).

In these processes, reflexivity enacts a methodological value that underlies many interpretive criteria (in particular, those concerned with checking researcher sense-making during data generation and analysis): transparency of knowledge generation.[17] Consider, for example, Gina Reinhardt's experiences having her marital status constantly challenged while she was in Mozambique, miles away from her fiancé in the US. This led her to make some key choices about her research. Reflecting on gender, race, the values that were important to her personally, and the choices she subsequently made, Reinhardt (2009: 297) writes:

> I ended up spending the majority of my time with people who had shown they would respect my engagement [despite her fiancé's absence from the scene]. Ultimately, this meant the four organizations I closely followed during the year were not chosen randomly or with a "most similar" or "most different" case design.

In making her reasoning transparent, Reinhardt invites the reader to consider the extent to which her research choices might have affected the knowledge claims she advances in presenting her data and in their analysis. Paradoxically, reflexivity can serve to enhance the trustworthiness of the researcher's knowledge-generation processes even as its use might reveal research activities that challenge that trustworthiness. A reader may decide that what is revealed through such transparency weakens the knowledge being advanced—but its presence enables that judgment. Without such transparency, assessment of knowledge claims would be impaired. It is a key to the legitimacy of interpretive sense-making: rather than making the connection between process and conclusions appear seamless, reflexivity reveals and, where possible, *analyzes* the consequences of a reliance on a "human" research instrument.[18]

There is considerable variation in the practice of reflexivity, as it is still an emerging methodological idea with norms that vary by discipline (e.g., it is expected, and accepted, more in anthropology than in political science) and field (e.g., more in feminist research than in policy studies). Variation may also be due to debates over the extent to which the researcher's voice should be on display in a research manuscript. Such debates recognize the stakes involved in self-disclosure, including the power of the researcher at the deskwork and textwork stages to (re)present her knowledge claims, as well as varying degrees of comfort with self-revelation.[19]

Choices concerning reflexivity enact the researcher's accountability to those studied, to the evidence as he understands it, and to the value of transparency for reviewers and potential readers of the study. Rather than being (or being seen as) an exercise in vanity or self-indulgence, reflexivity should be understood and treated as a scientific activity at the heart of interpretive research. Reflexivity enacts the systematicity of interpretive research in a manner that is consistent with an interpretive logic of inquiry, and it puts researcher presence in the field site and the subjectivity of interpretation front and center for critical consideration, rather than trying to mask or ignore it. It is a significant marker of quality in interpretive research because it makes the research process and its claims more transparent, thereby maximizing the trustworthiness of the researcher's claims to knowledge as voiced in a research manuscript. Until the centrality of reflexivity to interpretive science is more widely understood, its anticipation in various aspects of a research project and explicit discussion in research designs (and later, in methodology or methods sections of research manuscripts) is desirable.

Checking Researcher Sense-Making during Data Generation and Analysis

Because (as noted in Chapter 4) the major "instrument" for the conduct of interpretive research is the researcher him- or herself (as compared to the scripts and protocols that control positivist researchers as well as their "subjects"), skeptics ask: "How does the reader know that the researcher didn't look *only* for confirmatory evidence?" (Schwartz-Shea 2006: 104, original emphasis).

Investigators have developed a variety of strategies and techniques to check their sense-making processes during both data generation and data analysis phases of a research project. Because data generation and analysis are not entirely separable stages but are intertwined, researcher sense-making begins the moment the researcher enters the field, if not before,[20] and continues after she exits and settles down to the deskwork and textwork that are, in other, front-loaded forms of research, traditionally considered the data analytic stage. A plethora of data analytic techniques may be brought into play during the fieldwork, deskwork, and textwork phases, depending on the research question and the form(s) of the data, e.g., metaphor analysis for word data or spatial analysis for spatial data. Space limits preclude taking up the particularity of these distinctive techniques here (for a listing of a couple dozen possibilities, see Yanow and Schwartz-Shea 2006: xx).[21] These techniques and strategies vary in the extent to which they are designed to be used in both fieldwork and deskwork (e.g., Becker's, 1998, recommended strategy of searching for negative cases) or only or primarily during textwork (e.g., deconstruction). They also vary in the extent to which they assume it is possible or necessary to return to the field to generate more evidence (e.g., some forms of grounded theory; see Charmaz 2006).

Because interpretive researchers do not seek to mirror the world, their primary concern in checking their own meaning-making is not focused on "getting the facts right," as if there were only one version of that social reality. Rather, they are looking to articulate various experiences or viewpoints on the topic under investigation, in order to be able to understand its nuances more fully. Because they expect to learn about these over time, their task in checking their own sense-making concerns finding ways to suspend judgment or to avoid a "rush to diagnosis," that is, to prevent themselves from settling too quickly on a pattern, answer or interpretation.

No single umbrella term has emerged as a label for the many techniques that have been developed to check researcher sense-making while analyzing data in the field, at the desk, or in writing. For example, Frank (1999: 97–8) describes how student teachers can learn to delay interpretation by dividing their fieldnotes between "notetaking" (descriptions) and "notemaking" (analytic comments)—although we hold that even in the process of describing persons, settings, events, and so on, the researcher is selecting which details are significant in terms of the research question, and such choice-making is at heart itself analytic. Others include "following up surprises" in the data (during the deskwork phase; Miles and Huberman 1984: 262) and searching for "negative cases" (during both phases; Becker 1998: 192–4) or for "tensions" in the emerging explanation (also during both phases; Soss, personal communication, 27 February 2011; for a review, see Schwartz-Shea 2006). The general idea is that the researcher consciously searches for evidence that will force a self-challenging reexamination of initial impressions, pet theories or favored explanations. Although not always articulated in terms of a "check" on researcher sense-making, some specific data analytic techniques, e.g., semiotic squares, operate in analogous ways (see Feldman 1995).

These techniques are aided by other interpretive research practices—the continual testing and revising of initial expectations, drawing on attention to inconsistencies arising from intertextuality and to silences in the data, i.e., what the researcher is not hearing in the field or seeing at the desk. Unlike the single test characteristic of front-loaded research (e.g., administering the survey that will test hypotheses established a priori), field and archival settings provide the researcher with many opportunities for "testing" developing understandings of research puzzles while the research is under way.

An effective research design should demonstrate awareness of these general strategies and specific techniques for checking researcher sense-making. The researcher can indicate one or more that might be drawn on in the course of the research, as appropriate to the proposed methods of generating and/or analyzing data. Demonstrating familiarity with these practices marks the researcher as aware of the general issue of concern, as well as of the variety of field and archival methods that might be used to support and challenge sense-making at both the data generation and data analysis stages, even when particular practices to be used might not be specifiable at the design phase.

Checking Researcher Sense-Making through "Member-Checking"

"Member-checking" refers to the practice of sending or bringing written material involving the people studied back to them. These are commonly transcripts of interviews conducted with them; segments of a research manuscript (or a completed manuscript) reporting on an event in which they were involved or including something they said; or follow-up, face to face conversations over similar materials. The intention is to see whether the researcher has "got it right" from the perspective of members "native" to the situation or setting under study.[22] Where appropriate, an interpretive design should indicate whether the researcher plans to conduct "member-checking" and, if so, why.

Going back to others is more than the journalistic practice of "fact-" or "quote checking," which implies that there is a singular social reality that can be captured by the reporter, as does the idea of getting the research narrative "right" or "wrong." Neither of these is the sense in which this check on sense-making is used by interpretive researchers. Instead, it is used in recognition that research settings and sense-making of them may be quite complex, involving, for example, tacit knowledge, local vocabularies with local meanings, and/or positioned understandings of events and other things studied, the situated meaning of any of which the researcher may or may not have grasped well. The practice enacts the commitment to knowledge that takes into account situational actors' own understandings of their experiences.

There is, however, considerable methodological debate over the details of this practice (e.g., Miles and Huberman 1994: 275–7, Emerson and Pollner 2002, Schwartz-Shea and Yanow 2009), including over whether some of its forms are inappropriate for some modes of research. One difficulty is that given the variety of perspectives in the field, seamless agreement among all group members about whether the researcher has "got it right" is improbable. D. Mosse's (2005, 2006) account of his efforts at member-checking in his ethnography of aid policy and practice in development organizations showcases the extent to which researcher purposes and situated interpretations may be embraced by some actors in the field and vigorously rejected by others. Project managers in one non-governmental organization took "strong exception" to his account (2005: ix), later filing formal objections with his university and then the professional anthropology association to which he belonged, even as some staff and workers elsewhere were sympathetic to his analyses.

Moreover, the language of "checking" with situational members implies that if they object to what the researcher has written, their understanding will prevail. This denies the researcher any epistemological purchase that might arise from information gleaned from exposure to other parts of the setting, adding layers of understanding that are not available to the objecting individual, or from the academic literature and the debates taking place there. We have not found methodological discussions advancing this approach that engage the variety of responses a researcher might expect from members "checked" or how these responses might be engaged in the written manuscript (for discussion, see Schwartz-Shea and Yanow 2009: 70–2). For one example, Liebow (1993) published his informants' comments on his text in his footnotes, even when they took issue with his representations. Another difficulty is that the interpretive stance of inviting research participants to share what they feel and think on their own terms is in tension with the ultimate authority and power of the researcher at the text-making stage to present her theoretical and empirical arguments without consultation with members or their participation. And even when writing is jointly conducted, it is typically the academic researcher who wields the pen, so to speak (cf. Down and Hughes 2009).

Given these debates, whether member-checking is appropriate to a particular project should be carefully considered. It may not be feasible if the distance between the field site and the researcher's home base makes returning there prohibitively expensive—and mail or email may not always be an appropriate substitute for a face to face visit. It may not be desirable if sharing a manuscript or parts of one with some research participants might threaten anonymity or the confidentiality of others. It may be most appropriate to the sorts of participatory-action research (PAR) projects in which participants come close to the status of co-investigators (see, e.g., Cahill *et al.* 2004, Cahill 2007, Greenwood and Levin 2007, Berg and Eikeland 2008, Sykes and Treleaven 2009)—and in fact, PAR designs may sidestep this issue entirely. Despite these complications—or, perhaps, because of them—we think the issue worth thinking through in a research design.

Doubt, Trustworthiness, and Explanatory Coherence

The interpretive attention to researcher sense-making responds to a key issue in the broader context within which scientific research is conducted—its central concern with the trustworthiness of researcher claims vis-à-vis the knowledge presented in the research manuscript. As examined in this chapter, this concern plays out in different ways in positivist and interpretive methodological perspectives, each approach responding to this challenge by developing practices to address doubt, trustworthiness, and—by implication—the quality of any study.

In positivist methodology, the attitude of doubt is enshrined in one of its most powerful design concepts—falsifiability. Its widespread acceptance means that reviewers of research projects and designs often apply this standard to *all* research studies, regardless of their philosophical underpinnings. As discussed in

Chapter 5, this concept rests on the idea that research can objectively mirror or measure its study domain, a presupposition not accepted within interpretive research (because what constitutes data is understood as generated by the research question and co-generated with research participants).

The falsifiability standard also shows up less formally in a question that is often posed to researchers: *What evidence would convince you that your analysis is wrong?*[23] When asked by scholars working from a positivist perspective (e.g., King *et al.* 1994), this question voices a Popperian sensibility about how best to assess (causal) hypotheses that make up particular theoretical models (Hawkesworth 2006a). The question presumes that a model's hypotheses can be specified, tested, and assessed with precision against something in the externally observable world. This objectively "collected" evidence (as contrasted with the interpretive perspective on evidence as co-generated) can then be used by the researcher to evaluate the model's posited causal relationships, such that these can be shown to be erroneous.

The expectation is that researchers should be able to spell out the empirical implications of their theoretical models[24]: for example, that in producing a collective benefit, male subjects will cooperate less than female subjects, implied by a sex-differences model tested in social dilemma experiments (Eckel and Grossman 1996, Schwartz-Shea 2002); or that chosen candidates will move their platform promises closer to the median voter's position for the general election, implied by the model of voting behavior theory (Downs 1957). By referencing the evidence from an experiment or from the historical record, the researcher can answer the question concerning whether he has been wrong in his characterization of the world (as represented in that a priori model). If male and female experimental subjects cooperate at the same rate or if a political candidate fails to move her platform positions toward the median voter (and yet still wins the election), the models' predictions have been falsified, and the researcher knows he was wrong. (For a critical assessment of this logic, see Shapiro 2004: 28–36.)

In both research approaches, the question seeks to inquire into the trustworthiness of the researcher's analysis. The purpose of interpretive research, however, is not model testing, but the understanding of human meaning-making in context; the goal is not to erase ambiguities, but to understand their sources. For this approach, with its emphasis on immersion in human meaning-making in the field and in archives and its iterative sense-making processes, the question pursues a different reasoning. Asked from an interpretive perspective, it seeks to inquire into the logic and explanatory coherence of the analysis, rather than the "goodness" of the model: *How would you know if there were something else afoot in this situation that might be a better explanation of the puzzle you are seeking to explain?*

Framed in this way, the issue is the adequacy of explanation and analysis—the explanatory coherence of the argument. To address this question, an interpretive researcher will point to (1) the consistency of evidence from different sources (the intertextuality of the analysis), (2) the ways in which conflicting interpretations have been engaged, and (3) the logic with which the argument has been developed. The first of these, consistency of evidence from different sources, builds on all the design themes laid out in these chapters which engage an orientation toward meaning-making and its ambiguities, particularly mapping to enable exposure and intertextuality. The second, engaging conflicting or contradictory interpretations, involves the deskwork and textwork in which the researcher points out, discusses, and analyzes the different interpretations (enabled by item 1) in terms of participants' locations and identities, as well as the researcher's, using the many "clues" recorded and assembled in the fieldnotes. Conflicting interpretations are engaged in such a way that the research puzzle is "made sense of"—the "plot" is "resolved," so to speak. The connection between the second and third items is "methodological" in its fullest sense: that is, method alone can never produce the denouement of entangled interpretations; that calls for authorial judgment and theorizing.

Answering this question, then, means recognizing evidence (generated through mapping for exposure and intertextuality) that might challenge the researcher's explanation, engaging it in the text, and accounting for in the analysis. In Becker's words (1998: 210), the reason for searching out and engaging such inconsistencies is "to refine the portrait of the whole—in order to offer, in the end, a convincing representation of its complexity and diversity." As in the other logic of inquiry, the researcher turns to a marshalling of evidence—only here, the answer rests more on the logic of argumentation, its overall explanatory coherence, than on the logic of statistical analysis.

"Researcher Contamination" and "Bias" Revisited

For the methodological practices associated with positivism, researcher presence and judgment are problematic. From the perspective of these practices, it appears that the ideal researcher would be invisible to those she studied ("disembodied") in order to minimize her impact on them (see Pachirat 2009b). She would also be emotionally insulated from their reactions to her, as well as from her reactions both to them *and* to whether the results of empirical tests supported her theoretical expectations. Because this ideal is not humanly possible, positivist methodologies set up "controls" on research, researchers, and research subjects to contain or, ideally, entirely avoid researcher contamination and bias.

Given the positivist goals for knowledge—to achieve universal, a-historical causal laws—these methodological controls make sense. In contrast, from an interpretive logic of inquiry in which the researcher him- or herself is the primary "instrument" of data generation and sense-making and where iteration is intrinsic to the research process, these sorts of controls may stymie research or even stop it before it can get started. Research designs that seek to control for "contamination" and "bias" do not fit interpretive methodological concerns. The unsuitability of control-based design for interpretive research does not mean, however, that interpretive researchers are not concerned about the trustworthiness of their research. In the preceding section and previous two chapters, we have shown the sorts of methodological practices developed by interpretive research communities for achieving trustworthy research, yielding evaluative criteria that fit an interpretive logic of inquiry. These criteria, however, pose challenges for positivist understandings of and expectations for research design which often affect the evaluation of interpretive designs at the hands of reviewers of various sorts. In closing out this chapter, we engage some of these, showing how they appear differently with respect to matters of bias and research trustworthiness in the light of these two very different logics of inquiry.

Take, for example, the positivist methodological concern that researcher presence will interfere with the path to knowledge, threatening causal inference, in particular. In interpretive methodology, researcher presence is understood as inevitable and in some cases invaluable! For instance, should a researcher, whether in all ignorance or by intention, violate local expectations that attach to one or another of his demographic characteristics (e.g., sex, class), the resulting response may well be a key learning experience. This is a central concept in ethnomethodological and other norm violation research, and it is in keeping with Kurt Lewin's idea that the best way to understand something (e.g., an organization) is to try to change it (a point also made by feminist researchers, e.g., Cancian 1992: 633). Shehata (2006) illustrates this in noting that his intrusive presence and the extent to which he challenged social class taboos, often inadvertently, contributed greatly to how he came to understand the operation of social class in Egypt.

Another positivist concern is that research participants will "perform" for the researcher—act in ways that they would not naturally act if the researcher were not present. The intentional masking of "backstage" views, attitudes, and opinions by research participants is possible, perhaps even likely in some circumstances, as all persons (including researchers!) make decisions about what, and how much, to reveal about themselves, sometimes with strategic intent. With prolonged observation, researchers can come to see participants and their words and acts in context, which will put "performing for the observer" into perspective (Lincoln and Guba 1985: 304–5). Or, as Liebow (1993: 321) remarked, in the context of participant observation studies, ". . .one returns day after day and month after month to the study situation, and lies do not really hold up well over long periods of time."[25]

But more than that: to underscore a point raised in Chapter 5, interpretive researchers are less likely to understand "performance" as a problem than to see it as data. Invoking Goffman's (1959) backstage–frontstage distinction advances one perspective on the matter: all of us foreground a "presentation of self," seeking to keep other forms of self-knowledge private. The implication that is sometimes brought into play when this language is invoked—that backstage identity is somehow more real than frontstage presentation, or performance—is unwarranted from the perspective of interpretive research. When participants do "put on a show," that response is itself of intrinsic interest to the researcher. For example, reading across interviews and observations intertextually, Allina-Pisano (2009) and Agar (1986) both found that research participants had exaggerated certain claims. Allina-Pisano (2009: 68) described the exaggerations she encountered in a rural village in Russia as "part of broader social narratives and a liturgy of lamentation that is shared above all with outsiders." Agar (1986) analyzed the discrepancy between widespread trucker complaints about specific problems (which they contrasted with the then-popular movies portraying independent truckers as cultural heroes) and his observations of the rarity of these problems as he traveled with them and analyzed industry accident data. Treating these exaggerations as data enabled both authors to understand their study settings in ways they might not otherwise have been able to do.

Even more importantly, interpretive presuppositions contest the assumption that there exists some "pure" or "authentic" conduct on the part of research participants. Instead, *all* human conduct is understood in terms of the myriad historically constituted power relations that are part of all social settings. (For a theoretical framework that elaborates these ideas, see Scott 1990.) Researcher presence deserves attention and analysis, and whether it poses a problem or presents an opportunity should be assessed according to situational, contextual, and theoretical factors, rather than being assumed automatically to be an obstacle to trustworthy knowledge claims.

And then there is the concern about confirmation bias, that the researcher searches *only* for evidence that confirms her preferred answer to the research question. First, interpretive research does not, and cannot, rest on a search for or selection of data in any kind of perfectly controlled *or* random sense. Researchers give up such control when they enter research participants' worlds; and randomization is impossible because of the limitations on compiling a complete list (the "sampling frame") of everything that occurs in the field. Instead, *by intentional strategy and design*, interpretive practice means mapping the *variety* of people, places, events, texts, etc., to expose the researcher to *multiple* perspectives on the research question. Researchers offer "situated knowledges" (Haraway 1988), each related to location: knowledge from somewhere. Reading intertextually across the many forms of evidence (spatial, text-based, visual, numerical, experiential, etc.) attunes researchers to the complexities of lived experience. In the archives as well, the multiple "voices" from the texts of, for instance, individual authors, organizational task forces or community manifestos attest to struggles over meaning-making and narratives. Most pertinent to the concern with confirmation bias are the long-standing practices and checks on researcher sense-making discussed in this chapter. Interpretive researchers, too, search for "disconfirming evidence." That this practice is not consistent with falsifiability, Type I and Type II errors, or other aspects of the positivist framework of knowing does not mean it is less systematic (or rigorous). Instead, these overlapping checks and research practices enact a methodological rigor consistent with a logic of inquiry focused on the interpretive purpose of understanding meaning-making.

Second, the question about researchers intentionally choosing evidence that supports their argument while ignoring evidence that undermines it evinces an anxiety that is not unique to interpretive research: researchers working in other methodologies are also capable of "cooking the books" (and there are plenty of examples of that from laboratory research; see, e.g., Resnik 1998). What keeps researchers honest is an unwritten, unspoken, yet nonetheless tacitly known and communicated ethical code, largely articulated only when it is broken. Interpretive scientists are as committed to honest practices as any other kind of scientist; deceitful practices know no methodological borders. Moreover, acknowledging issues in knowledge generation, interpretive researchers continue to strive for transparency in their sense-making, including through reflexive checks on those processes. Demonstrating familiarity with interpretive research sensibilities and practices in a research design signals that the researcher is aware of these many issues.

The central methodological point that we are seeking to underscore here is that interpretive researchers are not captives of what they see, hear, or read—they are not *trapped* by what people tell them any more than they are by their prejudices. They are alert to the possibility of partial knowledge and multiple perspectives. Neither of these can be avoided or controlled for. But they *can* be acknowledged, engaged, and analyzed. Reflexivity aids in this process as researchers ask not only about their own meaning-making but also about what they are *not* hearing, about the silences in their interviews, readings, and observations. Inquiring into the meanings of such silences, whether chosen or imposed, is a major marker of quality in interpretive research. This is not to claim that reflexivity is a panacea for the issues raised by knowledge that is perspectival, any more than positivist controls can achieve that logic's ideal of objectivity. No one can be fully transparent to herself (Fay 1996, Luft and Ingham 1955), and all research endeavors proceed based on some set of presuppositions. The interpretive commitment is to increase understanding of the ways in which the characteristics of individual researchers and their academic communities affect the production of knowledge in the human sciences. Research designs that discuss the role of reflexivity in the project communicate this commitment to reviewers and other readers.

Summing Up

Table 6.1 summarizes the discussion presented in Chapters 3 through 6, bringing together design concepts that are particular to a specifically interpretive research project (the first column) with those that commonly appear in discussions of research designs in general but which are, in fact, specific to positivist methodological assumptions (the second column).

TABLE 6.1 Contrasting approaches to research and its design

	Interpretive Methodology	Positivist Methodology
Research orientation	• meaning-making • contextuality (in re. knowledge) • hermeneutic–phenomenological sensibility: explanatory description (answering "why?") • constitutive causality	• measurement • generalizability (in re. knowledge) • prediction tied to causal laws (answering "wherefore?") • mechanical causality
Design attitude	• abductive logic of inquiry: iterative, recursive, starting from surprise/ puzzle/tension deriving from expectations vs. lived experiences • prior knowledge, expectations (experiential, theoretical) • dynamic flexibility in implementation of design as learning occurs • participants = agents with valued local knowledge; researchers as experts in processes of inquiry • research as "world-making"	• deductive logic of inquiry; inductive logic as precursor to deductive inquiry • clarity of model; prior experiential knowledge deemed irrelevant or potentially biasing • fixed, a priori design; control • participants = subjects, informants; researchers as subject-matter experts • objective description
Getting going	• educated provisional sense-making; start with prior knowledge > the hermeneutic circle-spiral • investigating • access questions; choices: of settings, actors, archives, documents, . . . (relational turn in field research; ethical and power dimensions; active learning in the field)	• theories > concepts > hypotheses > variables • testing • case selection; researcher in control (access is subordinated to selection)
In the field or archives	• mapping for exposure and intertextuality • bottom-up, in situ concept development (learning) • exploration of concepts in ordinary language, local knowledge terms • revise design as needed	• sampling • a priori concept formation (separated from operationalization) • operationalization of concepts • changed research question requires research re-design and re-start
Analysis of evidence	• hermeneutic sensibility: coherence, logic of argumentation, . . .	• falsifiability
Evaluative standards	• trustworthiness • systematicity • reflexivity, transparency; engagement with positionality	• validity, reliability, replicability • rigor • objectivity

The table shows the rough equivalences between the concepts and phrases that are central to these two different logics of inquiry and their enactment in research designs. The order of the entries from top to bottom represents, very roughly, the broad orientations of these two approaches to knowledge, the generation and analysis of evidence, and associated evaluative standards. This order, however, does not necessarily reflect the dynamic processes that characterize the actual conceptualization and implementation of research designs.

The table, particularly the comparison of the two columns, can assist those new to interpretive methodologies to understand and respond effectively, in a non-defensive way, to positivist interlocutors. For example, if a researcher's objectivity were challenged, that entry in the table under the positivist methodology column would lead him to an interpretive response opposite it under the interpretive methodology column: he might explain that, given that his research purpose focuses on meaning-making, his task is about understanding research participants' worlds from their perspectives, rather than portraying an objective reality from a point outside their worlds. Or, if an interpretive study's "sampling" procedure is challenged, the table would lead the researcher to a discussion of mapping for exposure and intertextuality—concepts that can be used to flesh out the ways in which interpretive researchers search out variability and multiplicity (even as they lack the type of control implied by the sampling term).

The contrasts in terminology highlight some of the ways in which the concepts or phrases in the right-hand column, grounded as they are in positivist philosophical–methodological presuppositions, are inadequate for interpretive projects and at times even detrimental to their goals and sensibilities. The entries under the interpretive methodology column have a long history in interpretive literatures and research practices, although not all of them have been used in these ways before. We introduce them in this comparative context, drawing on interpretive methodological traditions, in ways that emphasize their continuity and consistency within an interpretive approach. We recognize that newer design concepts are bound to feel and sound strange by contrast with those that have been habitual research-speak. Only with widespread usage can new concepts acquire the recognition and legitimacy that will resolve this difficulty.

7

DESIGN IN CONTEXT

From the Human Side of Research to Writing Research Manuscripts

Thinking about research design does not end with access and other issues or its production on paper. There are more things still to think about: planning beyond the research itself, in both space and time. Field research, of whatever sort, has its own physical and emotional entailments, little talked about in the research design literature; to one extent or another, a researcher can anticipate and plan for these. These days, researchers need to anticipate ethics reviews; but particular issues arise when interpretive methodologies confront protections for human participants. Moreover, renewed demands for data archiving loom on the horizon, posing challenges for interpretive research: archiving invokes the matter of replicability (discussed briefly in the previous chapter), which raises ethical and methodological concerns of its own. Lastly, research designs lay the groundwork for the research manuscript: how might a researcher anticipate that in thinking about the parts of a proposal?

The Body in the Field: Emotions, Sexuality, Wheelchairedness, and Other Human Realities

Much as Weberian bureaucracy theory carries many unspoken assumptions about sex and gender, class, and so forth (Ferguson 1984), so, too, are there a lot of unspoken assumptions embedded in ideas about doing field research. One set of these concerns its "Western" dispositions, regarding, for example, openness with respect to scientific inquiry, along with an implied impartiality and accuracy of governmental and other sorts of data, something touched on in Chapter 4.[1] A second concerns emotional, sexual, and physical entailments. Methodological treatments, including the research design literature, irrespective of the methodological approach followed, have not yet taken on board the vast variety of researchers engaged in field and archival research. Where are the explicit engagements with race-ethnic issues in the field? Gender? Sexuality? Physical ability? Class? It is as if the researcher body is (still) male, middle class, Caucasian-European, capable of unfettered physical mobility, and a-sexual.[2]

We bring these topics in here not only for the benefit of researchers who do not fit this outdated stereotype, many of whom likely already know quite well what arrangements they would need to make in order to live their lives while conducting research, but for advisors and methods instructors, who, like us until recent years, have not been fully cognizant of the assumptions of ablebodied-ness, in particular, built into field research methods and their discussions. Here, it is we—instructors, advisors—who need to think more fully in contemplating research designs! This is also why we have set this discussion aside as a separate section, rather than integrating it into the "regular" discussion of design issues in earlier chapters: until it becomes a more normalized feature of the research meth-ods community, such that all methods discussions engage emotions, sexuality, wheelchairedness and other bodily dimensions as a matter of course, it needs to be flagged for attention. Several of these matters need to be anticipated and planned for, in ways that can involve advisors, too (and perhaps even department heads). Although we speak here specifically to those engaged in field research, some of what we say pertains to working in archives.

One common taboo in methods texts and design discussions concerns speaking openly of the emotional roller-coaster that, if unanticipated, can catch the field researcher unawares. Even knowing that it can affect some researchers does not necessarily prepare one for it oneself. Far from home, in a strange place, without a support network of family, friends, and well-worn weekend newspaper and cap-puccino routines, loneliness and homesickness can hit at odd moments of the day. Even discussions of "culture shock," much present in anthropological texts, at least, typically do not focus on these sorts of "ordinary emotions," dealing instead with the initial anger at and later acceptance of differences in the organization of life—different shopping hours, different food stuffs, different work habits, and so on. The initial emotional response to that is often: Why can't they do things the way we do them back home?

That is rather different from attacks of fear, or loss, from missing one's fiancé (Reinhardt 2009), one's spouse, parents, friends, and so on (see Ortbals and Rincker 2009, Henderson 2009). Modern technologies—the internet, email, VOIP (Voice Over Internet Protocol) set-ups such as Skype, video links, less expensive telephone connections, etc.—have diminished the sense of detachment relative to what it was in even the recent past (well into the 1990s, depending on location), when one might wait for the post for days or weeks on end. Particular research topics, too, may pose their own challenges (see, e.g., Whiteman 2010) and require even greater self-monitoring and self-care. Field research on vari-ous forms of violence—domestic, institutional, or political, such as insurgency-related events—may expose the researcher to physical and/or emotional brutalities which he has not anticipated. As Soss advises (2006: 143, emphasis added), researchers need to recognize that "the researcher role is a *human* role"; they need to learn and know their personal limits. For those heading into field settings marked by violence or its potential, planning for their own protection and safety—along with that of research participants which is the concern of US IRBs and other states' boards and policies (see discussion below)—must be carefully undertaken.

The extent to which these issues are made an explicit part of a research design is up to the researcher (and perhaps advisors), but they are well worth thinking through. Planning for time out of the field, if and where feasible, or for regular, ongoing support from others may be key to the on-going conduct of physically or emotionally taxing research. Fieldnotes provide a place to reflect on such issues; reflexivity calls for their discussion in research manuscripts, although a kind of tough field researcher identity seems often to preclude such narratives. Sometimes, just knowing that research has an emotional side, even if this is not commonly written or talked about (other than in informal conference settings, such as the corridor chat or the bar, long after the fact), is enough to assuage the strength of the feelings when they do hit.[3]

Methodologists have for some time discussed the ethnocentric, even racist, and class-biased character of ethnography and participant observer research: field researchers from the Northern hemisphere studying inhabitants of (former) colonies in the Southern hemisphere (Harrell 2006), as well as American Indians on reservations, a clear, if unspoken, analogue to more explicitly colonial situations (see Bruyneel 2007); and participant observers from wealthier classes studying the poor, the deviant, the outcasts in marginal domestic neighborhoods and communities. It is only in recent years that anthropologists have begun to speak openly of heterosexual relations, sometimes leading to marriage, between themselves and their "informants" in the field (Lewin and Leap 1996); yet Walby (2010: 641) remarks on ongoing silence among sociologists with respect to "the sexual politics of research" in general. That there is something worth thinking about in methods talk with respect to gay, lesbian, bisexual, transsexual, and queer research identities—whether "out" or closeted—is only beginning to be admitted as worthy of consideration and to be discussed explicitly (Lewin and Leap 1996, Wilkinson 2008). The question of whether to become involved in emotional or sexual relationships with research participants while in the field rehearses similar issues regardless of sexual identity, some of them echoing discussions in US universities about professor–student relations with respect to uneven power dimensions (see, e.g., Paludi 1996).

Whether to be out about non-heterosexual identity in field settings adds other dimensions to the discussion. As with other aspects of researcher identity, there is no single answer: at times it might aid access (see Wilkinson 2008), at others, hinder it (see also Walby 2010). In situations in which being out might endanger the researcher, or research participants, other layers of concern kick in.

(See criticisms of Humphreys' research, 1970, in which he took the automobile license plate numbers of gay men frequenting public bathrooms, pickup spots for casual sexual encounters, and followed them home; e.g., Humphreys and others 1976.) Some exploration of these parameters in advance of entering the field setting might be possible; certainly, thinking them through in advance is advised. Whether one includes these thoughts explicitly in a research proposal (and later, in the research manuscript, most likely in the methods section) is a matter of individual judgment, as it will depend on imagined and anticipated readers and local situations, as well as the researcher's own proclivities toward self-disclosure.

As silent as research design treatments, methods textbooks, and other discussions have been about emotions and sexuality, they have been even more so about assumptions of ablebodiedness built into the conduct of research, especially field research. Entire discussions of research design, including this one to this point, do not engage the sorts of considerations required by "wheelchairedness," as Mike Duijn puts it (personal communication, Fall 2008), the aging body in the field, so to speak, or other forms of physical limitation. Moreover, even when disability is engaged as a topic in field research, it has usually been with respect to studying wheelchaired, learning disabled, autistic, and other "impaired" people (e.g., Casper and Talley 2005), not the challenges posed to researchers.

Whether one is wheelchair-bound, for reasons of accident, genetics, illness, or age, or ambulatory but constrained by blindness (Krieger 2005a, b), rheumatoid arthritis (Felstiner 2000), multiple sclerosis, cerebral palsy, or some other sense impairment or movement disorder (Howe 2009, Mogendorff 2010, Robillard 1999), one may need to give additional consideration to the research settings in which one wants to position oneself and to the role(s) one wants to assume there. At a very basic level, are the buildings and rooms in which one will conduct interviews or read archived materials accessible? Although some nations' laws now require that buildings, within certain constraints, be made disability-accessible, these stipulations and their implementation are by no means universal. How does one handle toilets that are not designed to accommodate the wheelchaired? If one is sight-limited, how will observation and note-taking be conducted? If one's hearing capacity is limited, does that suggest the use of recording devices that other researchers might disparage (on the argument that they interfere with participant openness and rapport)? If one's speech is impacted, how will one conduct interviews? If one no longer has the agility of a 28-year-old, how will one negotiate seven flights of stairs or hillier, rockier climbs? And so forth.

None of these is *ipso facto* prohibitive for conducting field research, and we know a handful of researchers who have successfully completed field research projects under such constraints. But as they and others are aware, it takes forethought and planning, and incorporating the outcomes of both into the research design. It may require educating one's advisor(s), if one is a graduate student, to the constraints under which one works and the additional plans one needs to undertake. It may require additional line items in a research grant: much as those limited by language draw on translators, who need to be paid, some of the wheelchaired and others may draw on aides, who also need to be accommodated in a research budget. Physical access to and within archives—Are the shelves reachable? Are the study tables usable?—can be equally challenging, requiring planning, various sorts of accommodations, and budgeting for the same.

There is an even more fundamental, methodological as well as material, question: Does one "pass," a possibility for those with physical limitations that are not (immediately) visible?[4] Or does one let research participants know ahead of time that one needs some form of accommodation? As with other sorts of researcher demographic attributes, which enable access in some situations and block it in others, this question has no universal answer. "Common sense" might suggest advanced notice as part of planning, e.g., for an interview: making sure ahead of time that the participant knows what one's access, seating, drinking, toilet, and other needs are. But at least one action research ethnographer we know at times intentionally does not apprise prospective interviewees of his wheelchairedness, feeling that the surprise factor—and their ultimate need to arrange to carry him physically up the stairs where there is no (functioning) elevator—can work to his advantage in the subsequent interview (Mike Duijn, personal communication, October 2008). Shah (2006: 216, emphasis added) comments on both methods and methodological issues when she writes:

> Although I carried out the interviews, a non-disabled support worker was present to facilitate access to fieldwork settings, ensure the data collection tools (i.e., mini disc recorder) were working, and assist with any problems that emerged. She could also reflect on the visual dynamics that were shaping the discussions between the interviewer and participant, and take additional field notes when required. . . . On the few occasions where I could not make myself understood to the participant, the support worker would amplify my voice and repeat the question for the participant, thus changing the dynamics between the three people and *enriching* the interview situation. However, from the outset it was agreed that the support worker should have her own strategies to avoid being drawn into the formal discussion between the researcher and the young person. She did this by positioning herself out of the young person's visual range.

It is worth underscoring her comment that the aide's interventions, far from harming (biasing?) the interview, enriched it! Although Shah presents her comment in the context of "the methodological privileges available to a disabled researcher doing disability research" (2006: 217), we see no reason that these advantages cannot apply also to research on other topics. We look forward to a day when these issues are a central, yet unremarkable aspect of research design thinking.[5]

Interpretive Research and Human Subjects Protections Review

It is increasingly required that scholars formalize their research ideas as soon as they conceive of them as potential research projects and submit them for some form of ethics review. Unlike journalists who, in the US, enjoy First Amendment protections that allow them to follow the trail of a story interviewing whoever will agree to it, social science researchers today must submit research proposals for prior review to Institutional Review Boards (IRBs) in the US or to similar committees elsewhere that bear the responsibility of assessing whether the researcher has taken adequate measures to protect the rights of human research participants (and animals, in other arenas of the research world). In this section, we address the specific concerns that arise when an interpretive project involving human participants is reviewed by an IRB in the US. We are aware of parallel policies pending in EU member states, as they develop their own "code of researcher conduct" review committees, largely modeled on their image of US policies and procedures. Other states—Australia, Canada, and the UK among them—have their own boards and policies, which may or may not raise similar concerns. A full comparative analysis is beyond the scope of this volume, but as this is a major concern in a significant part of the research world, we outline the issues here, with US IRBs as our case, in the thought that it may be enlightening for others submitting research for review to ethics and other committees elsewhere.

We begin with a brief summary of the historical background of US policy, as the EU member states' policies we have seen, which claim to be modeled on the US approach, appear to be ignorant of the ways in which this history, much of which they do not share, has shaped that policy. And the specific privacy laws of the EU and its member states, which drive their data protection policies, are different from US IRB preoccupations. IRB policy is potentially of concern to non-US scholars, too, who collaborate with US researchers. As we have noted elsewhere, US institutions are increasingly requiring non-US research partners to provide documentation of equivalent review at their home institutions (Yanow and Schwartz-Shea 2008). We anticipate that this will influence EU and other non-US policymaking in the near future.

Institutional Review Boards were created in the US as part of federal policymaking that developed between the 1970s and the late 1990s in response to perceived violations of research ethics.[6] The "pre-history" of this legislation started with international response to the experimentation on human subjects conducted by Dr. Josef Mengele, in particular, and others during the Nazi regime in Europe. Three international resolutions—the 1947 Nuremberg Laws, the 1948 Declaration of Geneva, and the 1964 Declaration of Helsinki (the latter two from the World Medical Association)—sought to define and protect the rights of human subjects by articulating general ethical principles to guide research (respect for persons, beneficence, and justice). The more immediate antecedents to US legislation were specific to the US: medical and psychological experiments conducted by scientists in US institutions, often with federal funding, which came to light or drew attention in the 1970s–1980s. These included the 1928–1972 Tuskegee syphilis experiments (conducted by the US Government Public Health Service);[7] the 1951–1974 Holmesburg pharmaceutical tests (funded by the CIA, US Army, Dow Chemical, Johnson & Johnson, and over 30 other federal agencies and commercial companies); Stanley Milgram's 1961 and later psychological experiments (on subjects' compliance with orders); and Philip Zimbardo's 1971 Stanford prison experiment studying abuse of authority (funded by the US Office of Naval Research). Some would also include Humphreys' 1965–1968 sociological observation of gay male bathhouse behaviors.

This history led to a series of legislative acts and policy documents: the 1974 National Research Act, which created the National Commission for the Protection of Human Subjects of Biomedical and Behavioral Research; the latter's 1979 Belmont Report (*Ethical Principles and Guidelines for the Protection of Human Subjects of Research*); the 1991 Federal Policy for the Protection of Human Subjects, the so-called Common Rule; and the 2001 National Bioethics Advisory Commission (NBAC) *Ethical and Policy Issues in Research Involving Human Participants* (Volume I) report. Although created at the federal level, these US policies rest on their implementation at local levels, through university-based or private "institutional review boards" (where the broad policy name comes from). This includes determining the content of the consent form that participants are required to sign indicating awareness of the possible harms they might incur from participating in the research, as well as deciding whether or not the researcher must administer such a form.

Initially designed on the basis of an underlying, albeit unarticulated experimental research design, the Common Rule has extended IRB oversight to other research designs starting in 1991, including field research and even, in some cases, oral history and other forms of humanities research. As part of IRB assessments, board members in some places, at some times, also evaluate the scientific merits of the proposal—*despite the fact that this is not part of the federal policy mandate that created these boards*. Research designs can figure prominently in such judgments.[8] This has become a problem for those conducting interpretive research (and, in some places and times, qualitative field research), when board members are familiar with and expect an experimental research design (with its formal hypotheses, specified variables, and testing, validity, and reliability specifications) but, instead, are confronted with a research design with a very different character.

To recap what we have laid out in previous chapters: experimentalists have, on the whole, more control over their laboratory settings and research subjects than field researchers have over their field settings and research participants. This, plus the specifics of their kinds of research and types of subjects or participants, means that experimentalists typically have more power in and control of their research settings than field researchers do of theirs, especially when the latter are conducting research among societal, political, and organizational leaders, experts, and other elites. The open dynamism and requisite flexibility of interpretive research designs, the fact that participants may choose a different form of participation than that initially envisioned by the researcher, the potential risks faced in some projects by researchers, the fact that interpretive research at times begins, in effect, long before the researcher even envisions doing research on that topic, the lack of researcher controls over settings, events, and persons—none of these conforms to expectations of designs that approximate experimental research or to IRB procedures that in effect control for both researcher and participant agency. This does not mean that interpretive (and qualitative) researchers should be let off the hook with respect to protecting research participants; on the contrary! But it does mean that their concerns, and the kinds of permissions and release forms they need to use, are different.

For example, field researchers working in contested terrains, whether among insurgents or among perpetrators and survivors, or among risk-seeking populations and/or practices, such as drug users and graffiti taggers (Librett and Perrone 2010: 739), need to take precautions with respect to inadvertently having their participants tagged as collaborators, traitors, and the like, endangering their well-being and their lives. Requiring signed consent forms under such circumstances would likely achieve the opposite of IRB protection purposes. Oscar Salemink (2003: 4) relates three such incidents, among them the story of Georges Condominas, a French anthropologist working in Vietnam who described a man's marriage in a subsequent publication. Some two decades later, Condominas learned that the subsequent, illegal translation of that book by the US Department of Commerce distributed to the Green Berets (a US Special Forces unit) had led one of its officers to identify and torture the man. As Salemink suggests, such outcomes can be the result of researcher naiveté as much as of oversight. This account highlights the extent to which publication may pose a far greater risk to participants than researcher "interventions," despite having signed consent forms—or perhaps even because of them.

US IRB procedures are highly ethnocentrically biased. They assume a population of literate, research-savvy, English-speaking, well-off participants, with access to modern technologies regardless of where in the world they are located. One undergraduate, working on her BA honors thesis, was required by her university board to write her consent form in English, despite the fact that the people she was interviewing were not English-speaking.[9] The form had to include a US telephone number which participants could phone should they have concerns about the research—despite the dearth of telephones in their homes and town, the unaffordable expense of a trans-oceanic telephone call had they been able to access a phone, and the fact that no one at the US end of that telephone number spoke their language and they had no access to translators or the ability to pay them.

One feature of interpretive research poses a particular challenge to IRB policies: the fact that research projects often originate in aspects of the researcher's non-academic life, turning into formal research only after the researcher has already gained access, established relationships (although non-research in character), and become familiar with the setting and its "inhabitants" (discussed in Chapter 2). As soon as scientists conceive of their ideas as potential research projects, IRB policy would require them to formalize these ideas as research designs in order to submit them to human subjects protection review. How a board would handle the prior contact common in some interpretive research is unknown, indicative of the ways in which these policies are out of synch with interpretive research practices.[10]

A second, procedural matter arises out of the flexible openness of interpretive research designs requiring on-the-spot response to what might transpire in the field, but it is a potential issue shared with other forms of research: the extent to which design implementation varies from design plans, and the stated intent of some IRBs to begin to require the equivalent of an "exit license" (Schwartz-Shea, fieldnotes, 19 September 2006). This would explore the extent to which researchers in the field carried out what they said they were going to do in their proposals, in particular (we imagine) with respect to human participant protections. Until now, such oversight has not been enacted, as far as we know, and the threat appears to go far beyond federal policy. Moreover, the extent to which actual research conforms to protocols is at issue in laboratory research itself (one of several problems in pharmaceutical trials reported in Hill *et al.* 2000, for example), where the image is that conformance is not only the ideal but the reality. If local IRBs begin to institute these sorts of post-review reviews, the ripple effects of this cast stone will echo far beyond the ponds of interpretive and qualitative social science.[11]

Facing IRB practices, there is little that interpretive (and qualitative) researchers can do at this point other than to be knowledgeable about federal policy, to be aware of the kinds of challenges they might face, and to prepare themselves to respond. There has been little uniformity in local IRB policies and practices from one university to another—federal policy rests on local implementation—and no set of case law and precedent, although this may be changing with the advent of accrediting associations for IRBs.[12] Various social science associations, as well as individual scholars, have begun to pay attention to these matters and to try to educate the oversight agencies at the federal level to the needs of non-experimental social science research designs.[13] In Librett and Perrone's words concerning ethnographers, "If [researchers] are to return from the pale of academic deviance, a better effort must be made to engage and explain the relevance of interpretive research in an academic milieu obsessed with prediction" (2010: 744).

We hope that this brief discussion might assist researchers engaging in these conversations at the local level. Understanding the differences between what federal policy mandates and what is left to local interpretation and implementation might help as they respond to issues that might arise when boards examine interpretive research with an experimental design in mind. We also hope that this might alert researchers in other parts of the world to the potential

complications that may arise in their own locations from research regulation policies that are built on experimental research designs alone, as well as to possible
difficulties arising from collaborations with US scholars operating under present
research regulation regimes.[14]

Data Archiving and Replicability

Replicability—the ability of another researcher to repeat a research project, repro-
ducing the process through which data were initially generated, with the same
results—has become a central feature of certain kinds of science. It is increasingly
being heralded in the social sciences, along with—and perhaps influenced by—
the development of large databases. In service of the positivist ideal of research
replicability and as it is costly in both money and time to collect large amounts
of quantitative data, pressure is increasingly being brought to bear on researchers
who have built databases out of their own collected data to archive these. This,
in order to enable other researchers to develop their own research by replicating
the archived research or by reusing archived data to address different research
questions. The archived data become, for all intents and purposes, self-standing,
context-independent databases. Indeed, some journals, such as the *American
Journal of Political Science*, have recently announced editorial policies limiting publication of accepted empirical research manuscripts to those for which authors
make the data available to other researchers.

   This practice raises all sorts of concerns for both qualitative–positivist and
qualitative–interpretivist researchers, given the ethical considerations raised by
their having promised confidentiality in the process of acquiring and generating
information. Some sources of data are impossible to disguise: known figures (e.g.,
the Minister of Immigration during a particular regime or era); unique organizations (e.g., the only major interstate bridge-building mega-project connecting
two countries), especially when understanding what has gone on in the research
setting requires knowing cultural or sociopolitical information about it or unique
socio-political or other group features (e.g., the Black Panthers; Davenport 2010).
If confidentiality has been offered and accepted and disguise is not possible, archiving runs the risk of violating that promise as other researchers—and, potentially,
not only researchers—have access to the data.[15]

   With respect to fieldnotes, aside from questions of the confidentiality of
materials contained in them, archiving in order to make them available to other
researchers makes little sense. For one, they are typically, literally, *notes*: scratches
of ideas and thoughts and records of conversations, observations, and so forth,
made by a researcher—often in a hurry, under fieldwork, rather than deskwork,
conditions—as an *aide de memoire* to jog recollections later when, under calmer,
quieter, and more reasonable working conditions, she can sit down to work them
out in more narrative form in the research manuscript.[16] Those notes are not
likely to be meaningful to a researcher who did not experience what the notes

summarize. Julian Orr (personal communication, 13 November 2010), draws a useful contrast with "the records of an archaeological excavation, in which the point is to record the exact location in three dimensions of every artifact, while also detailing the changing soils."[17] But the differences between studying unmoving, nonreactive potsherds and moving, reacting people are clear. Moreover, some IRBs require researchers to destroy their fieldnotes after a time, as further protection of participants, a common requirement in The Netherlands and other EU member states under "personal data protection" or other privacy laws. This would prohibit archiving altogether (and pose problems for cross-continental collaborations with clashing US and EU institutional rules).

Furthermore, there are important questions to be asked about the quality of the databases that are made so readily available to other researchers. McHenry (2006), for instance, analyzes the entries for India in the Cross-National Time-Series Data Archive (CNTS) developed by Arthur S. Banks, specifically the three categories that represent domestic conflict: general strikes, riots, and antigovernment demonstrations. These three do not reflect lived experience in India itself: living and working there, McHenry found at least nine different kinds of disturbance, a far more nuanced picture than that suggested by the database—leading one to think that research using CNTS might be seriously flawed.[18] As Becker (2009: 549) writes, "[R]esearchers can use statistics others have gathered, but only when they have independently investigated their adequacy for a theoretically defined purpose, something that can never be taken for granted." We suggest this holds not only for data in statistical form.[19]

For interpretive researchers, aside from the ethical and data quality concerns posed by data archiving, other research process features make replicability itself— the reason for data archiving—less appropriate and less thinkable. For one, it assumes a cut and dried, fixed research process, rather than a dynamic, flexible design: the former promises clear, specified steps which are, at least in principle, capable of replication, whereas the latter, given its variability in response to local conditions and specific persons, is much less replicable. Moreover, even if research processes were, in principle, replicable based on the researcher's fieldnotes and other tracking records kept for the purposes of reflexivity and transparency, interpretive researchers assume that competent researchers must respond to field contingencies. These are not likely to be replicable, and they may well reflect the identity and persona of the researcher, as well as that of participants, who cannot be counted on to reappear—or even to articulate the same views in the same words or tone of voice. Another researcher, different research circumstances—quite aside from what might be called, turning the table on its head, "participant effects," "setting effects," "event effects," and so forth (and not just "interviewer effects" or "researcher effects")—all limit the extent to which field experiences can be replicated. As with other matters, this difficulty is caused not by researchers who are not "objective," but by the dynamic character of social life. Unfortunately, the willingness to archive for the purposes of replication has been conflated with the research value of transparency (e.g., Lamont and White 2009: 85, Albright and Lyle 2010: 17). This means that interpretive researchers may need to clarify that they are not opposed to transparency even as they contest the norm of replicability as applicable to all forms of research and, in particular, to their logic of inquiry.

Many scholars who archive their data are likely to see such actions as a service to the research community because their data are then available to other scholars. Moreover, independent archiving by non-state actors and the enhanced availability of some data sets may also be important to transparency in democratic systems because, as Sadiq (2009: 37) argues, "every state, democratic or authoritarian, suppresses information about certain groups or phenomena."[20] We concur with Sadiq and Monroe (2010: 35) that the scholarly community needs to pay more attention to the "politics of data collection" and, by implication, archiving. Where archiving is voluntary and do-able conceptually, ethically, and methodologically, we have no quarrel with it. To the extent that the matter is coming into greater play in the context of publishing practices, it is worth thinking through in a research design (as well as more widely in methodological circles), even if it is not taken up there.

Writing Research Designs and Manuscripts

So much time and effort is put into preparing a research design that new researchers might well wonder whether it is "wasted" effort—work done only for the proposal and then forgotten once that has been accepted and the research project launched. As more experienced researchers know, that is far from the case! And so we provide a brief guide for newer researchers as to the "recyclability" of sections of their research designs. We begin with the general structure of a research manuscript as that is produced in many social science fields and show how the sections of the design develop into chapters.

Although in some subfields of some disciplines, experimentation in writing is accepted (e.g., in those fields that draw on more performative methods, such as play-acting, painting, and autoethnography, as used in some areas within educational and allied health studies), many other disciplines—sociology, geography, public policy, international relations among them—still expect fairly traditional written work, even when the methods used are "less traditional," interpretive forms. Within these fields, the "plotlines" of much empirical written work—conference papers, journal articles, dissertations, book manuscripts—often follow a common logic. Moving from a broader focus in the "literature review" to a more narrow one in the "data presentation" back out to a broader engagement in the concluding section or chapter, the shape resembles an hourglass (see Figure 7.1).[21]

The data section (III) is the narrowest part of the hourglass in the sense that it is the most detailed, the most grounded, in its focus. The "literature review" (I) is, by comparison, broader in that it sketches out the domain within which the

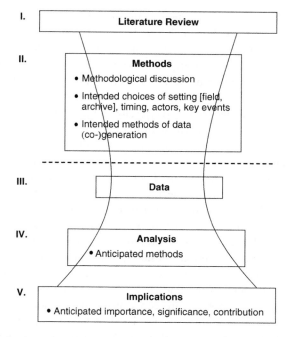

FIGURE 7.1   The hourglass shape of a traditional research manuscript as it relates to a research design. Sections I and II are common in content across research designs and manuscripts; below the dotted line, design contents are different, as indicated from the perspective of the design. Title page, table of contents, acknowledgments, notes, bibliography are not indicated. Original graphic design, Dhoya Snijders, Ph.D. candidate, VU University, Amsterdam; revision, Akiko Kurata, Ph.D. candidate, University of Utah.

conversation concerning the research question is taking place. The methodology/ methods section (II) focuses down from that, in presenting the knowledge-making rationale underlying the data that follow and legitimating the knowledge that will be claimed on their basis. The analysis section (IV) broadens out from the data, explaining to the reader how the data just presented (in III) bear on the specific research question (developed in I) and make sense of its puzzle. And the concluding section (V) explains the significance of the analysis (IV) in terms of the broader context of the research question laid out in section I.

The literature review in the research design, which explains and justifies the research question (the puzzle) and its significance, typically becomes section or chapter 1 of the research manuscript. The proposal's methods section, which presents the actual design of the research project—its "where," "when," "who," "what," "how?"—and whatever methodological explanation and/or justification, typically becomes section or chapter 2, although what is presented in the proposal with a future "I will . . ." orientation becomes the past "I did . . ." in the writing up.[22] (That section or chapter would also include key decisions related to unexpected turns in the field, which have been recorded in the researcher's field-notes.) The remainder of the research proposal—the timetable, plans for disseminating the findings, etc.—is clearly future-directed planning and drops away in writing the research manuscript. Section III is not included in the research design, given that data can only be presented once they have been generated, and the discussion of their intended sources is typically included in section II. But sections IV and V do have their counterparts in the design, at the level of anticipation: what forms of analysis might the researcher use, and what might be the analytic importance, theoretical significance, or other contributions of that analysis?

Some researchers feel that the methods discussion, focusing as it does on the nuts and bolts of the research project, is a logical misfit in this second position, interrupting the flow of exposition that seemingly should run directly from its theoretical argumentation and situating to the data presentation. (And indeed, one sometimes finds the methods section in an appendix, rather than in the main body of a manuscript.) When one considers, however, that the argumentation in the methods chapter serves to legitimate, to authorize, the evidence presented in the subsequent chapter and the knowledge claims advanced in the analysis and concluding chapters, its position in second place makes logical sense. Its placement in this position contributes at the level of logical exposition to research transparency in that this chapter explains the knowledge-generating assumptions on which the presented data rest.

While the general construction of a research manuscript may follow the traditional hourglass model depicted in Figure 7.1, the "feel" characteristic of an interpretive research manuscript is quite different from that of a positivist–quantitative (and perhaps even –qualitative) manuscript, built as it commonly is around a table or tables containing findings in statistical form. The table(s) signal(s) to reviewers and other readers that the researcher has followed the expected steps and processes characteristic of positivist research—the initial threshold after which detailed assessment of the manuscript's quality begins. Interpretive manuscripts also communicate that their authors have followed the criteria and standards appropriate to their methodological approach, but do so in different ways. Some aspects of this signaling begin already in the research design. For instance, a researcher signals the intent to map for exposure and intertextuality, to be open to revising research plans as the need arises (including what some of these circumstances might be and how they might be handled), and to be reflexive about positionality in the plans for various methods of data generation (and perhaps analysis) discussed in the research design. The enactment of reflexivity, though, along with other standards (notably, thick description), is woven into the writing of the manuscript itself, along with the manifestations of other criteria or standards that have been followed (Schwartz-Shea and Yanow 2009, Yanow 2009).[23]

Might there be other ways of writing interpretive manuscripts? Scholars writing autoethnographic research have broken a fair amount of ground on this front (see, e.g., Ellis and Bochner 2000); others have explored performative styles of writing. Laurel Richardson (2000) has called for treating writing itself as a method of inquiry. One of us argued for a different dissertation structure with her advisor. She wanted to begin with the story of the organization being analyzed—its history, development, structure, actors, key events, and so on. As her own sense-making and theorizing about the case had emerged from that evidence, how would a reader be able to make sense of the theorizing without having the data presented first? Her advisor argued to the contrary: how could a reader make sense of the case material without a sense of the theoretical hooks through which its presentation was constructed? Being a dutiful graduate student, she complied, coming eventually to see the wisdom in that argumentation. In recent years, however, she has sought to begin papers and articles with a brief narrative of key empirical events, to set the stage for the theorizing. After all, story-telling captures an audience's attention, as we know from the relevant research literature (e.g., Boje 2008, Czarniawska 2004, Gabriel 2000, Hummel 1991). As (co-)authors, the two of us now often use carefully chosen epigraphs to the same desired end. As more and more social scientists experiment with breaking the frame of traditional, realist–objectivist writing, including greater use of the authorial "I," we may see changes in this hourglass model.

8

SPEAKING ACROSS EPISTEMIC COMMUNITIES

This book has been an effort not only to elucidate what it means to conduct research informed by an interpretive approach, but also to enable scholars from different epistemic communities to converse with one another. For the sake of scientific discourse about substantive research topics that matter to their researchers, scholars need not only to be able to recognize distinctive research approaches, including those designed from an interpretive perspective; they need also to be able to communicate with one another about the varied contributions of the research, even when—or perhaps especially when—those conversations cross epistemic communities and their respective methodological presuppositions.

At the beginning of the book we deferred one methodological topic that, in some of its uses, calls for putting interpretivism and positivism in direct engagement with each other: mixed methods. We pick that up now, briefly, engaging both its referential clarity and its challenges to logics of inquiry, and then turn to another arena of conversation that potentially crosses epistemic communities: research design reviews. In conclusion, we pick up some threads woven throughout the book, including the matter of the abilities and training required to conduct interpretive research.

Designing for "Mixed Methods" Research

In some research arenas, primarily those in which interpretive or qualitative methods are still challenged as not fully legitimate modes of doing science (i.e., labeled as "soft" or treated as useful only as a preliminary stage subordinate to the "hard," quantitative research), arguments have arisen on behalf of "mixed methods." What it means, precisely, to "mix" methods—or, even more specifically, what the use of the phrase "mixed methods" signals—is, however, not always spelled out, leading to one sort of potential confusion originating in linguistic meanings, both denotative and connotative. A second sort of confusion emerges at a methodological level.

At the denotative level of language, ethnographic and participant observation practices in the various disciplines that use them (whether in positivist or in interpretivist approaches), for example, have long "mixed" "methods"—if by methods one means the three fundamental processes drawn on in generating data: observing (with whatever degree of participating), talking to people (including more formal interviewing), and examining research-relevant materials. As these kinds of approaches have not been thought of as mixing methods, this insight points to one of the difficulties in parsing the meaning of the term. Does "mixed methods" refer only to mixing methods of data generation, as when realist interviews are used in combination with a survey questionnaire in a single research project? Or does it mean "mixing" at analytic stages, as well, as in the combination of semiotic squares and category analysis? Or "mixing" in the same project and research question, or across projects and questions addressing the "same" research topic?

In one stream of work, the term "mixed methods" has come to denote combinations of "quantitative" and "qualitative" methods in the same research project, at whatever phase (data collection, analysis). In this context, what is "mixed" has acquired a wide range of specific referents. In the inaugural issue of the *Journal of Mixed Methods Research*, for instance, editors Tashakkori and Creswell (2007a: 4) list seven types of mixing. Their categorization scheme includes techniques that combine data collection and data analysis (e.g., focus groups and surveys; statistical and thematic analyses), as well as different forms of data (e.g., numerical and textual), types of sampling procedures (probability and purposive), and "two types of conclusions (emic and etic representations, 'objective' and 'subjective,' etc.)."[1] Another exploration of mixed methods (R. Johnson *et al.* 2007) identifies nineteen different definitions. The term has also been used, particularly in the comparative politics subfield of political science, in reference to the admixture of distinctive forms or traditions of research in the same study, such as the combination of case study methods with either formal modeling or statistical analysis (Ahmed and Sil 2009, Chatterjee 2009).

Still other forms of mixture appear under the name "multiple methods," promoted in particular by Nobel Laureate Elinor Ostrom and her colleagues (Poteete *et al.* 2010). Poteete (2010), who uses "multi-method research" seemingly with the same meaning, adds, in our reading, two other ways of defining the combining of methods. In one, the mix entails tacking back and forth between different traditions of research while focusing on the same research topic (common pool resources, for Ostrom and her co-authors). In Ostrom's research agenda, for example, findings derived from field observations were reformulated as formal models and then tested in a laboratory setting. For Poteete (2010: 29), this means that "the generality [a.k.a. generalizability] of field observations [from their setting of origin to another] can be evaluated using experiments." In a second usage, multiple methods refers to teams of researchers with expertise in different methods who collaborate on a large project—a design common in clinical research—each team contributing its particular methods expertise to the study of a common question. Poteete (2010) describes multi-disciplinary research teams, such as the International Forestry Resources Institutions research program that combines the work of natural scientists, economists, and others who "conduct field research in forest sites using a common set of data-collection protocols and contribute data to a common database" (Poteete, 2010: 32), as well as multi-sited research teams investigating gender–state relations, such as the Research Network on Gender Politics and the State.[2]

Beyond its jumble of denotative uses, the term also conveys other meanings. "Mixed methods" appears to be held out in some research communities across the social sciences as a solution to the perceived crisis concerning the scientific status of traditional qualitative—i.e., interpretive—methods. In this use lie both a move to combine quantitative and qualitative or interpretive methods in the same research project and an implicit strategic rationale for that move. This strategy can be seen in the editorial statement of the new *Journal of Mixed Methods Research*, begun in 2007, which defines both its aims and "mixed methods" quite broadly as the publication of articles that "explicitly integrate the quantitative and qualitative aspects of the study" as used in "collecting and analyzing data, integrating the findings, and drawing inferences using both qualitative and quantitative approaches or methods" (*Journal of Mixed Methods Research* 2007).[3] The strategic rationale can also be heard in less formal discussions of the need for mixing methods. What is animating this movement is not necessarily the needs of a research question that calls for such mixing, but a climate in many social sciences today that disparages qualitative research, not to mention interpretive research. In some disciplines, this seems to be a response to the challenge posed by King *et al.* (1994) to make qualitative research resemble more strongly the scientific apparatus those authors present, normatively, as characteristic of natural and physical science (the singular used intentionally). The feeling among those who adopt this view appears to be that adding quantitative methods to research projects whose approach is, at heart, qualitative or interpretive will somehow still critiques of them as "lesser" forms of science.[4]

In some disciplines, debates about "mixed methods" appear to be increasing. Some, such as Poteete (2010: 28, emphases added), assert claims about the desirability of multi-method research as if they were uncontroversial:

> The complementarities of qualitative and quantitative research *are well known*. In multi-method research, *the strengths of one method can compensate for the limitations of another*. Furthermore, confidence in findings increases when multiple types of evidence and analytical techniques converge.

This statement assumes that those strengths and weaknesses are self-evident and widely accepted, as well as that their pairing will cancel out each other's limitations. Although we argued (in Chapter 5) that intertextuality, in drawing on multiple types and/or sources of evidence, can enhance the trustworthiness of an interpretive analysis, we do not imagine this author or other advocates of mixed methods have this kind of mixture within an interpretive approach in mind.

For other scholars, mixed-methods inquiry promises to be a new paradigm for research, although they recognize that it still poses many unresolved questions (Greene 2008). Specifically, some argue that these various types of combinations of methods create additional problems for the scientific quality of such research. Ahmed and Sil (2009: 2, original emphases), for instance, worry that the emphasis on multi-method research "is quickly turning into a new dogma that researchers *must*, or *ideally should*, incorporate 'all means available' to validate their work." Arguing that "there is no epistemologically sound reason to elevate [multi-method research] above others" (meaning single-method approaches to research; 2009: 3), they speculate that the movement to advance the mixing of methods "may ultimately hurt the quality of scholarship, producing thin case studies, shoddy datasets, and unsophisticated models" (2009: 5).

This concern points to a second kind of confusion, one raised by the use in a single research project of methods underpinned by different ontological and/or epistemological premises. From our perspective, mixing methods within a single methodology (e.g., combining a survey with regression analysis, or metaphor analysis with semiotics) is, on the face of it, unproblematic. But when the methods that are mixed rest on different, and conflicting, notions of social realities and their know-ability, the mixing can produce research that is not logically consistent or philosophically coherent (a point made also by Blaikie 2000 and P. Jackson 2011: 207–12). To wit, it requires accommodating both realist and constructivist ontological positions and objectivist and interpretivist epistemological ones within research addressing a single question, and these mixings pose tremendous difficulties of logic. A researcher who uses a survey instrument, for instance, with its a priori concept formation and analytic presuppositions of a singular reality, along with its promise of producing results that closely mirror social realities, would be violating those principles by also drawing on data-generating and analytic methods grounded in local knowledge and multiple social realities—in addressing the same research question. That is, in such a combination, the search for the singular truth would require disregarding or dismissing the very ambiguities and multiplicities of meaning-making on which interpretive research questions often center. And vice-versa, a researcher who is interested in a meaning-focused inquiry exploring the lived experiences of particular persons in particular settings or as recounted in archived documents would be contradicting the ontological and epistemological presuppositions underlying those approaches in turning to a data analytic technique (e.g., quantitative content analysis) that strips away that very context.

In such situations, we have "mixed methodologies" more than "mixed methods." It is hard, if not impossible, to square research that rests on constructivist ontological presuppositions and interpretive epistemological ones with research that rests on realist ontological and objectivist epistemological ones. Blaikie (2000: 274) makes the same point in saying,

> [W]hat cannot be done is to combine data that are produced by methods that each deal with different (assumed) realities. It is not possible to use data related to a single "absolute" reality to test the validity of data related to multiple "constructed" realities, regardless of what methods are used in each case.

Ontological and epistemological presuppositions affect the very articulation of a research question itself. In the "combining" or "mixing" of approaches, the question is likely to transmogrify. It can happen that a researcher wants to explore a research *topic* that encompasses several research *questions*, each of which necessitates adopting a different approach. We see this, for example, in research exploring changes in social welfare policies (the research topic), in which the researcher wants to measure the economic impact of the changes on various categories of recipients (a quantitative research question), as well as to understand what the new policy means to welfare recipients from the perspective of its effects on their everyday lives (an interpretive or qualitative research question; see, e.g., Schram 2002). In such a situation, *the specific research question itself shifts*, and along with it, the design that outlines a plan to address that question. Blaikie (2000: 274) also sees the possibility of taking up what he terms qualitative and quantitative methods in sequence, "possibly with switches between approaches/paradigms," as long as the ontological assumptions within each are the same. The resulting research can be said to mix methodologies within a single research topic, and perhaps to mix methods within a single methodology; *but it does not mix methodologies within a single research question.*[5]

Equally important is the implication for interpretive methods of some methodological discussions of mixed methods research, in which the preeminent design issue concerns the appropriate sequencing of methods to be mixed. The mixture under discussion in this particular literature clearly concerns qualitative (or interpretive) and quantitative components of a study. The central question is whether qualitative/interpretive and quantitative components are to be undertaken simultaneously or sequentially, and if the latter, in which order. But in these discussions the distinctions between approaches (i.e., positivist–qualitative and interpretive–qualitative) are submerged in ways that tend to emphasize a logic of inquiry and nomenclature that is more positivist than interpretive in tone (e.g., invoking the need for "sampling" and "consistency"; see Collins *et al.* 2007, Tashakkori and Creswell 2007b). Such treatments not only subordinate qualitative or interpretive research to quantitative research. They leave little room for fleshing out the interpretive component's logic of inquiry in the research design, including its associated standards (such as reflexivity), to the fullest, depriving interpretive–qualitative methods of their scientific grounding. The consequence is a weakening of their scientific standing, precisely the opposite of what the mixed methods movement has stipulated as its intended achievement.

We hasten to note that advocating for "methodological pluralism" is not the same as arguing for mixed or multi-methods research. The former constitutes an appeal within a discipline to give equal standing to all research that draws on one or more of the full range of methods in use within that discipline. Within human or social geography, for instance, it would mean accepting research conducted on the basis of qualitative methods, such as walking the terrain (e.g., Hall 2009), as well as research using quantitative methods, as having claims to equal scientific standing. When interpretive purposes and presuppositions, and their scientific status, are not well understood, confusions of methodology and methods with respect to what is getting mixed, and what is mixable, are more likely to occur.

Crossing the Boundaries of Epistemic Communities: Proposal Review and Epistemic Communities' Tacit Knowledge

With a draft of the research design in hand, researchers of all epistemological persuasions may seek feedback from interlocutors, whether from classmates or a thesis or dissertation advisor (in the case of graduate students) or from a mentor or colleague. In order to focus on matters methodological in these sorts of "reviews," we bracket such issues as the significance of the research question and the adequacy of the literature review, each of which will be judged within the context of the specific area of research being proposed, and look instead at the kinds of questions a research design might raise in general.

The following kinds of questions are commonly on the minds of many readers of all manner of research designs, including those proceeding along interpretivist methodological lines:

- What is the purpose of your research?
- What is the relationship between theory and empirical research (or data) in your project?
- Where are your independent and dependent variables?
- Where is your control group?
- What sorts of causal relationships does your research intend to explore?
- What manner of prediction can/will you make on the basis of this project?
- Are your findings going to be generalizable?

We hope the preceding chapters of this book make clear that all but the first two of these questions are inappropriately asked of an interpretive research project—and that the inability of the researcher to engage those questions is not a fault of the research design or a manifestation of the unpreparedness and inadequacy of the researcher. Instead, this kind of cross- or mis-communication is a manifestation of what happens when designs for interpretive research are read by members of other sorts of epistemic communities who are unfamiliar with their methodological grounding.

Assessments of the design will be shaped by its readers' assumptions about the general purposes of research and the forms of explanation that are accepted within the discipline in which it is proposed—that is, within which the particular conversation about the topic and its problematics is taking place—and at times, even within an epistemic community within that discipline. As we have noted, research designs present choices, along with the argumentation that explains and justifies their selection among alternatives, in light of the intended purposes of the research project. Readers will be looking for decisions and choices—of settings, events, actors, times of year for the study, and so forth—that are justified in light of the stipulated research question and which make sense as ways of addressing and exploring it. An interpretive researcher might be asked, for example, for additional justification for the choice of a particular participant role or of a particular archive as a starting point, given the research question defined. In advancing their rationales, authors communicate certain things to their readers, frequently without spelling those out. Often, these are not spelled out because the author is writing for members of the epistemic community of which she is a member, and these ideas are part of the tacit knowledge they share and therefore need not be said.

Within a single epistemic community, with its shared understandings of research purposes and customary practices, feedback will likely be appropriate to the methodological presuppositions underlying the research design. When proposal readers and reviewers come from epistemic communities other than the one in whose presuppositional context the researcher has been working and writing, however, communication may be stymied by any of the sorts of issues we have taken up so far. This can happen when readers-evaluators and author do not share the assumptions and presuppositions common within an epistemic community concerning what constitute appropriate and expected research procedures for the question at hand. A deductive, positivist approach, for instance, with its operationalized variables and promise of refuted or supported hypotheses, implies an architectural or engineering blueprint that can be executed with precision (assuming the competence of the researcher). An abductive, interpretive approach, with its recursive–iterative flexibility and promise of substantive insights about a particular case, implies a more improvisational tack to be taken in response to local, situational social, political, and cultural realities. When the latter sort of research design is read by those expecting the former, who are not attuned to its own logic of inquiry, it may be negatively assessed (as may its written "products" later on when submitted for journal review, etc.) for not meeting the criteria of the first sort of methodological approach.

Such judgments can be made, for instance, when what constitutes the purpose(s) of research is a matter of disagreement across epistemic communities—from contributing to generalizable knowledge to providing insights about the case under study to providing knowledge that will aid in emancipation. Imagine, for instance, how a reader familiar with survey research design, with its orientation toward realist–objectivist knowledge, might be surprised by an ethnomethodological design focusing on the details of participants' meaning-making practices in their daily lives. Interpretive projects may be put at a disadvantage if funders or other reviewers expect interpretive research designs to include positivist methods (or a justification for their absence, a possible outcome of increasing attention to "multi-method research"). Given standard research proposal page limits, it can be challenging both to fully develop the logic of inquiry for an interpretive project and to explain the methodological inconsistency of positivist methods with the articulated research question (and, hence, their absence). We note that quantitative researchers are seldom asked for such explanation, although it might equally be an occasion to ask them to explain why they are not also using interpretive or qualitative approaches to address their research question.

Depending on research purpose, "design" can be understood as an unvarying roadmap or as a flexible plan for guiding situated improvisation in response to local circumstances. Social science reviewers outside of cultural-social anthropology often have not understood the methodological centrality of design flexibility and its necessity for the proposed research project (see, e.g., Ragin *et al.* 2004, Lamont and White 2009; cf. Becker 2009). In the current environment of methodological multiplicity, intended purposes need to be carefully communicated by proposal writers *and* attended to by proposal reviewers in their assessments. Increased awareness of the scientific grounding of these several methodological approaches should lead to proposals being evaluated according to the standards appropriate to the specific logic of inquiry of each.

Should there remain doubters among our readers as to the scientific grounding and contributions of interpretive research—something we have until this point asserted implicitly, without making it the explicit subject of argumentation—should such skeptics still be reading at this point, we have one thing more to say. You may have noticed that at the same time that we have been citing recently published literature, we have also cited works published in the 1940s through 1960s. What they, at the time of publication, called qualitative research and which we have been calling interpretive, such as Becker *et al.*'s on physicians (1977/1961), Dalton's on managers (1959), Roy's (1959) on shop floor workers, Whyte's on the social organization of neighborhood life (1955/1947), and others of that vintage, remains widely read and cited, outstanding examples of what can be achieved through interpretive research methods. Liebow's *Tally's Corner* (1967), for instance, not only remains in print, but "has been translated into multiple languages and has sold more than a million copies" (J. Kelly 2011). As one of the reviewers of this manuscript remarked, these works "have stood the test of time—still read, still taken seriously, after all these years." This is, he noted, a criterion "that is so often proposed by positivist [researchers] as the mark of real science. . . . [That these older works are still] being read now, so many years after their publication, gives a strong warrant for the methods by which they were done."

Practicing Interpretive Research: Concluding Thoughts

A certain degree of mythologizing characterizes discussions of research design. Across the social sciences, the equivalence between "promises" made in formal research designs and what appears in published research is variable.[6] Experienced researchers know that what gets done in the field or in the archive often does not match what was proposed in the research design. Formal methodological discussions contrast with what researchers know "informally," in practice, and what they reveal when they talk among themselves (or "let down their guard," as Gerring, 2007: 148, puts it). Defining scientific purposes exclusively in terms of generalizable knowledge may contribute to such mythologizing among those disciplines or epistemic communities that hold on to that image of science. Research methods textbooks and course syllabi, and perhaps course discussions as well, in some cases also convey this notion that "science" is uniform, and universal, in its prosecution. IRB practices on many US campuses add to this sense of the timelessness and placelessness of science: the imagined ideal-typical form of scientific inquiry is being further reified and mythologized, extended as fact to the non-experimental social sciences. Moreover, as discussed in Chapter 7, campus IRBs may make efforts to control the variability across research designs and their implementation as they seek to assess finished research projects at random against the designs that had been approved.

Still, as noted at the outset of this book, research designs are central to the scholarly gate-keeping processes that characterize the modern university system. Others decide whether the individual achieves the Ph.D., obtains time off from teaching to pursue a project, or receives the grant for travel and other expenses necessary to conduct the research. Independent scholars unaffiliated with universities, colleges, or research organizations are also likely to be subjected to such gate-keeping processes when they seek support for their endeavors. A research proposal with a coherent logic of inquiry articulated in its design is more likely to pass muster with such gatekeepers if there is broader understanding of the scientific bases for both interpretive and positivist approaches.

Given its density, we have not delved deeply in this book into the philosophical terrain which provides the ontological and epistemological underpinnings of the unspoken assumptions behind the reviewers' evaluative questions listed above. We hope that at this point, it is clear that these questions are not generic, applicable to all research designs, but are, rather, reflective of particular philosophical—methodological—assumptions about reality and its know-ability; about the possibility of standing outside that which one is studying and generating scientific knowledge of it from that point; indeed, about the very meaning of "science" and the character of being "scientific." On the one hand, the differences between positivist and interpretive approaches presented and discussed in this book may seem subtle—a "mere" tweaking of such terms as "validity" and "trustworthiness." On the other hand, these differences reflect radically different conceptions of the role of the social sciences in society, perhaps best captured by entertaining the idea of the social sciences as "human sciences" (Pachirat 2006, Polkinghorne 1983).

We hope to have provided a way to think about the differences in logics of inquiry across various approaches to science and a conceptual vocabulary for naming and talking about those differences. As we said at the outset, we are pluralists: we do not think that interpretive research designs hold for all modes of doing science any more than we think that positivist ones are universal in their application. Although all scientists may share a belief in and a value orientation toward the systematicity and suspension of faith to be followed in the pursuit of knowledge, the ways we go about enacting both systematicity and doubt, along with the standards and criteria we hold up to evaluate those processes, vary across epistemic communities. We do not wish a world of inquiry governed by "methodism," the slavish attention to the dictates of technological, methodological, and philosophical purity, but we do wish a social scientific world that makes a place at its table for interpretive and qualitative modes of doing research alongside other modes. With meaning-making and the understanding of ambiguity and multiplicity at their center, interpretive methodologies make essential contributions to knowledge. Research design concepts and processes that recognize these aspects better serve those researchers committed to them.

Finally, some scholars who recognize the skill that is needed to do "sophisticated quantitative research"—we can point to several "boot camps" set up to train graduate students in statistics and other "advanced" analytic methods—hold that "anyone" can do interpretive (or qualitative) work, no special training required. We are hopeful that the discussion in this volume shows that this is far from the case—that knowing how to observe, how to listen, how to ask, including of archival materials, and which choices these entail and how to think about and make them are learned skills, mastered only with repeated practice. Carol Cohn (2006: 106–7) remarks on the fit between her personal proclivities and her choice of research methods: she is genuinely interested in others, she says, temperamentally; a listener, conflict-avoidant, attentive to feelings, and compelled to honest openness about her views—all traits related to skills used in interpretive research. We join with Forsey (2010: 560) in holding that there are "important links between methodology and the personality traits of a social researcher." There are reasons beyond the merely intellectual that some are led to master and enjoy regression analyses, while others are led to master and enjoy narrative analyses. Such a view is in keeping with research on various kinds of intelligence, not all of them held in equal measure by all (Gardner 2006, Goleman 1995). In seeking to explicate the concepts and processes entailed in designing interpretive research, we have engaged in skill-related discussions only briefly (in Chapter 4). We encourage interested scholars to seek out the kinds of readings, courses, and exercises that foster such learning, which will in itself lead to a greater understanding, from the inside, of the interpretive research design concepts and processes we have explored here.

NOTES

Introduction

1 Often, these social science fields or subfields assume that this approach characterizes work in the natural and physical sciences; and given the sense of inferiority carried by many social scientists vis-à-vis those other modes—captured in the language of "soft" versus "hard" sciences—they seek to emulate what they perceive as "true," and better, scientific practices. (In French, interestingly enough, the distinction is drawn between *sciences dures* (hard) and *souples* (literally, supple), the latter fitting nicely with the notion of flexibility in interpretive research.) That many of those other sciences do not conduct their work following the steps of "the scientific method" goes unnoticed. We do not have space to pursue this fully here, but we return to the point at the end of the chapter when we take up textbook presentations of research methods versus their practice.

2 This formulation omits the possibility of a critical realist perspective (see, e.g., A. Collier 1994), which we do not take up in this volume for reasons of space and because we think that, for purposes of research design, the critical realist would unlikely find traditional, positivist designs problematic. For alternative perspectives on critical realism and design, see Blaikie (2000).

3 That this is not a tale only of behavioralism triumphant is clear in Mirowski's (2003) analysis of post–World War II US developments in science and its curriculum, with growing implications for social science worldwide under pressure, today, to follow the US model.

4 Although both qualitative–positivist and qualitative–interpretive methods use one or more of the same three methods in generating data—observing(-participating), talking (interviewing), reading documents—the difference between them is most clearly seen in what they do with data once they have them in hand. If one looks closely, however, one can see that either positivist or interpretive sensibilities inform what researchers indeed do—not only in analyzing data, but also in generating them; so even the orientation toward and enactment of data generation methods is different, as the example of interviewing, above, illustrates.

5 We intentionally cite Ferguson's book here, for several reasons: it is a useful example as it crosses disciplinary boundaries both because of its feminist theoretical argumentation

and because several disciplines trace their theoretical origins to Weberian bureaucracy theory; and it is an interesting bit of interpretive theoretical work that has profound implications for empirical analyses of and interventions in organizations and management practices.

6 See, e.g., Mihic *et al.* (2005). We do know it is also an issue in others of the human sciences (How 2011).

7 We note that the Western Political Science Association has an organized section entitled "Political Theory and Its Applications." The section "welcomes papers at the intersection of political theory and empirical concern, creating a critical dialogue between theory and practice in which events push our thinking further and intellectual labor is performed to conceptualize historical and contemporary developments." Many of the methods of analysis used by political theorists are also used by field researchers analyzing linguistic materials generated from observations, interviews, and other sources: deconstruction, semiotics, poststructuralism, and other exegetical ways of treating texts. Much like anthropologists learning their research methods, these scholars learn and manifest their methods in implicit ways, through the reading, discussing, and writing of texts, rather than through methods courses. Perhaps for these reasons, as well as structural ones having to do with the political science discipline, "theorists" are not recognized as having methods. Our thanks to Mary Bellhouse, Anne Norton, and Elizabeth Wingrove for educating us in these matters.

8 The term "positivism" encompasses the three initial nineteenth-century schools of positivist thought—social positivism, evolutionary positivism, and critical positivism (or empirio-criticism)—along with the early-twentieth-century logical positivism that surpassed them, which emphasizes verification, and mid-twentieth-century post-Popperian neopositivism, which emphasizes falsifiability (see Hawkesworth 2006a, P. Jackson 2011). Reading across disciplines today, we find both verificationist and falsificationist philosophies present, and so we have chosen to use the broader positivist label here. It is often the case that methods texts that treat their subject in keeping with positivist presuppositions make no mention of it.

9 The term "interpretivism" encompasses a broad array of schools with a variety of specific methods that are united by their constructivist ontological and interpretive epistemological presuppositions. For discussion, see Chapter 2.

10 John Van Maanen (2011) has recently added a fourth term to this trilogy—headwork—in reference to the conceptual work that informs research. This includes prior knowledge of both a theoretical–academic and an experiential kind, which we take up in subsequent chapters, although without his terminology.

11 Paradoxically enough, in some influential feminist political theory, to be a "subject" implies having existence and agency. Ella Myers (personal communication, 1 November 2010) notes that Judith Butler, drawing on Foucault, argues that "the status of . . . 'subject' always carries a double-meaning: . . . one is simultaneously 'subject to' constraining conditions and a 'subject' (not object) who is capable of action within those conditions (which are enabling and not only constraining)." This makes agency "a key dimension of what it is to be a subject, even within a social constructionist frame such as Butler's." As Butler (1997: 17) writes, power both initiates the subject and constitutes the subject's agency, so that the subject is "neither fully determined by power nor fully determining of power (but significantly and partially both)." Our thanks to Ella Myers for help on this point.

12 We acknowledge that there are other forms of positivist research that are not overtly variables-based, such as some forms of historical analysis. (To see the extent to which some positivist historical analysis follows a variables-based logic, see the brief discussion by Falleti, 2006.) Still, we have not experienced challenges to interpretivist researchers along the lines of why they did not undertake process tracing or how they dealt with selection bias with respect to choices of period or event, whereas we have witnessed

many such encounters concerning variables and have heard even more stories about such challenges from others.

13 In doing so, we hear political scientist Raymond Duvall's words in our ears, and we thank him for continuing to sound this caution!

14 Nor do we delve into whether practicing positivist or interpretivist researchers can articulate their philosophical presuppositions, beyond the brief discussion on page 4. The extent to which members of each group do so reflects, to some extent, the hegemonic position of the former and the "minority" position of the latter. In "bicultural" fashion (see Bell 1990), interpretivists need to be conversant with the culture and language of the majority as well as with their own. Whereas scholars doing positivist research are rarely called upon to articulate the methodological presuppositions underlying their research, interpretivists often, if not usually, need to do so. We would hope for a certain "bilingualism" and the ability to "code-switch" for both groups, in the name of better communication.

 We also do not discuss whether researchers believe in these presuppositions. As a colleague expressed to one of us, in his experience, it is rare at a conference to hear claims of general laws from positivist, behavioral researchers. Instead, they recognize their studies as imperfect descriptions of a complex world.

15 For an interesting historical fictional account of this period, based in 1630s Oxford, see Pears (1997).

1 Wherefore Research Designs?

1 In other words, settings do not determine methodology! Many kinds of settings, as well as methods, can fit either positivist or interpretivist approaches.

2 Just to be clear, we see a distinction between understanding the broad treatment of a concept in a particular body of research literature, on the one hand, and a priori concept formation, on the other.

3 One exception is the fifth edition of Singleton and Straits (2009), whose revised chapter on ethics, repositioned more prominently from near the end of the book in previous editions to the third chapter, goes somewhat beyond IRB issues.

4 For those who assume that ethics concerns do not apply to their form of research because they are not interacting directly with living human beings, see the cautionary tales in Marks (2005) and Wylie (2005).

5 We are indebted to Lee Ann Fujii for helping us bring out these implications.

2 Ways of Knowing: Research Questions and Logics of Inquiry

1 Our thanks to Markus Haverland for noting that this needs saying—and for saying it!

2 These cases of research questions developing after the research has, in a sense, already started to pose problems for many US IRBs, although it is a long-common way of doing participant observer research and is not (yet) problematic for EU member states. We take this up in Chapter 7.

3 We thank Joe Soss for help drawing out this point.

4 Patrick Jackson (personal communication, Toronto, 1 September 2009) notes that we should be cautious in invoking Peirce's ideas for interpretive methodological purposes, given their origins in positivist thought. Peirce's ideas about abduction, however, apparently changed between his early writings and his later ones (Benjamin Herborth, personal communication, Potsdam, 12 September 2009). (Friedrichs and Kratochwil, 2009: 715, also imply contending interpretations of Peirce's intended meaning.) We suspect that Herborth's point resolves Jackson's. What is presented here would seem to be in keeping with Peirce's later views. Jackson's point, however, supports the

research reality that non-interpretive research can also begin with a puzzle or surprise. But abductive reasoning enables methodologists to articulate a number of characteristics particular to interpretive research which the logic and language of inductive reasoning do not explain, such as the focus on puzzles as the starting point and the iterative–recursiveness of the research process.

5 See also Glynos and Haworth (2007) on retroduction, used synonymously; but see Blaikie (2000) for a usage that distinguishes between the two. For historical background, see Menand (2001). Kuhn's notion of "puzzle-solving" (1996/1962, chapter 4) appears to be a rather different activity from the puzzling that launches abductive inquiry.

6 Thanks to Xymena Kurowska (personal communication, 16 July 2010) for suggesting a turn to etymology and metaphoric meaning to "normalize" the resonance of abduction as a concept.

7 As discussed in Chapter 6, researchers assess these provisional explanations using various checks on their own sense-making.

8 Once again, Joe Soss has helped us articulate what was just below the surface.

9 Although Campbell (1989: 8, original emphasis), in his foreword to a revised edition of Yin's widely read text on case study research, claims that hermeneutics means "*giving up* on the goal of validity and abandoning disputation as to who has got it right," it does not follow from the hermeneutic circle that disputation is abandoned: even among members of an interpretive community who share an understanding as to how data are to be interpreted, disagreements over interpretations are possible. They would be resolved, however, by appeal to those shared understandings (e.g., by appeal to ethnographic data, rather than to statistical analyses). Contra Campbell, this general reasoning about disputation applies to *both* interpretive and positivist research: there can be different ways to interpret statistical results, for example, and such disagreements are resolved by logic and argumentation within a shared epistemological framework.

10 Hatch and Yanow (2008) used the metaphor of painting styles to try to evoke differences in research approaches, seeing in Jackson Pollock's drip paintings this same trace or echo of human action which interpretive researchers seek to grasp.

11 This "front-loading," i.e., working out issues in advance of data collection, means that quantitative research can be comparatively easy to write up, by contrast with both qualitative and interpretive research. Statistical testing means that the "logic" advanced in the design is either supported or refuted, and "writing up" means reporting and assessing the implication of the "results." Without the apparatus of significance testing, both qualitative and interpretive research requires different kinds of attention to the meaning of the evidence, such that writing is, literally, less "formulaic." Finally, as is well recognized, quantitative research also tends to take up less space because "findings" are often presented as equations rather than in the "word" detail necessary to many forms of qualitative and interpretive research.

12 This is one of the things that distinguishes research interpreting theoretical texts—e.g., readings that seek to make sense of Aristotle or Arendt—from the interpretive analysis of empirical data, including the documentary texts that might be drawn on in either historical or contemporary research.

13 See also Sandberg and Alvesson (2011) on what they call "gap-spotting" in existing literature as the source of research questions.

14 Our thanks to Lee Ann Fujii for the analogy and other help articulating this point.

15 In positivist social science traditions, theorizing is understood as "formal" in language and logic, with mathematical systems that are abstract and impersonal still considered the ideal in several disciplines (although see Whitehead, 1997/1925, on the "fallacy of misplaced concreteness": the notion that mathematical formulations are more concrete than descriptions of lived experience). These systems are often described by their creators and advocates as "parsimonious" or "elegant," displaying a clarity in

their postulated causal relationships that other modes of theorizing supposedly cannot achieve. See Lincoln (2010) on these differences and their connections to knowledge accumulation.

16 This does not mean that positivist modes of research do not begin with puzzles, too. But textbook discussions of design, even if they do mention puzzles as sources of research questions, typically do not engage abductive logic. They are more likely to emphasize the "stages" of research, presented in a linear fashion (e.g., Singleton and Straits 1999).

3 Starting from Meaning: Contextuality and Its Implications

1 Others include the historical turn (McDonald 1996), cultural turn (Bonnell and Hunt 1999), pragmatist turn (S. K. White 2004), and so on. What they share is a repositioning of meaning-expression and -communication, along with interpretation, at the center of theorizing about ways of seeing (J. Berger 1972) and knowing.

2 There is an extensive literature on proper question construction and phrasing in survey instruments, intended to control for "interviewer effects" and other forms of researcher influence on participants' responses, something that does not trouble interpretive researchers in the same way, given their different methodological presuppositions about social realities and the ways in which these can be known. We discuss these points further in Chapter 6.

   We do not mean to suggest, however, that survey researchers are completely unconcerned with context. They are, for instance, attuned to changes in meaning over time and whether, with repeated surveying, this would require changing questionnaire language as particular phrases or words become outdated. For instance, in a 2012 version of a survey initially conducted in 1972, should the researcher replace "women's liberation," used when the question was first asked, with the more common contemporary phrase "the women's movement" (Conway *et al.* 2005)? A survey researcher would be concerned with whether "women's liberation" means the same thing in 2012 as it did in 1972 or if it has dropped out of use altogether, thereby rendering the question useless.

   Less discussed are the cultural assumptions underlying survey methodology. Standard techniques may not be possible in countries or with populations that have little experience with surveys. Tessler and Jamal (2006: 436) describe how, in Egypt, those they approached "wanted to think through their responses very carefully" (which was hugely time-consuming), asked for follow-up explanations, or wanted to hear the surveyor's opinion before responding—things not customarily accepted in survey research. And random selection also worried them! Rudolph (2005) describes administering a survey in rural India in 1957, assuming the interaction would involve only one resident and one "woman within" as respondent—only to discover that it took a village, so to speak, to deliberate over the questions and provide answers. See also Chabal and Daloz (2006: 177–84).

3 Williams contests the value of this approach: "There is nothing [in the text] to help the reader decide what is of value in the situation, what they [sic] will find insightful, or on what basis they [sic] might do so" (2000: 219). From our perspective this position misses the point of thick description in this specific situation, which is to enable readers to compare the study context to their own. Moreover, the criticism paints a rather passive portrait of readers that is inconsistent with seeing them as more active meaning-constructors, as suggested by reader-response theory (e.g., Iser 1989) and other interpretive presuppositions.

4 These purposes have been discussed across a wide range of theoretical and methodological fields, among them feminist theorists and researchers (e.g., Cancian 1992, Ackerly *et al.* 2006, Hawkesworth 2006b); critical legal studies (e.g., Halley and Brown

2003); critical race theory (e.g., Crenshaw 1995, Delgado and Stefanic 2001); critical theory (e.g., Prasad 2005, Ch. 9); and action research (e.g., Greenwood and Levin 2007).

5 Williams (2000: 215) argues that interpretive researchers do generalize in a form he calls "moderatum generalization." Noting that Geertz wants to "say something of something" (p. 213), he argues that Geertz is "inferring from specific instances to the characteristics of a wider social milieu" (p. 212). We do not dispute this understanding of generalization, but we note how it is tied to context and, as important, is *not* in the service of building general, a-historical, a-cultural theory. For a brief discussion of Geertz' understanding of the value of the general in relation to the particular, see Adcock (2006: 60–3).

6 This orientation toward contextual meaning-making is seldom acknowledged in general research methods texts, leading their treatment of design to be implicitly, if not explicitly, positivist (Schwartz-Shea and Yanow 2002). Interpretive researchers consulting such texts will find little guidance for producing designs that link meaning and context, along with some advice (e.g., the need to define concepts a priori) that would sever that connection.

7 It is important to note, also, that "thickness" is a relative measure, not an absolute one. For one, both the level and the kind of detail have to be pertinent to the research question: one would not likely report the number of tiles in the ceiling, for instance, in a research project focused on, say, a school principal's management style. Additionally, one needs to take account of one's readers and what they already know, or can be reasonably assumed to know, about the subject. Such judgments lead to accounts that may be "thicker" in some parts than in others.

8 "Local knowledge" is often credited to Geertz (1983), but it has many conceptual antecedents, especially in the field of urban, regional, and international (development-related) planning and its 1970s emphasis on participation in planning and design (see, e.g., Arnstein 1969, Gans 1968, Peattie 1970, and Piven and Cloward 1977).

9 "Formal" models include game-theoretic and other forms of theorizing using mathematical tools. We are not sure how it is that mathematical theorizing has claimed exclusive ownership of the adjective "formal." Referring to other modes of theorizing as "non-formal" (see, e.g., Aldrich *et al.* 2008: 834) is presumptuous, at best.

10 This choice of terminology may confuse those readers acquainted with parallel debates in the field of International Relations. In an influential article, Wendt (1998) distinguished *between* causal and "constitutive" theorizing. Wendt, however, argued for and used a constructivist ontology combined with an objectivist epistemology—putting him at odds with the constructivist ontological and interpretivist epistemological approach articulated in this book.

11 Some scholars identified with interpretive research have used the language of "mechanisms" in their efforts to explain the distinctive ways that qualitative or interpretive research can contribute to causal explanation (see, e.g., Lin 1998). Informed as we are by the arguments developed here, however, we do not find this approach to be helpful. It is also not clear how "mechanisms" in that literature is different from its meaning and use by positivist–qualitative researchers in the comparative case study literature.

4 The Rhythms of Interpretive Research I: Getting Going

1 For a thought experiment on a positivist reviewer's encounter with an interpretive manuscript, see Schwartz-Shea (2006: 90–1).

2 This is the case even when conducting a pilot study, whose results may be used to modify the research instrument prior to beginning the full research project.

3 There are exceptions to this separation of data collection and analysis among positivist–qualitative researchers, most notably in work by Ragin (1997) and Brady and Collier

(2010). As the latter put it, ". . . many qualitative researchers view the *iterated refinement of hypotheses* in light of the data to be essential" (2010: 329, original emphasis). This view has not, however, been incorporated yet in most research design textbooks or course discussions, which tend to articulate the more classic model.

4 This is the sort of advanced preparation and practice undertaken by improvisers in theater and music (Renaissance, jazz, and other forms), which lays the groundwork on which flexible, adaptive responses in the field can be built. See discussion at the end of this chapter.

5 For a comparison between positivist–qualitative and interpretive(–qualitative) ethnography, see Schatz (2009). The fact that ethnographic, case study, and some other forms of research can be informed by either positivist or interpretive presuppositions is what has given rise to the terminological distinction between qualitative and interpretive methodologies, a point discussed in this book's introduction.

6 But see Russell *et al.* (2002: 14) on rapport and its conceptual difficulties: "[N]eo-positivist claims about the technical function of rapport in field research rest on assumptions about the possibility of collecting 'accurate' or 'unbiased' data from and about one's subjects."

7 Paying participants is a debated topic in academic ethics, with practices varying across the social sciences. In experimental research in psychology and economics, it is accepted practice to pay subjects for their participation; in psychology, undergraduate student subjects often receive course credit for participating in experiments. In field settings in other social sciences, it is usually frowned upon (not only by IRBs). That Walby (2010) paid the men he interviewed is of note.

8 This perspective on researcher identity is a far cry from the common positivist view that factors such as personal contacts or language skills are methodologically irrelevant to case selection: "[T]hese features of a case have no bearing on the validity of the findings stemming from a study" (Gerring 2007: 150). That perspective follows from the methodological assumption that "the case should stand for the population" (Gerring 2007: 147), a position consistent with the goal of building general theory, which leads to the severing of a "population" from its context. From an interpretive perspective, this denial of the embodied aspects of research obscures the ways in which researcher characteristics—gender and race-ethnicity, but also ablebodiedness, age, and other factors—may affect access (and, ultimately, the character of social science knowledge).

This is a point that has been central to feminist theory and methods, including the debates on standpoint, as well as to science studies (see Haraway 1991, Harding 1993, Hartsock 1987, Hawkesworth 2006a). Gerring (2007: 146) does recognize that the contemporary social science knowledge base is skewed by attention to "a few 'big' (populous, rich, powerful) countries." He goes on to argue that "a good portion" of the disciplines of economics, political science, and sociology, in particular, is built primarily on familiarity with one country, the US. One might consider the extent to which not treating contacts and language skills as methodologically relevant is responsible for producing this skewing and how seeing such access-related issues as linked, methodologically, to knowledge claims might remedy the problem.

9 She traces her ability to deal with stressful experiences in this way to prior experience as intake director at a crisis center for homeless teens in New York City—another example of the unanticipated ways in which prior knowledge can play a role in research.

10 Our thanks to Lee Ann Fujii, Tim Pachirat, Joe Soss, and Dorian Warren for pointing us to these and other sources.

11 A rhizome is a plant form which reproduces by sending out shoots underground, each of which might give rise to a new plant. The term was introduced by Deleuze and Guattari (1987) as a way of highlighting features that entail connections among multiple nodes which can be entered at any point (a concept theorized also as "networks"). It has since caught on as a way of describing a form of research process.

12 We note that conducting survey research among hard-to-reach groups (e.g., those trying to avoid calling attention to themselves, such as immigrants without official papers) poses its own difficulties.

13 "Small n" research is used across many fields, from sociology (Ragin 2005) to business (S. Jackson 2008), from history (Snow *et al.* 2004) to medicine (Cowan *et al.* 2004). In the field of comparative politics, the literature devoted to the proper selection of cases is voluminous. What constitutes "a case" is the first question; the possibilities include individuals, decisions, social groups, events, and countries, among others. For an overview of the nine possible selection techniques suited to a "small n" case study approach, see Gerring (2007, Chapter 5). The concern with "selection bias" in the choice of country case studies was classically articulated by Barbara Geddes (1990; see also D. Collier *et al.* 2004).

14 Additionally, the selection of cases according to "most similar" or "most different" design logics assumes that what is "similar" and "different" can be determined by an external judge, the researcher. As one of the manuscript reviewers put this point, in reference to the epigraph at Chapter 3: "[T]he fact that we don't know whether or not Indians prefer cold milk in the morning also means that we don't really know what a similar or different case *is*, in most circumstances, at least not without an already-established 'thick' knowledge of contextual factors" (original emphasis). Our thanks to the anonymous reviewer for this key point.

15 We note the implicit and completely unreflective bias in methods textbooks and discussions towards "Western" values of openness when it comes to scientific inquiry, as well as to the implied impartiality and accuracy of governmental and other sorts of data. Tessler and Jamal (2006) and other essays in "Field Research Methods in the Middle East" (2006) provide several examples. See also Sadiq and Monroe (2010).

16 Compiling a complete sampling frame is challenging in other areas as well. US pollsters once found landline phone lists to be comparatively complete for certain tasks (e.g., predicting voting patterns), but cell phones have eliminated this possibility. For particular populations, such as the homeless, immigrants, or others who fear authorities, complete lists are also problematic. Fear of authorities can also have a historic reference point: synagogue and other groups in The Netherlands do not compile lists of members today because of what was done with those lists during World War II.

17 By this positivist logic, a researcher can and should be concerned only with choosing the "best case" for testing theoretical propositions developed a priori. This is not to say that positivist researchers don't encounter obstacles to achieving this ideal (e.g., available sampling frames are inadequate or panel data are distorted by attrition), but that these obstacles are not theorized in relation to researcher identity. (Our thanks to an anonymous reviewer for pushing us toward a more subtle treatment of these points.) For a related discussion of the relevance of researcher identity to knowledge generation, see Note 8, this chapter.

18 This point is what the title of Lincoln and Guba's (1985) seminal text *Naturalistic Inquiry* emphasizes—investigating research participants in their "natural" settings. We have not used this terminology for reasons explained in the introduction.

19 The matter of researcher control seems not to be problematized in methods discussions of these kinds of research, an unintended consequence, perhaps, of extending experimental logic to such settings.

20 The citation is to Charles Ragin. 1987. *The Comparative Method: Moving Beyond Qualitative and Quantitative Strategies*. 164–71. Berkeley: University of California Press.

21 On listening skills in interviewing and sense-making, see, e.g., Forester (2006), Spradley (1979), and Weiss (1994). Forsey (2010) calls for a shift of emphasis to include "participant listening," and not just participant observing.

22 Use of multiple interviewers or research assistants is still relatively rare in US interpretive research, although it is more common in Europe, with the demands of EU

funding driving multi-state studies. The time- and labor-intensive nature of the work for the primary investigator means that "measures of productivity" that are increasingly being developed to assess university researchers, which are attuned to survey and laboratory work, may systematically undervalue interpretive research and researchers.

5 The Rhythms of Interpretive Research II: Understanding and Generating Evidence

1 Thus far, neo-positivists, i.e., those endorsing Popperian falsifiability over logical positivism's verification criterion to demarcate science from non-science, would agree; our discussion is consistent with the idea that observation is theory-laded. (For a clever explication of this relationship, see Shapiro's, 2004: 26, example of questions and evidence about a woman saying "I do" in a conventional marriage ceremony.) However, neopositivists do not take the next step, to the co-generation of data, which is elaborated in the rest of this section.

2 This is a point where our introductory caveats matter! We are drawing attention to the implications of the commonplace notion of the "collection" of data and to the positivist philosophical presuppositions that imply that scientists' theories (can) "mirror" the world. No doubt many practicing positivist scientists are aware of the ways in which the research questions they formulate "create" or "generate" their data. Experiments are purposely set up by scientists to produce data relevant to their questions. Survey researchers emphasize the ways in which their phrasing of survey questions produces particular answers (e.g., Zaller 1992, Walsh 2009). Yet it does not follow that they have necessarily rejected the overarching goal of approximating "reality" through objectivist means.

3 "Pure" autoethnography, in which the researcher uses his own experience in the setting in question as a vehicle for understanding, is a key exception to the idea of data that are co-generated. But some autoethnographies also incorporate others' sense-making. See, for example, Greenhalgh's (2001) study of her own experiences with illness and medical diagnoses. In other respects, autoethnographies generally follow the lines sketched out in these chapters for thinking about research design, and we do not otherwise single them out.

4 The first citation is to J. L. Austin. 1962. *How To Do Things with Words*. Oxford: Oxford University Press. Watson's argumentation with respect to the implications of a speech-acts-and-presentation-of-self take on field research is that it is only the context of daily, ethnographic immersion in a setting that enables researchers to situate what they hear in interviews: ". . . the people who supply us with information would be far more circumspect about what they tell us if they saw us as a person they knew and encountered everyday in the workplace rather than as 'that researcher from the university up the road'" (2011: 210, on organizational ethnography). This leads him to doubt the utility of interviews for understanding, when those interviewed are only encountered in interview events. On the tradeoffs between interviewing and ethnographic research, see Soss (2006).

5 We note in passing that little has been written about the "lies" that researchers tell in the field, typically in the context of masking parts of their non-research identity. See Ellis (1995).

6 This produces what Harding (1993) has called "strong" objectivity—strong because prior knowledge and embodiment are theorized, rather than ignored. We discuss objectivity further in Chapter 6.

7 Although we have not found a published statement to the effect that qualitative (i.e., non-numerical) data are inferior, that quantitative data are better appears to be a tacit assumption among many positivist researchers. This inference is based on the emphasis on measurement in standard methods texts, the ubiquitous equation of science with

"measurement," the unreflective privileging of "hard" over "soft" data, the apologetic tone of some qualitative researchers when presenting their work at conferences, and qualitative researchers' efforts to model their research after quantitative practices. For example, King *et al.* (1994: 23, 25) state that data "can be qualitative or quantitative in style," but they then proceed to discuss the need for *improving* the character of qualitative data in terms of their measurability.

In the second edition of their edited volume, Brady and Collier (2010: 325) state that a "piece of [qualitative] data that begins as an isolated causal-process observation can subsequently be incorporated into a rectangular data set"—presumably in order to improve the status of word-data by rendering them in tabular form similar to that of quantitative data sets. Ragin (1997) has been one of the most forceful voices speaking against this oft-tacitly accepted ideal.

8 Our thanks to Shaul Shenhav for helping us draw out the implications of our thinking.

9 Shaul Shenhav (personal communication, 2 June 2011) draws a distinction between intertextuality in interpretive methods and in positivist ones. In the former, it is "a process of interaction between the scholar's mind and the object of investigation, . . . a living process where the researcher brings whatever he has [acquired] . . . to help him to understand the object of investigation or to address the [research] questions he has. In [positivist] methods this process is rather different. You have many predefined guidelines, the potential arenas are much more narrow, creativity is bounded by pre-defined procedures, [and so on]. In other words, intertextuality in [positivist] methods is restricted to predefined arenas (data sets, statistical procedures, accepted visualizations . . .). Obviously, it affects the mapping and exposure. . . . While both in quantitative and qualitative [positivist and interpretive] methods you have to work very hard to make sense of what you find, in qualitative–interpretative approaches the human efforts for each study start right at the beginning when you [begin to look for this kind of] intertextuality. . . . The difference is not about numbers or the deductive-inductive dichotomy and it is different from Charles Ragin's way of seeing the two approaches. It is more a question of mind-set or cognitive schemes applied while doing research."

10 This does not mean that interpretive researchers do not study similarities. They often ask: What are the shared, yet tacitly known assumptions of members of this group, that make for common ground? Sir Geoffrey Vickers (n.d.) once observed, in fact, that social scientists pay more attention to the "mismatched signal" than they do to the "matched signal"—i.e., to differences, rather than to the shared assumptions and values, including with respect to what needs to remain unspoken, that make a social unit work.

11 "Auditing" also appears in interpretive methodological discussions to designate a similar process of keeping track of major decisions during the research. The term derives from anticipating an "audit" of one's manuscript by future reviewers (Schwartz-Shea 2006).

12 This is one among many reasons why the sort of "data archiving" championed by quantitative and some qualitative scholars ("Data Collection and Collaboration" 2010) is problematic for interpretive research. Additional considerations include the sheer volume of notes generated in the field, the cost of transcription, issues of academic freedom, and, most important, ethical concerns, including promises of confidentiality and the need to protect participants from possible harm. See Chapter 7.

6 Designing for Trustworthiness: Knowledge Claims and Evaluations of Interpretive Research

1 Debates over the general utility of significance testing have even spilled over onto the pages of the *New York Times* (Carey 2011). For a scholarly review see Gill (1999).

2 The problem of construct validity is especially clear in secondary data analysis where researchers adapt indicators that were created by another researcher for her specific purposes to their own research needs. This problem is relevant to data archiving, discussed in Chapter 7. (For an in-depth, nuanced discussion of different measures of construct validity, see Adcock and Collier, 2001.)

3 A National Science Foundation report on standards for assessing qualitative research describes replicability thus: "The description of the methodology should be sufficiently detailed and transparent to allow other researchers to check the results and/or reanalyze the evidence. All reasonable efforts should be undertaken to make archival and other data available to scholars" (Lamont and White 2009: 85). As discussed in this section, "checking the results" presumes a "mirroring of the world" and the irrelevance of researcher identity (see also Chapter 4, Note 8).

4 See, e.g., King *et al.*'s (1994: 31–2, 151–68) emphasis on estimating and reporting uncertainty attributable to "measurement error," a preoccupation for positivist researchers that drives their research design. Behind this assumption lies an aspect of the "unity of science" debates—that the social world can be understood through the same sorts of general, a-historical, a-cultural laws that are understood to characterize the natural and physical sciences. This is an older, and now generally rejected, understanding of how those sciences do their work. For more, see Cat (2010).

5 Although the degree of stability of social phenomena is an empirical question, the positivist gestalt, in searching for causal laws, encourages a neglect of context that often produces a-historical, presentist research agendas.

6 Although some interpretive researchers might emphasize the stability of reified patterns and institutions in their studies, at the more philosophical level these are also understood as humanly constructed and historically constituted and, therefore, potentially changeable, although not necessarily with ease. See P. Berger and Luckmann (1966) for the classic discussion of objectification and reification in the context of social construction processes.

7 This is a methodological point that we do not have the space to discuss in detail, although we emphasize that it concerns interpretation and interpretive communities, not the character of human "nature" (as in the "rational man" arguments in economics). For a philosophical treatment of this understanding of interpretive processes as similar across humans, see Fay (1996), Chapters 1, "Do you have to be one to know one?" and 4, "Do people in different cultures live in different worlds?"

8 The relationship between forms of distance and types of bias has not been engaged in textbook discussions of objectivity. On the other hand, this is the idea at the heart of the notion of "going native" which textbook discussions of qualitative methods so often warn against: that a researcher, in dwelling physically in close proximity to those being studied, would lose the cognitive–emotional "distance" required to study them. All manner of epistemological assumptions are built in to this phrase, as well as ontological ones concerning the character of "member" and "stranger," not to mention a residual colonialist paternalism or even racism (Nencel and Yanow 2011).

9 Experiments have found confirmation bias to affect the judgment of research subjects such as "political experts" (e.g., intelligence analysts, Tetlock 2005), as well as of psychologists and other research scientists (e.g., Shadish 2007). In their report on the National Science Foundation Workshop on Interdisciplinary Standards for Systematic Qualitative Research, Lamont and White (2009: 85–6) treat confirmation bias as a problem in the analysis of qualitative data, presumably because of this experimental literature, although they neither cite that literature nor clarify why confirmation bias should be a specific concern in qualitative research. To guard against it they suggest that researchers test their "novel insights or facts" against evidence gathered independently from the case under study or taken from other cases developed by other researchers.

10 Ethnographers and participant observers often draw on observations of the sort that Webb *et al.* initially designated "unobtrusive" (e.g., noting the amount or character of laundry hanging to dry on a line behind an apartment building as indicative of the kinds of people living there, their age, size of families, etc.). But the original 1966 *Unobtrusive Measures* was retitled in the 1981 edition as *Nonreactive Measures in the Social Sciences*, and the discussion in the text itself clearly signals that the authors were aiming not only at an unobtrusive observer, an accustomed role for participant observers, but one who could achieve uncontaminated, objective observations. Title and text also signal that they intended "measures" to be taken more literally than as a synonym for indicators, for instance.

Reactivity is also understood as a threat to "external validity" (Campbell and Stanley's, 1963, phrase for generalizability): if reactivity combines with the independent variable to cause an effect in the experimental or quasi-experimental setting, the findings of that research may not generalize to, or obtain in, other settings or groups in which researchers are not present. Placebos and their measured effects in medical research, on which there is an extensive literature, are a standard way in which positivists assess reactivity.

11 As survey researchers know, however, respondents often are perplexed by survey questions or categories when these seem not to fit their experiences or views, and they try to get the researcher to clarify them in ways that would mean adapting or adjusting the questionnaire. Researchers in those areas of the world where surveys are not commonly part of the societal culture may find their expectations of respondents' compliance thwarted, with various impacts on their research timetables as they are asked not only to explain questions that are not understood, but to offer their own personal answers to the questions so that respondents can know better how to frame their answers (Tessler and Jamal 2006; see also Rudolph 2005). Researchers who alter or explain the questions to survey respondents have, within the methodological parameters of survey research, introduced bias into their survey results. In this view, researchers are not meant to make "*ad hoc*" responses to individuals even if, in the researcher's judgment, such responses facilitate respondent understanding of what they are being asked.

12 Again, this is an idea that carries over from experimental research design, in which researchers certainly do not—to the best of our current knowledge—interact with cells in petrie dishes, for instance, affecting research outcomes (although this is precisely the point that Heisenberg, in his "uncertainty principle," was articulating with respect to measuring distances in physics and the ways in which the act of measuring itself affects that which is being measured).

13 The concept of reflection also has a place in practice studies and, even more specifically, in management studies, due to the writings of Donald Schön on reflective practice (e.g., 1983). Although methodological reflexivity shares a sense with reflective practice—both of them, after all, are intended to turn the reflector's attention back onto prior acts and to attend to sense-making in and of those acts—reflexivity as a methods practice has received much more elaboration and specification than reflective practice, and they are not identical in their implementation.

14 For instance, one of us is relatively short in height, which, combined with her gender, leads some people in US settings to "see" her as non-threatening and to open up in conversations. But the same traits lead others to question her competence as a researcher. She has learned to anticipate such construals of her identity and to prepare ahead of time a variety of possible responses.

15 Just to underscore the point, we hold that hearing or listening should have equal standing with seeing—what Forsey (2010) calls "a democracy of the senses"—and that emotions can also be a source of knowing and knowledge generation. Consider the interview participant who, seeing the interviewer's eyes well up with tears in response to a pain-filled narrative, decides to open up even further and share additional per-

sonal experiences that she might have otherwise withheld (see, e.g., Bayard de Volo 2009).

16 This approach to reflexivity is associated with Bourdieu, who does not emphasize reflection by the researcher on how her personal characteristics may have affected data generation and analysis processes. Instead, he emphasizes "the systematic exploration of the 'unthought categories of thought which delimit the thinkable and predetermine thought' [citation to Bourdieu], as well as guide the practical carrying out of social inquiry. . . . What has to be constantly scrutinized and *neutralized, in the very act of construction* of the object, is the collective scientific unconscious embedded in theories, problems and (especially national) categories of scholarly judgment" (Bourdieu and Wacquant 1992: 40, original emphases).

17 To the extent that those working with others' databases do not investigate and report how those data were originally generated, they fail to enact this key value.

18 Conflating transparency with replicability, as in the NSF Report (Lamont and White 2009, quoted in Note 3, this chapter), is unwarranted because it is logically possible to be committed to transparency (i.e., being forthcoming about how one did one's research) without assuming that others can duplicate either the reported research processes or their associated results. Interpretive research endorses transparency as essential to science even as it sees the standard of replicability as inconsistent with interpretive presuppositions.

19 Harrell (2006) has a brief, but very useful overview of the evolution of the methodological debates in anthropology concerning the ways in which the researcher represents those studied. Starting from a third-person authoritative voice, criticized as "colonial" and "patronizing" in its treatment of "natives," anthropology underwent a "crisis in representation" in which researchers doubted whether they could "speak for others" (Alcoff 1991, Clifford and Marcus 1986; for overview and analysis, see Atkinson *et al.* 2003).

   Reflexivity in research manuscripts can appear stunted or seamless depending on, perhaps, author uncertainty over these unresolved methodological issues and, frankly, the writing talents of particular authors. Researchers in various fields have tried self-consciously experimental reporting styles and degrees of self-revelation in their reflexive accounts, some of which have been criticized by other interpretive methodologists as narcissistic navel-gazing. We find Alvesson and Skolberg's (2000: 246) critique on this point useful: they are "against the type of self-reflection that leaves little energy left over for anything else," a highly subjective assessment which, if we understand it, is a position we ourselves tend to share.

20 We would, in fact, argue that it begins before, at least during the proposal development stage of research, if not even earlier during degree-related coursework and even in prior experiences, to the extent that these inform the subsequent development of a research question. Lest this line of thinking lead to an infinite pre-research regress, however, we formulate our discussion in the context of a researcher formally developing and carrying out a research project.

21 Forthcoming volumes in this series will engage several of these, including postcolonial analysis, narrative analysis, interviewing, and ethnography.

22 Transcripts of interviews or sections of texts may also be sent back when the initially negotiated permission to quote or cite needs to be confirmed, e.g., when promised confidentiality cannot be kept. This is not what the US literature on member-checking typically refers to, although it is one aspect discussed in the German-language literature (Beate Littig, personal communication, January 2011).

23 King *et al.* (1994: 19, n. 6) note that this "is probably the most commonly asked question at job interviews in our department and many others."

24 We take this specific language, "empirical implications of theoretical models" (EITM), from the National Science Foundation-funded summer institutes that offer training in this approach. See Aldrich *et al.* (2008).

25 Shah (2006: 212), quoting Howard Becker, remarks that "'putting on a show' becomes difficult to sustain for individuals who tend to be more drawn in by the social reality that is more important to them than the researcher's presence." Watson (2011: 210–12) argues a similar point in noting that the researcher's ongoing presence makes the "manufactured data" of one-shot interviews and focus groups less likely to occur.

7 Design in Context: From the Human Side of Research to Writing Research Manuscripts

1 The Western "imperialism" of categories (Rudolph 2005) and concepts (see Schaffer 1998) is another, albeit related matter.

2 Malinowski's diaries, published in 1967, were shocking at the time because the texts revealed the fieldwork methods pioneer of anthropology to have had racist and perhaps classist attitudes, along with an active sexual imaginary. See Geertz (2010: 15–20).

3 Attention to sexual harassment and rape of women in the US military and among news journalists as we were preparing the final version of this manuscript, in Spring 2011, reminds us that both the event and one's emotional responses to it are also silenced in the methods literature, along with other dimensions just discussed. That both are real is known among researchers. We think it time that this conversation, too, come out of the closet, at the very least to prepare newer field researchers so they can think carefully about their movements in the field.

4 Which is not to say that those who can pass unnoticed (or who are "forced to pass," as Hamilton puts it) are not themselves challenged, at times, by the unfetteredly able for *not* being visibly "handicapped"! As Karen Mogendorff (2010: 330) writes, in answer to why she declines to use the bus seat reserved for the disabled, "[A]s long as I am walking it is apparent to everyone in the bus that I am entitled to sit in the seat reserved for disabled people. It is when I sit in the seat reserved for disabled people that my right to sit there is sometimes contested; then it is not visible to the untrained eye that I am entitled to use disability arrangements." See M. Jones (1997), Hamilton (1997), Lingsom (2008).

5 Such "normalization" may, in fact, be beginning. As we were preparing this book, we learned of a new field of study, "crip theory" (McRuer 2006; thanks to Lisa Johnson for pointing us toward the idea and this work). Growing out of disability studies, most of this work is being conducted in philosophy, literary theory, and intersections with feminist and queer theories. But its methodological and methods implications cannot lag far behind (e.g., M. L. Johnson 2011). Historian Mary Felstiner's (2000) essay, concerned with rheumatoid arthritis, illustrates other issues of physical impairment (for its implications for research, see the section entitled Shift Key, 278–80). For a personal account of growing blindness and research, see Krieger (2005a, b). In the book, she wrote: "Because my vision has been gradually growing worse, last summer I took a series of lessons in the use of a blind person's white cane. . . . A man came out to my house. He walked with me along the streets nearby, showing me how to use the cane, feel the sidewalk, go up and down steps, know if a car was parked across a driveway and then how to get around it. *As I walked with him, I learned to listen*" (Krieger 2005b; emphasis added). Another area of silence in design and methods discourses concerns aging bodies in the field, a topic suggested by Harry Wels in light of the research of social gerontologist Kees Knipscheer on aging dancers. This and other discussions, in particular with Mike Duijn and sparked by conversation with him and with Erwin Engelman, led to a 2009 methodological seminar, "The body in the field," organized by Wels and the second author (VU University, Amsterdam, 3 April).

6 The rest of this section draws on research published in Yanow and Schwartz-Shea (2008).

7 These are widely understood as having harmed participants, who were selected along

racial lines among prisoners; but recent research (Shweder 2004) calls this view into question. We do not have the space here to review this more fully.

8 On IRB "mission creep," see Gunsalus *et al.* (2007).

9 We accept the point raised by one reader of an earlier draft that an English version of the form makes sense for an English-reading board. But the same evaluative purpose might have been served through a summary of the form's contents, which are usually fairly standard; a full, formal translation seems unnecessary—and it is in keeping with the ethnocentric myopia and thoughtlessness of the required US telephone number.

10 As a result of IRB policies, US field researchers enjoy less autonomy today than they did in the past. Unlike the journalists mentioned in the section's opening, field researchers must obtain ethics approval before proceeding—even if the ultimate decision is that their research is of minimal risk and therefore adjudged to be "exempt" from some or all IRB requirements. Under these strictures, it is possible that some earlier, path-breaking interpretive field research would have been disallowed. Some scholars (e.g., Shweder 2006) also question whether the current review system has unnecessarily curtailed the principle of academic freedom so central to US higher education (and elsewhere).

11 Most IRBs have "amendment" procedures if researchers decide they need to change their study designs. For example, the University of Utah website states: "The IRB requires an amendment to note any changes related to an approved study. The amendment must describe the modification(s) requested including reasons for the change, whether the modification will increase or decrease the risk of harm to the subject, and whether the consent form requires modification" (http://www.research.utah.edu/irb/submissions/amendments.html, accessed 9 July 2011). If "any changes" is read literally, it would clearly make interpretive research infeasible. If the logic of interpretive research design (and the ways in which flexibility and researcher judgment may be essential to the protection of research participants) were understood by IRB reviewers and staff, such language would have to be modified.

12 See the Association for the Accreditation of Human Research Protection Programs, Inc. (AAHRPP) website at www.aahrpp.org/www.aspx (last accessed 9 July 2011).

13 The burgeoning literature includes several special issues of journals across disciplines and practice areas, among them *The ANNALS of the American Academy of Political and Social Science* (in 2005), *Northwestern University Law Review* (in 2007), *Qualitative Inquiry* (various), and *Social Science & Medicine* (in 2007). For an optimistic view of the possibility of educating one's IRB about the particularities of ethnographic research, see Librett and Perrone (2010). Among other things, they decry IRB conflation of ethics with research validity (p. 737), a key point with which we fully agree.

14 As this book goes to print, existing IRB policies are under federal review. We do not know whether they are likely to be changed and if so, how these changes might affect what we have written.

15 Advocates of archiving argue that "user-access controls" can protect confidentiality (Elman *et al.* 2010). Yet releasing information *to an archivist* could be understood as violating the researcher's promise to her research participants. Requiring interpretive researchers to archive their research materials—e.g., interview transcripts and field notebooks, the forms that their "data" come in—could make certain kinds of research projects undoable as it limits the kinds of confidentiality promises that researchers can legitimately make.

16 Elman *et al.* (2010: 23) proposes that a variety of electronic forms of qualitative data might be archived, including "interview tapes, text files (transcripts from interviews, focus groups, and oral histories; case notes; meeting minutes; research diaries), scans of newspaper articles, images of official documents, and photographic, audio, and video materials." To the extent that data archiving is mandated rather than voluntary,

such policies raise issues of academic freedom. They also imply an unlimited research budget, something not available to all researchers and privileging those at elite schools with greater access to such funding and outside grants, as well as those doing more traditional forms of research for which such funding is more readily available.

17 He also observes that some archaeologists, revisiting previous excavations, have made some interesting reinterpretations of such detailed fieldnotes.

18 McHenry further notes that the database was not developed on the basis of direct experience of events in India, being based, instead, on reportage in the *New York Times*.

19 As mentioned in Chapter 6, Note 2, a key question when researchers reuse indicators developed for other research purposes is construct validity—whether the existing indicator is congruent with the new user's own theoretical understandings of the concept so measured. One contributor to the American Political Science Association's Political Methodology Section's listserve argued: "Grabbing someone else's numbers and running analyses on them should no longer be acceptable in political science (or anywhere else, for that matter)" (Monday, 10 January 2011, 2:20 pm, POLMETH list). This position would seemingly put him at odds with those in the same association advocating for data archiving.

20 See Sadiq (2009: 35–7) on the limitations of data quality in non-Western settings.

21 One of us heard the hourglass notion in 1981–1982 from her dissertation advisor Suzanne R. Thomas-Buckle, then at MIT.

22 Why we should speak of "writing up" field research notes is an oddity. Police "write one up" for an offense by describing the event in detail; a "write-up" is a summary; "write this up" means to turn informal language into formal language, or notes into a formal report. Perhaps it is another way of referring to the detailed character of this sort of writing.

23 The best way for those endeavoring to learn more about the crafting of interpretive research writing is to read published interpretive research, as so much depends on disciplinary traditions, particular journals or book publishers, and genres (i.e., article- versus book-length manuscripts). Methods chapters also make for excellent ways to learn, inductively, about what is required in such research. William Foote Whyte's appendix to the second edition of his *Street Corner Society* (1955) is a classic, and we have recently become enamored of Liebow's (1993) appendix, too (thanks to Reviewer 1 of this manuscript). To some extent this is a matter of personal reading preferences, but our own favorites include Pierce's (1995) and Lin's (2000) appendices, Fujii's (2009) second chapter, Shehata's (2006) and Pachirat's (2009a) explanations of why they did what they did in their ethnographies (Shehata 2009, reproduced there as Chapter 6; Pachirat 2011), and Soss's (2006) on how he thinks about interview-based and other field research.

8 Speaking across Epistemic Communities

1 They also name two other forms of mixed methods: having both quantitative and qualitative research questions; and developing research questions in participatory fashion and having research questions that are "preplanned."

2 She claims that multi-method team research balances "internal validity and external validity . . ., gaining comparative breadth without sacrificing qualitative depth" (Poteete 2010: 33).

3 There is also a double-blind, peer-reviewed, online *International Journal of Mixed Methods for Applied Business and Policy Research* based in Australia and published by Academic Global Publications; but as of this writing, it seems not to have published any articles since its 2009 inception, and its domain statement does not add any further clarification of what is meant by "mixed methods."

4 This is manifested, for instance, in conversations between non-anthropology doctoral students wanting to do ethnographic research and their advisors, who raise the specter of lowered job prospects if the students are not able to demonstrate mastery of quantitative methods alongside their field research. The misunderstanding repeated in King *et al.* (1994) and other works concerning natural and physical sciences as they are actually done and the role of "the scientific method" within them has been critically assessed by others (see, e.g., Becker 2009), and we will not repeat those analyses here. We note, however, the negative effect of such misunderstandings on research designs in discussions of proper sequencing of research "segments," discussed below.

5 This might appear to be similar to the "multiple methods" advocated by Ostrom and her collaborators. In their research, however, the mixing all takes place within a positivist framework for the purpose of lessening the assumed tradeoff between internal validity/causal inference and external validity/generalizability (see Poteete 2010).

6 Empirical research shows that the same variability holds for randomized clinical trials (e.g., Epstein 1996).

REFERENCES

"A Humanist Who Knows Corn Flakes." 2005. *Harvard Magazine* 108/1: 64–5.

Abolafia, Mitchel Y. 2010. "Narrative Construction as Sensemaking: How a Central Bank Thinks." *Organization Studies* 31/3: 349–67.

Ackerly, Brooke A., Stern, Maria, and True, Jacqui, eds. 2006. *Feminist Methodologies for International Relations*. Cambridge: Cambridge University Press.

Adcock, Robert. 2006. "Generalization in Comparative and Historical Social Science: The Difference That Interpretivism Makes." In *Interpretation and Method: Empirical Research Methods and the Interpretive Turn*, edited by Dvora Yanow and Peregrine Schwartz-Shea, 50–66. Armonk, NY: M E Sharpe.

Adcock, Robert and Collier, David. 2001. "Measurement Validity: A Shared Standard for Qualitative and Quantitative Research." *American Political Science Review* 95: 529–46.

Agar, Michael H. 1986. *Speaking of Ethnography*. Newbury Park, CA: Sage.

Agar, Michael H. 1996/1980. *The Professional Stranger: An Informal Introduction to Ethnography*, 2nd ed. New York: Academic Press.

Agar, Michael. 2010. "On the Ethnographic Part of the Mix: A Multi-Genre Tale of the Field." *Organizational Research Methods* 13/2: 286–303.

Ahmed, Amel and Sil, Rudra. 2009. "Is Multi-Method Research Really 'Better'?" *Qualitative and Multi-Method Research* [Newsletter of the American Political Science Association Organized Section for Qualitative and Multi-Method Research] 7/2: 2–6.

Albright, Jeremy J. and Lyle, Jared A. 2010. "Data Preservation through Data Archives." *PS: Political Science and Politics* 43: 17–21.

Alcoff, Linda. 1991. "The Problem of Speaking for Others." *Cultural Critique* (Winter): 5–33.

Aldrich, John H., Alt, James E., and Lupia, Arthur. 2008. "The EITM Approach: Origins and Interpretations." In *The Oxford Handbook of Political Methodology*, edited by Janet M. Box-Steffensmeir, Henry E. Brady, and David Collier, 828–43. Oxford: Oxford University Press.

Allina-Pisano, Jessica. 2009. "How to Tell an Axe Murderer: An Essay on Ethnography,

Truth, and Lies." In *Political Ethnography: What Immersion Brings to the Study of Power*, edited by Edward Schatz, 53–73. Chicago: University of Chicago Press.

Allwood, Paul. 2004. "Handwashing among Public Restroom Users at the Minnesota State Fair." St. Paul, MN: Division of Environmental Health, Minnesota Department of Health. www.health.state.mn.us/handhygiene/stats/fairstudy.html (accessed 25 February 2011).

Alvesson, Mats. 2009. "At-Home Ethnography: Struggling with Closeness and Closure." In *Organizational Ethnography: Studying the Complexities of Everyday Life*, edited by Sierk Ybema, Dvora Yanow, Harry Wels, and Frans Kamsteeg, 56–74. London: Sage.

Alvesson, Mats and Skolberg, Kaj. 2000. *Reflexive Methodology: New Vistas for Qualitative Research*. London: Sage.

Anderson, Benedict. 2006 [1991]. *Imagined Communities: Reflections on the Origins and Spread of Nationalism*, rev. ed. London: Verso.

Arnstein, Sherry R. 1969. "A Ladder of Citizen Participation." *Journal of the American Institute of Planners* 35: 216–24.

Athens, Lonnie. 2010. "Naturalistic Inquiry in Theory and Practice." *Journal of Contemporary Ethnography* 39/1: 87–125.

Atkinson, Paul, Coffey, Amanda, and Delamont, Sara. 2003. "From Styles of Reporting to Poetics and Beyond." In *Key Themes in Qualitative Research: Continuities and Change*, edited by Paul Atkinson, Amanda Coffey, and Sara Delamont, 165–86. Walnut Creek, CA: Alta Mira Press.

Avenier, Marie-José. 2010. "Shaping a Constructivist View of Organizational Design Science." *Organization Studies* 31: 1229–55.

Barley, Stephen R. 1983. "Semiotics and the Study of Occupational and Organizational Cultures." *Administrative Science Quarterly* 28: 393–413.

Barley, Stephen R. 1986. "Technology as an Occasion for Structuring: Evidence from Observations of CT Scanners and the Social Order of Radiology Departments." *Administrative Science Quarterly* 31/1: 78–108.

Bayard de Volo, Lorraine. 2003. "Service and Surveillance: Infra Politics at Work among Casino Cocktail Waitresses." *Social Politics: International Studies in Gender, State, and Society* 10/3: 346–76.

Bayard de Volo, Lorraine. 2009. "Participant Observation, Politics, and Power Relations: Nicaraguan Mothers and U.S. Casino Waitresses." In *Political Ethnography: What Immersion Brings to the Study of Power*, edited by Edward Schatz, 217–36. Chicago: University of Chicago Press.

Becker, Howard S. 1963. *Outsiders: Studies in the Sociology of Deviance*. New York: The Free Press.

Becker, Howard S. 1967. "Whose Side Are We On?" *Social Forces* 14: 239–48.

Becker, Howard S. 1998. *Tricks of the Trade: How to Think About Your Research While You're Doing It*. Chicago: University of Chicago Press.

Becker, Howard S. 2009. "How to Find Out How To Do Qualitative Research." *International Journal of Communication* 3: 545–53.

Becker, Howard S., Geer, Blanche, Hughes, Everett C., and Strauss, Anselm L. 1977 [1961]. *Boys in White: Student Culture in Medical School*. New Brunswick, NJ: Transaction Publishers.

Beech, Nic, Hibbert, Paul, MacIntosh, Robert, and McInnes, Peter. 2009. "'But I Thought We Were Friends?' Life Cycles and Research Relationships." In *Organizational Ethnography: Studying the Complexities of Everyday Organizational Life*, edited by Sierk Ybema, Dvora Yanow, Harry Wels, and Frans Kamsteeg, 196–214. London: Sage.

Bell, Ella L. 1990. "The Bicultural Life Experience of Career-Oriented Black Women." *Journal of Organizational Behavior* 11: 459–77.

Bellah, Robert N., Madsen, Richard, Sullivan, William M., and Swidler, Ann. 2007 [1985]. *Habits of the Heart: Individualism and Commitment in American Life.* Berkeley: University of California Press.

Bellhouse, Mary L. 1991. "Visual Myths of Female Identity in Eighteenth-Century France." *International Political Science Review* 12/2: 117–35.

Bellhouse, Mary L. 2011. "Under the Eaves of the Louvre: Political Theory Research in American and European Art Museums, Art Collections, and Art Libraries." Western Political Science Association Annual Conference, San Antonio, TX (21–23 April).

Bentz, Valerie Malhotra and Shapiro, Jeremy J. 1998. *Mindful Inquiry in Social Research.* Thousand Oaks, CA: Sage.

Berg, Anne Marie and Eikeland, Olav, eds. 2008. *Action Research and Organization Theory.* Frankfurt am Main: Peter Lang.

Berger, John. 1972. *Ways of Seeing.* London: British Broadcasting Corporation and Penguin.

Berger, Peter L. and Luckmann, Thomas. 1966. *The Social Construction of Reality.* New York: Anchor Books.

Bernstein, Richard J. 1978. *The Restructuring of Social and Political Theory.* Philadelphia: University of Pennsylvania Press.

Bevir, Mark and Kedar, Assaf. 2008. "Concept Formation in Political Science: An Anti-Naturalist Critique of Qualitative Methodology." *Perspectives on Politics* 6/3: 503–17.

Black, Nick. 2001. "Evidence Based Policy: Proceed with Care." *British Medical Journal* 323 (4 August): 275–9.

Blaikie, Norman. 2000. *Designing Social Research: The Logic of Anticipation.* Malden, MA: Polity Press.

Blau, Peter. 1963 [1953]. *The Dynamics of Bureaucracy.* Chicago: University of Chicago Press.

Blee, Kathleen M. 2002. "Introduction: Crossing a Boundary." In *Inside Organized Racism: Women in the Hate Movement,* 1–24. Berkeley, CA: University of California Press.

Bogner, Alexander, Littig, Beate, and Menz, Wolfgang, eds. 2009. *Interviewing Experts.* Houndmills, Basingstoke: Palgrave Macmillan.

Boje, David M. 2008. *The Storytelling Organization.* London: Sage.

Bonnell, Victoria E. and Hunt, Lynn, eds. 1999. *Beyond the Cultural Turn.* Berkeley: University of California Press.

Bourdieu, Pierre and Wacquant, Loïc J. D. 1992. *An Invitation to Reflexive Sociology.* Chicago: University of Chicago Press.

Brady, Henry E. and Collier, David, eds. 2010. *Rethinking Social Inquiry: Diverse Tools, Shared Standards,* 2nd ed. Lanham, MD: Rowman and Littlefield.

Brandwein, Pamela. 1999. *Reconstructing Reconstruction: The Supreme Court and the Production of Historical Truth.* Durham, NC: Duke University Press.

Brandwein, Pamela. 2000. "Disciplinary Structures and 'Winning' Arguments in Law and Courts Scholarship." *Law and Courts* [Newsletter of the Law and Courts Section, American Political Science Association] 10/3: 11–9.

Brandwein, Pamela. 2006. "Studying the Careers of Knowledge Claims: Applying Science Studies to Legal Studies." In *Interpretation and Method: Empirical Research Methods and the Interpretive Turn,* edited by Dvora Yanow and Peregrine Schwartz-Shea, 228–43. Armonk, NY: M E Sharpe.

Brandwein, Pamela. 2011. *Rethinking the Judicial Settlement of Reconstruction*. New York: Cambridge University Press.

Brown, Richard Harvey. 1976. "Social Theory as Metaphor: On the Logic of Discovery for the Sciences of Conduct." *Theory and Society* 3/2: 169–97.

Browne, Malcolm W. 1989. "Physicists Debunk Claim of a New Kind of Fusion." *The New York Times* (3 May). http://partners.nytimes.com/library/national/science/050399sci-cold-fusion.html (accessed 25 February 2011).

Bruyneel, Kevin. 2007. *The Third Space of Sovereignty: The Postcolonial Politics of U.S.-Indigenous Relations*. Minneapolis: University of Minnesota Press.

Bryneel, Kevin. 2011. *Postcolonial Theory and Analysis in Political Studies*. New York: Routledge (draft manuscript).

Büger, Christian and Gadinger, Frank. 2007. "Reassembling and Dissecting: International Relations Practice from a Science Studies Perspective." *International Studies Perspectives* 8: 90–110.

Burgess, Robert G. 1989. "Grey Areas: Ethical Dilemmas in Educational Ethnography." In *The Ethics of Educational Research*, edited by Robert G. Burgess, 60–76. London: Routledge.

Burkhart, Geoffrey. 1996. "Not Given to Personal Disclosure." In *Out in the Field*, edited by Ellen Lewin and William L. Leap, 31–48. Urbana: University of Illinois Press.

Butler, Judith. 1997. *The Psychic Life of Power: Theories in Subjection*. Palo Alto, CA: Stanford University Press.

Cahill, Caitlin. 2007. "The Personal Is Political: Developing New Subjectivities in a Participatory Action Research Process." *Gender, Place, and Culture* 14/3: 267–92.

Cahill, Caitlin, Arenas, Erica, Contreras, Jennifer, Jiang, Na, Rios-Moore, Inra, and Threatts, Tiffany. 2004. "Speaking Back: Voices of Young Urban Womyn of Color: Using Participatory Action Research to Challenge and Complicate Representations of Young Women." In *All About the Girl: Culture, Power, and Identity*, edited by Anita Harris, 233–44. New York: Routledge.

Calhoun, Craig. 2007. "Sociology in America: An Introduction." In *Sociology in America: A History*, edited by Craig Calhoun, 1–38. Chicago: University of Chicago Press.

Campbell, Donald T. 1989. "Foreword." In Robert K. Yin, *Case Study Research: Design and Methods*, rev. ed., 7–9. Newbury Park, CA: Sage.

Campbell, Donald T. and Stanley, Julian C. 1963. *Experimental and Quasi-Experimental Designs for Research*. Boston, MA: Houghton-Mifflin.

Cancian, Francesca M. 1992. "Feminist Science: Methodologies that Challenge Inequality." *Gender and Society* 6/4: 623–42.

Carey, Benedict. 2011. "You Might Already Know This." *The New York Times* (10 January). www.nytimes.com/2011/01/11/science/11esp.html?_r=1&scp=7&sq=Carey%2C+Benedict&st=nyt (accessed 25 February 2011).

Casper, Monica J. and Talley, Heather Laine, eds. 2005. "Special Issue: Ethnography and Disability Studies." *Journal of Contemporary Ethnography* 34: 115–245.

Cat, Jordi. 2010. "The Unity of Science." In *The Stanford Encyclopedia of Philosophy* (Fall 2010 Edition), edited by Edward N. Zalta. http://plato.stanford.edu/archives/fall2010/entries/scientific-unity/ (accessed 12 February 2011).

Chabal, Patrick and Daloz, Jean-Pascal. 2006. *Culture Troubles: Politics and the Interpretation of Meaning*. Chicago: University of Chicago Press.

Charmaz, Kathy. 2006. *Constructing Grounded Theory*. London: Sage.

Chatterjee, Abhishek. 2009. "Ontology, Epistemology, and Multi-Methods Research."

Qualitative and Multi-Method Research [Newsletter of the American Political Science Association Organized Section for Qualitative and Multi-Method Research] 7/2: 11–5.

Clements, Dave. 2004. *What Counts? Interpreting Evidence-Based Decision-Making for Management and Policy.* Report of the 6th Canadian Health Services Research Foundation Annual Invitational Workshop, Vancouver, British Columbia (11 March). www. chsrf.ca/knowledge_transfer/pdf/2004_workshop_report_e.pdf (accessed 21 February 2006).

Clifford, James and Marcus, George E., eds. 1986. *Writing Culture: The Poetics and Politics of Ethnography.* Berkeley: University of California Press.

Cohn, Carol. 2006. "Motives and Methods: Using Multi-Sited Ethnography to Study US National Security Discourses." In *Feminist Methodologies for International Relations*, edited by Brooke Ackerly, Maria Stern, and Jacqui True, 91–107. New York: Cambridge University Press.

Collier, Andrew. 1994. *Critical Realism: An Introduction to Roy Bhaskar's Philosophy.* London: Verso.

Collier, David, Brady, Henry E., and Seawright, Jason. 2010. "Introduction to the Second Edition: A Sea Change in Political Methodology." In *Rethinking Social Inquiry: Diverse Tools, Shared Standards*, 2nd ed., edited by Henry E. Brady and David Collier, 1–10. Lanham, MD: Rowman and Littlefield.

Collier, David, Mahoney, James, and Seawright, Jason. 2004. "Claiming Too Much: Warnings about Selection Bias." In *Rethinking Social Inquiry: Diverse Tools, Shared Standards*, edited by Henry E. Brady and David Collier, 85–102. Lanham, MD: Rowman and Littlefield.

Collins, Kathleen M. T., Onwuegbuzie, Anthony J., and Jiao, Qun G. 2007. "A Mixed Methods Investigation of Mixed Methods Sampling Designs in Social and Health Science Research." *Journal of Mixed Methods Research* 1/3: 267–94.

Conway, Margaret M., Steuernagel, Gertrude A., and Ahern, David W. 2005. *Women and Political Participation: Cultural Change in the Political Arena*, 2nd ed. Washington, DC: CQ Press.

Cowan, Richard J., Hennessey, Mary L., Vierstra, Courtney V., and Rumrill, Phillip D., Jr. 2004. "Small-N Designs in Rehabilitation Research." *Journal of Vocational Rehabilitation* 20/3: 203–11.

Cramer, Renee A. 2008. "The Limits of Law in Securing Reproductive Freedoms: Midwife-Assisted Homebirth in California." Joint Meetings of the Law and Society Association and the Canadian Association for the Study of Law and Society, Montreal, Quebec (1–3 June).

Crenshaw, Kimberlé, ed. 1995. *Critical Race Theory: The Key Writings That Formed the Movement.* New York: New Press.

Czarniawska, Barbara. 2004. *Narratives in Social Science Research.* London: Sage.

Czarniawska-Joerges, Barbara. 1992. "Budgets as Texts: On Collective Writing in the Public Sector." *Accounting, Management & Information Technology* 2/4: 221–39.

Dalton, Melville. 1959. *Men Who Manage.* New York: Wiley.

Danjoux, Ilan. Forthcoming. *Political Cartoons and the Israeli-Palestinian Conflict.* Manchester: University of Manchester Press.

Danziger, Kurt. 1990. *Constructing the Subject: Historical Origins of Psychological Research.* Cambridge: Cambridge University Press.

Darnton, Robert. 1984. *The Great Cat Massacre and Other Episodes in French Cultural History.* New York: Basic Books.

Darnton, Robert. 2003. *George Washington's False Teeth: An Unconventional Guide to the Eighteenth Century*. New York: W W Norton.

"Data Collection and Collaboration." 2010. Symposium. *PS: Political Science & Politics* 43/1: 15–58.

Davenport, Christian. 2010. "Data from the Dark Side: Notes on Archiving Political Conflict and Violence." *PS: Political Science & Politics* 43: 37–41.

Davis, Natalie Zemon. 1983. *The Return of Martin Guerre*. Cambridge, MA: Harvard University Press.

Deleuze, Gilles and Guattari, Félix. 1987. *A Thousand Plateaus: Capitalism and Schizophrenia*. Translated by Brian Massumi. Minneapolis: University of Minnesota Press.

Delgado, Richard and Stefanic, Jean. 2001. *Critical Race Theory: An Introduction*. New York: New York University Press.

Devine, Patricia G., Hirt, Edward R., and Gehrke, Elizabeth M. 1990. "Diagnostic and Confirmation Strategies in Trait Hypothesis Testing." *Journal of Personality and Social Psychology* 58/6: 952–63.

Dilthey, Wilhelm. 1976. *Selected Writings*. Translated and edited by H. P. Rickman. Cambridge: Cambridge University Press.

Down, Simon and Hughes, Michael. 2009. "When the 'Subject' and the 'Researcher' Speak Together." In *Organizational Ethnography: Studying the Complexities of Everyday Life*, edited by Sierk Ybema, Dvora Yanow, Harry Wels, and Frans Kamsteeg, 83–98. London: Sage.

Downs, Anthony. 1957. *The Economic Theory of Democracy*. New York: Harper.

Drori, Israel and Landau, Dana. 2011. *Vision and Change in Institutional Entrepreneurship: The Transformation from Science to Commercialization*. Oxford: Berghahn.

Eckel, Catherine C. and Grossman, Philip J. 1996. "The Relative Price of Fairness: Gender Differences in a Punishment Game." *Journal of Economic Behavior and Organization* 30: 143–58.

Ellis, Carolyn. 1995. "Emotional and Ethical Quagmires in Returning to the Field." *Journal of Contemporary Ethnography* 24/1: 68–98.

Ellis, Carolyn and Bochner, Arthur P. 2000. "Autoethnography, Personal Narrative, Reflexivity." In *Handbook of Qualitative Research*, 2nd ed., edited by Norman K. Denzin and Yvonna S. Lincoln, 733–68. Thousand Oaks, CA: Sage.

Elman, Colin, Kapiszewski, Diana, and Vinuela, Lorena. 2010. "Qualitative Data Archiving: Rewards and Challenges." *PS: Political Science & Politics* 43/1: 23–7.

Emerson, Robert M. and Pollner, Melvin. 2002. "Difference and Dialogue: Members' Readings of Ethnographic Texts." In *Qualitative Research Methods*, edited by Darin Weinberg, 154–70. Malden, MA: Blackwell.

Emerson, Robert M., Fretz, Rachel I., and Shaw, Linda L. 1995. *Writing Ethnographic Fieldnotes*. Chicago: University of Chicago Press.

Epstein, Steven. 1996. *Impure Science: AIDS, Activism, and the Politics of Knowledge*. Berkeley: University of California Press.

Erlandson, David A., Harris, Edward L., Skipper, Barbara L., and Allen, Steve D. 1993. *Doing Naturalistic Inquiry*. Newbury Park, CA: Sage.

Falleti, Tulia G. 2006. "Theory-Guided Process-Tracing in Comparative Politics: Something Old, Something New." *CP-APSA* [The Organized Section in Comparative Politics of the American Political Science Association] *Newsletter* 17/1: 9–14.

Fay, Brian. 1996. *Contemporary Philosophy of Social Science: A Multicultural Approach*. Oxford: Blackwell.

Feldman, Martha S. 1995. *Strategies for Interpreting Qualitative Data*. Thousand Oaks, CA: Sage.

Feldman, Martha S., Bell, Jeannine, and Berger, Michele Tracy, eds. 2003. *Gaining Access*. Walnut Creek, CA: AltaMira.

Felstiner, Mary Lowenthal. 2000. "Casing My Joints: A Private and Public Story of Arthritis." *Feminist Studies* 26/2: 273–85.

Fenno, Richard F., Jr. 1986. "Observation, Context, and Sequence in the Study of Politics." *American Political Science Review* 80/1: 3–15.

Ferguson, Kathy. 1984. *The Feminist Case against Bureaucracy*. Philadelphia: Temple University Press.

Ferguson, Kathy. 2011. Presentation on "The Gift of the Archive." Panel on "Political theorizing in the archive," Western Political Science Association Annual Conference, San Antonio, TX (21–23 April).

Feynman, Richard P., as told to Ralph Leighton. 1988. *What Do You Care What Other People Think?* New York: W W Norton.

"Field Research Methods in the Middle East." 2006. Symposium. *PS: Political Science & Politics* 39/3: 417–41.

Forbis, Robert E. 2009. "Drill Baby Drill: An Analysis of How Energy Development Displaced Ranching's Dominance Over the BLM's Subgovernment Policymaking Environment." Unpublished Ph.D. dissertation, University of Utah.

Forester, John. 2006. "Policy Analysis as Critical Listening." In *Oxford Handbook of Public Policy*, edited by Robert Goodin, Michael Moran, and Martin Rein, 124–51. New York: Oxford University Press.

Forsey, Martin Gerard. 2010. "Ethnography as Participant Listening." *Ethnography* 11/4: 558–72.

Foucault, Michel. 1984. "Truth and Power." In *The Foucault Reader*, edited by Paul Rabinow, 51–75. New York: Pantheon.

Frank, Carolyn. 1999. *Ethnographic Eyes: A Teacher's Guide to Classroom Observation*. Portsmouth, NH: Heinemann.

Fraser, Nancy. 1995. "Pragmatism, Feminism, and the Linguistic Turn." In *Feminist Contentions*, edited by Seyla Benhabib, Judith Butler, Drucilla Cornell, and Nancy Fraser, 157–72. New York: Routledge.

Freire, Paulo. 1970. *Cultural Action for Freedom*. Cambridge, MA: Harvard Educational Review, monograph 1.

Friedrichs, Jorg and Kratochwil, Friedrich. 2009. "On Acting and Knowing: How Pragmatism Can Advance International Relations Research and Methodology." *International Organization* 63: 701–31.

Fujii, Lee Ann. 2008. "The Power of Local Ties: Popular Participation in the Rwandan Genocide." *Security Studies* 17: 569–97.

Fujii, Lee Ann. 2009. *Killing Neighbors: Webs of Violence in Rwanda*. Ithaca, NY: Cornell University Press.

Fujii, Lee Ann. 2010. "Shades of Truth and Lies: Interpreting Testimonies of War and Violence." *Journal of Peace Research* 47/2: 231–41.

Gabriel, Yiannis. 2000. *Storytelling in Organizations: Facts, Fictions, and Fantasies*. London: Oxford University Press.

Gadamer, Hans-Georg. 1976. *Philosophical Hermeneutics*. Translated and edited by David E. Linge. Berkeley: University of California Press.

Gamson, William A. and Lasch, Kathryn. 1983. "The Political Culture of Social Policy."

In *Evaluating the Welfare State*, edited by Shimon E. Spiro and Ephraim Yuchtman-Yaar, 397–415. New York: Academic Press.

Gans, Herbert J. 1968. *People and Plans*. New York: Basic.

Gans, Herbert. 1976. "Personal Journal: B. On the Methods Used in This Study." In *The Research Experience*, edited by M. Patricia Golden, 49–59. Itasca, IL: F.E. Peacock.

Gardner, Howard E. 1983. *Frames of Mind*. New York: Basic Books.

Gardner, Howard E. 2006. *Multiple Intelligences: New Horizons in Theory and Practice*. NY: Basic Books.

Geddes, Barbara. 1990. "How the Cases You Choose Affect the Answers You Get: Selection Bias in Comparative Politics." In *Political Analysis*, Vol. 2, edited by James A. Stimson, 131–50. Ann Arbor, MI: University of Michigan.

Geertz, Clifford. 1973. *The Interpretation of Cultures*. New York: Basic Books.

Geertz, Clifford. 1983. *Local Knowledge: Further Essays in Interpretive Anthropology*. New York: Basic Books.

Geertz, Clifford. 2010. *Life among the Anthros and Other Essays*. Edited by Fred Inglis. Princeton: Princeton University Press.

Gerring, John. 2007. *Case Study Research: Principles and Practices*. New York: Cambridge University Press.

Ghorashi, Halleh and Wels, Harry. 2009. "Beyond Complicity: A Plea for Engaged Ethnography." In *Organizational Ethnography: Studying the Complexities of Everyday Life*, edited by Sierk Ybema, Dvora Yanow, Harry Wels, and Frans Kamsteeg, 231–52. London: Sage.

Gill, Jeff. 1999. "The Insignificance of Null Hypothesis Significance Testing." *Political Research Quarterly* 52/3: 647–74.

Giorgi, Amadeo, Barton, Anthony, and Maes, Charles. 1983. *Duquesne Studies in Phenomenological Psychology*, Vol. 4. Pittsburgh, PA: Duquesne University Press.

Glaser, Barney G. and Strauss, Anselm L. 1967. *The Discovery of Grounded Theory: Strategies for Qualitative Research*. Chicago: Aldine.

Glynos, Jason and Howarth, David. 2007. *Logics of Critical Explanation in Social and Political Theory*. New York: Routledge.

Goffman, Erving. 1959. *The Presentation of Self in Everyday Life*. New York: Doubleday.

Goffman, Erving. 1963. *Behavior in Public Places: Notes on the Social Organization of Gatherings*. New York: The Free Press.

Golden-Biddle, Karen and Locke, Karen. 1993. "Appealing Work: An Investigation of How Ethnographic Texts Convince." *Organization Science* 4/4: 595–616.

Golden-Biddle, Karen and Locke, Karen. 1997. *Composing Qualitative Research*. Thousand Oaks, CA: Sage.

Goleman, Daniel. 1995. *Emotional Intelligence*. New York: Bantam.

Goodman, Nelson. 1978. *Ways of World-Making*. Indianapolis, IN: Hackett.

Gottlieb, Alma. 2006. "Ethnography: Theory and Methods." In *A Handbook for Social Science Field Research: Essays and Bibliographic Sources on Research Design and Methods*, edited by Ellen Perecman and Sara R. Curran, 47–68. Thousand Oaks, CA: Sage.

Green, Daniel M., ed. 2002. *Constructivism and Comparative Politics*. Armonk, NY: M E Sharpe.

Greene, Jennifer C. 2008. "Is Mixed Methods Social Inquiry a Distinctive Methodology?" *Journal of Mixed Method Research* 2/1: 7–22.

Greenhalgh, Susan. 2001. *Under the Medical Gaze: Facts and Fictions of Chronic Pain*. Berkeley, CA: University of California Press.

Greenwood, Davydd J. and Levin, Morten. 2007. *Introduction to Action Research: Social Research for Social Change*, 2nd ed. Thousand Oaks, CA: Sage.

Gunsalus, C.K., Bruner, Edward M., Burbules, Nicholas C., Dash, Leon, Finkin, Matthew, Goldberg, Joseph P., Greenough, William T., Miller, Gregory A., Pratt, Michael G., Iriye, Masumi, and Aronson, Deb. 2007. "The Illinois White Paper: Improving the System for Protecting Human Subjects: Counteracting IRB 'Mission Creep.'" *Qualitative Inquiry* 13: 617–49.

Gusfield, Joseph R. 1963. *Symbolic Crusade*. Urbana: University of Illinois Press.

Gusfield, Joseph R. 1976. "The Literary Rhetoric of Science: Comedy and Pathos in Drinking Driver Research." *American Sociological Review* 41/1: 16–34.

Gusfield, Joseph R. 1981. *The Culture of Public Problems*. Chicago: University of Chicago Press.

Gusfield, Joseph R. 1995. "The Second Chicago School?" In *A Second Chicago School? The Development of a Postwar American Sociology*, edited by Gary Alan Fine, vii–xvi. Chicago: University of Chicago Press.

Hall, Tom. 2009. "Footwork: Moving and Knowing in Local Space(s)." *Qualitative Research* 9/5: 571–85.

Halley, Janet E. and Brown, Wendy, eds. 2003. *Left Legalism/Left Critique*. Durham, NC: Duke University Press.

Hamilton, Amanda. 1997. "Oh the Joys of Invisibility." *Electric Edge: The Disability Experience in America* (July/August; web edition of *The Ragged Edge* 18/4). www.ragged-edge-mag.com/archive/look.htm (accessed 12 February 2011).

Hammersley, Martyn. 2008. *Questioning Qualitative Inquiry: Critical Essays*. Thousand Oaks, CA: Sage.

Hammersley, Martyn and Atkinson, Paul. 1983. *Ethnography: Principles in Practice*. London: Tavistock.

Hansen, Hans. 2007. "Abduction." In *The Sage Handbook of New Approaches in Management and Organization*, edited by David Barry and Hans Hansen, 454–63. London: Sage.

Hansen, Lene. 2006. *Security as Practice: Discourse Analysis and the Bosnian War*. New York: Routledge.

Haraway, Donna. 1988. "Situated Knowledges: The Science Question in Feminism and the Privilege of the Partial Perspective." *Feminist Studies* 14: 575–99.

Haraway, Donna. 1991. *Simians, Cyborgs and Women: The Reinvention of Nature*. New York: Routledge.

Harding, Sandra. 1986. *The Science Question in Feminism*. Ithaca, NY: Cornell University Press.

Harding, Sandra. 1993. "Rethinking Standpoint Epistemology: What Is 'Strong Objectivity'?" In *Feminist Epistemologies*, edited by Linda Alcoff and Elizabeth Potter, 49–82. New York: Routledge.

Harrell, Stevan. 2006. "Essentials for Ethnography: Ethnographic Methods." In *A Handbook for Social Science Field Research: Essays and Bibliographic Sources on Research Design and Methods*, edited by Ellen Perecman and Sara R. Curran, 163–8. Thousand Oaks, CA: Sage.

Hartsock, Nancy C.M. 1987. "The Feminist Standpoint." In *Feminism & Methodology*, edited by Sandra Harding, 157–80. Bloomington: Indiana University Press.

Hatch, Mary Jo and Yanow, Dvora. 2008. "Methodology by Metaphor: Ways of Seeing in Painting and Research." *Organization Studies* 29: 23–44.

Hawkesworth, M. E. 1988. *Theoretical Issues in Policy Analysis*. Albany, NY: SUNY Press.

Hawkesworth, Mary E. 2006a. "Contending Conceptions of Science and Politics: Methodology and the Constitution of the Political." In *Interpretation and Method: Empirical Research Methods and the Interpretive Turn*, edited by Dvora Yanow and Peregrine Schwartz-Shea, 27–49. Armonk, NY: M E Sharpe.

Hawkesworth, Mary E. 2006b. *Feminist Inquiry: From Political Conviction to Methodological Innovation*. New Brunswick, NJ: Rutgers University Press.

Henderson, Frances B. 2009. "'We Thought You Would Be White': Race and Gender in Fieldwork." *PS: Political Science & Politics* 42/2: 291–4.

Hergovich, Andreas, Schott, Reinhard, and Burger, Christoph. 2010. "Biased Evaluation of Abstracts Depending on Topic and Conclusion: Further Evidence of a Confirmation Bias Within Scientific Psychology." *Current Psychology* 29: 188–209.

Hiley, David R., Bohman, James F., and Shusterman, Richard, eds. 1991. *The Interpretive Turn*. Ithaca, NY: Cornell University Press.

Hill, Suzanne R., Mitchell, Andrew S., and Henry, David A. 2000. "Problems with the Interpretation of Pharmacoeconomic Analyses: A Review of Submissions to the Australian Pharmaceutical Benefits Scheme." *Journal of the American Medical Association* 283/16 (26 April): 2116–21.

Homan, Roger. 1991. *The Ethics of Social Research*. New York: Longman.

Hopf, Ted. 2002. *Social Construction of International Politics: Identities and Foreign Policies, Moscow, 1955 and 1999*. Ithaca, NY: Cornell University Press.

How, Alan R. 2011. "Hermeneutics and the 'Classic' Problem in the Human Sciences." *History of the Human Sciences* 24: 47–63.

Howe, P. David. 2009. "Reflexive Ethnography, Impairment and the Pub." *Leisure Studies* 28/4: 489–96.

Huggins, Martha K. 2002. *Violence Workers: Police Torturers and Murderers Reconstruct Brazilian Atrocities*. Berkeley, CA: University of California Press.

Hummel, Ralph P. 1991. "Stories Managers Tell: Why They Are as Valid as Science." *Public Administration Review* 51/1: 31–41.

Humphreys, Laud. 1970. *The Tearoom Trade: Impersonal Sex in Public Places*. Chicago: Aldine.

Humphreys, Laud and others. 1976. "Retrospect: Ethical Issues in Social Research." In Laud Humphreys, *The Tearoom Trade*, enlarged edition, 175–232. Hawthorne, NY: Aldine de Gruyter.

Iedema, Rick, Long, Debbi, and Carroll, Katherine. 2011. "Corridor Communication, Spatial Design and Patient Safety: Enacting and Managing Complexities." In *Organizational Spaces: Rematerializing the Workaday World*, edited by Alfons van Marrewijk and Dvora Yanow, 41–57. Cheltenham: Edward Elgar.

Iser, Wolfgang. 1989. *Prospecting: From Reader Response to Literary Anthropology*. Baltimore, MD: Johns Hopkins University Press.

Jackson, Patrick Thaddeus. 2002. "The West Is the Best: Occidentalism and Postwar German Reconstruction." In *Constructivism and Comparative Politics*, edited by Daniel Green, 230–64. Armonk, NY: M E Sharpe.

Jackson, Patrick Thaddeus. 2006. "Making Sense of Making Sense: Configurational Analysis and the Double Hermeneutic." In *Interpretation and Method: Empirical Research Methods and the Interpretive Turn*, edited by Dvora Yanow and Peregrine Schwartz-Shea, 264–80. Armonk, NY: M E Sharpe.

Jackson, Patrick Thaddeus. 2011. *The Conduct of Inquiry in International Relations: Philosophy of Science and Its Implications for the Study of World Politics*. New York: Routledge.

Jackson, Sherri. 2008. *Research Methods and Statistics*. Belmont, CA: Thomson/Wadsworth.

Jacobs, Sue-Ellen. 1996. "Afterword." In *Out in the Field*, edited by Ellen Lewin and William L. Leap, 287–308. Urbana: University of Illinois Press.

Johnson, Merri Lisa. 2011. Call for Papers: Crip Theory and/as Feminist Methodology. Association for Feminist Epistemologies, Metaphysics, Methodologies, and Science Listserve (posted 11 February, 13:24 Amsterdam time).

Johnson, R. Burke, Onwuegbuzie, Anthony J., and Turner, Lisa A. 2007. "Toward a Definition of Mixed Methods Research." *Journal of Mixed Method Research* 1/2: 112–33.

Jones, Megan. 1997. "'Gee, You Don't Look Handicapped . . .': Why I Use a White Cane to Tell People That I'm Deaf." *Electric Edge: The Disability Experience in America* (July/August; electronic edition of *The Ragged Edge* 18/4). www.ragged-edge-mag.com/archive/look.htm (accessed 12 February 2011).

Jones, Phil Ian, Bunce, Griff, Evans, James, Gibbs, Hannah, and Hein, Jane Ricketts. 2008. "Exploring Space and Place with Walking Interviews." *Journal of Research Practice* 4/2, Article D2. http://jrp.icaap.org/index.php/jrp/article/view/150/161 (accessed 22 February 2010).

Journal of Mixed Methods Research. 2007. "Aims and Scope." www.sagepub.com/journalsProdDesc.nav?ct_p=boards&prodId=Journal201775#tabview=aimsAndScope (accessed 19 November 2010).

Kanter, Rosabeth Moss. 1977. *Men and Women of the Corporation*. New York: Basic Books.

Katz, Arlene M. and Shotter, John. 1996. "Hearing the Patient's 'Voice': Toward a Social Poetics in Diagnostic Interviews." *Social Science & Medicine* 43/6: 919–31.

Kaufman-Osborn, Timothy. 2006. "Dividing the Domain of Political Science: On the Fetishism of Subfields." *Polity* 38/1: 41–71.

Kelly, Alison. 1989. "Education or Indoctrination? The Ethics of School-Based Action Research." In *The Ethics of Educational Research*, edited by Robert G. Burgess, 100–13. London: Routledge.

Kelly, John. 2011. "44 Years Later, Tally's Corner Is Revealed." *The Washington Post* (26 February). www.washingtonpost.com/wp-dyn/content/article/2011/02/26/AR2011022603483.html (accessed 3 July 2011).

Keohane, Robert O. 2009. "Political Science as a Vocation." *PS: Political Science & Politics* 42/2: 359–63.

King, Gary, Keohane, Robert O., and Verba, Sidney. 1994. *Designing Social Inquiry: Scientific Inference in Qualitative Research*. Princeton, NJ: Princeton University Press.

Klayman, Joshua and Ha, Young-Won. 1987. "Confirmation, Disconfirmation and Information in Hypothesis Testing." *Psychological Review* 94/2: 211–28.

Klotz, Audie and Lynch, Cecelia. 2007. *Strategies for Research in Constructivist International Relations*. Armonk, NY: M E Sharpe.

Krieger, Susan. 2005a. "Losing My Vision." *Qualitative Inquiry* 11/2: 145–51.

Krieger, Susan. 2005b. "Blindspots." In *Things No Longer There: A Memoir of Losing Sight and Finding Vision*, Ch. 10. Madison: University of Wisconsin Press. http://susankrieger.stanford.edu/tnlt/book.html#chapter10 (accessed 15 February 2011).

Kuhn, Thomas S. 1996/1962. "Normal Science as Puzzle-Solving." In *The Structure of Scientific Revolutions*, 3rd ed., 35–42. Chicago: University of Chicago Press.

Kunda, Gideon. 1992. *Engineering Culture*. Philadelphia: Temple University Press.

Kusenbach, Margarethe. 2003. "Street Phenomenology: The Go-Along as Ethnographic Research Tool." *Ethnography* 4/3: 455–85.

Lakoff, George. 2008. *The Political Mind: Why You Can't Understand 21st-Century American Politics with an 18th-Century Brain*. New York: Viking Penguin.

Lamont, Michèle and White, Patricia. 2009. "Workshop on Interdisciplinary Standards for Systematic Qualitative Research." Washington, DC: National Science Foundation, Cultural Anthropology, Law and Social Science, Political Science, and Sociology Programs. www.nsf.gov/sbe/ses/soc/ISSQR_workshop_rpt.pdf (accessed 2 February 2011).

Latour, Bruno. 1987. *Science in Action: How to Follow Scientists and Engineers through Society*. Cambridge, MA: Harvard University Press.

Latour, Bruno and Woolgar, Steve. 1988. *Laboratory Life: The Construction of Scientific Facts*, 2nd ed. Princeton, NJ: Princeton University Press.

Leap, William L. 1996. "Studying Gay English: How I Got Here from There." In *Out in the Field*, edited by Ellen Lewin and William L. Leap, 128–46. Urbana: University of Illinois Press.

Lewin, Ellen and Leap, William L., eds. 1996. *Out in the Field*. Chicago: University of Illinois Press.

Librett, Mitch and Perrone, Dina. 2010. "Apples and Oranges: Ethnography and the IRB." *Qualitative Research* 10/6: 729–47.

Lichterman, Paul. 2002. "Seeing Structure Happen: Theory-Driven Participant Observation." In *Methods of Social Movement Research*, edited by Bert Klandermans and Suzanne Staggenborg, 118–45. Minneapolis, MN: University of Minnesota Press.

Liebow, Elliot. 1967. *Tally's Corner*. Boston, MA: Little, Brown.

Liebow, Elliot. 1993. *Tell Them Who I Am: The Lives of Homeless Women*. New York: The Free Press.

Lin, Ann Chih. 1998. "Bridging Positivist and Interpretivist Approaches to Qualitative Methods." *Policy Studies Journal* 26/1: 162–80.

Lin, Ann Chih. 2000. "Appendix 2. On Being Who You Are: Credibility, Bias, and Good Research." In *Reform in the Making: The Implementation of Social Policy in Prison*, 186–94. Princeton, NJ: Princeton University Press.

Lincoln, Yvonna S. 2010. "'What a Long, Strange Trip It's Been . . .': Twenty-Five Years of Qualitative and New Paradigm Research." *Qualitative Inquiry* 16/1: 3–9.

Lincoln, Yvonna S. and Denzin, Norman K. 2003. "Introduction: Revolutions, Ruptures, and Rifts in Interpretive Inquiry." In *Turning Points in Qualitative Research: Tying Knots in a Handkerchief*, edited by Yvonna S. Lincoln and Norman K. Denzin, 1–16. Walnut Creek, CA: Alta Mira Press.

Lincoln, Yvonna S. and Guba, Egon G. 1985. *Naturalistic Inquiry*. Thousand Oaks, CA: Sage.

Linder, Stephen. 1995. "Contending Discourses in the Electric and Magnetic Fields Controversy: The Social Construction of EMF Risk as a Public Problem." *Policy Sciences* 28/2: 209–230.

Lingsom, Susan. 2008. "Invisible Impairments: Dilemmas of Concealment and Disclosure." *Scandinavian Journal of Disability Research* 10/1: 2–16.

Livingstone, David N. 2003. *Putting Science in Its Place*. Chicago: University of Chicago Press.

Locke, Karen. 1996. "Rewriting the Discovery of Grounded Theory after 25 Years?" *Journal of Management Inquiry* 5/3: 239–45.

Locke, Karen, Golden-Biddle, Karen, and Feldman, Martha S. 2008. "Making Doubt Generative: Rethinking the Role of Doubt in the Research Process." *Organization Science* 19/6: 907–18.

Longino, Helen. 1990. *Science as Social Knowledge*. Princeton, NJ: Princeton University Press.

Lorenz, Chris. 1998. "Can Histories Be True? Narrativism, Positivism, and the 'Metaphorical Turn.'" *History and Theory* 37: 309–30.

Luft, Joseph and Ingham, Harry. 1955. "The Johari Window, a Graphic Model of Interpersonal Awareness." *Proceedings of the Western Training Laboratory in Group Development*. Los Angeles: University of California at Los Angeles.

Luker, Kristin. 1984. *Abortion and the Politics of Motherhood*. Berkeley: University of California Press.

Luntz, Frank. 2007. *Words That Work: It's Not What You Say, It's What People Hear*. New York: Hyperion.

Lynch, Cecelia. 1999. *Beyond Appeasement: Interpreting Interwar Peace Movements in World Politics*. Ithaca, NY: Cornell University Press.

Lynch, Cecelia. 2006. "Critical Interpretation and Interwar Peace Movements: Challenging Dominant Narratives." In *Interpretation and Method: Empirical Research Methods and the Interpretive Turn*, edited by Dvora Yanow and Peregrine Schwartz-Shea, 291–9. Armonk, NY: M E Sharpe.

Lynch, Michael and Woolgar, Steve, eds. 1990. *Representation in Scientific Practice*. Cambridge, MA: MIT Press.

Marks, Jonathan. 2005. "Your Body, My Property: The Problem of Colonial Genetics in a Postcolonial World." In *Embedding Ethics: Shifting Boundaries of the Anthropological Profession*, edited by Lynn Meskell and Peter Pels, 29–45. New York: Berg.

Mathison, Sandra. 1988. "Why Triangulate?" *Educational Researcher* 17: 13–7.

Maynard-Moody, Steven, and Musheno, Michael. 2003. *Cops, Teachers, Counselors: Stories from the Front Lines of Public Service*. Ann Arbor, MI: University of Michigan Press.

Maynard-Moody, Steven and Musheno, Michael. 2006. "Stories for Research." In *Interpretation and Method: Empirical Research Methods and the Interpretive Turn*, edited by Dvora Yanow and Peregrine Schwartz-Shea, 316–30. Armonk, NY: M E Sharpe.

Mayo, Elton. 1933. *The Human Problems of Industrial Civilization*. New York: Macmillan.

McCloskey, Donald N. 1985. *The Rhetoric of Economics*. Madison, WI: University of Wisconsin Press.

McDonald, Terrence J., ed. 1996. *The Historic Turn in the Human Sciences*. Ann Arbor, MI: University of Michigan.

McDougall, Dennis M. 2006. "Recent Innovations in Small-N Designs for Research and Practice in Professional School Counseling." *Professional School Counseling* (June). http://findarticles.com/p/articles/mi_m0KOC/is_5_9/ai_n16689778/ (accessed 15 January 2011).

McHenry, Dean E., Jr. 2006. "The Numeration of Events: Studying Political Protest in India." In *Interpretation and Method: Empirical Research Methods and the Interpretive Turn*, edited by Dvora Yanow and Peregrine Schwartz-Shea, 187–202. Armonk, NY: M E Sharpe.

McRuer, Robert. 2006. *Crip Theory: Cultural Signs of Queerness and Disability*. New York: New York University Press.

Menand, Louis. 2001. *The Metaphysical Club: A Story of Ideas in America*. New York: Farrar, Straus, Giroux.

Meskell, Lynn and Pels, Peter, eds. 2005. *Embedding Ethics: Shifting Boundaries of the Anthropological Profession*. New York: Berg.

Mihic, Sophia, Engelmann, Stephen G., and Wingrove, Elizabeth Rose. 2005. "Making Sense in and of Political Science: Facts, Values, and 'Real' Numbers." In *The Politics of Method in the Human Sciences: Positivism and Its Epistemological Others*, edited by George Steinmetz, 470–95. Durham/London: Duke University Press.

Miles, Matthew B. and Huberman, A. Michael. 1984. *Qualitative Data Analysis: A Sourcebook of New Methods*. Beverly Hills, CA: Sage.

Mirowski, Philip E. 2003. "What's Kuhn Got to Do with It?" *Social Epistemology* 17/2–3: 229–39.

Moeran, Brian. 2009. "From Participant Observation to Observant Participation." In *Organizational Ethnography: Studying the Complexities of Everyday Organizational Life*, edited by Sierk Ybema, Dvora Yanow, Harry Wels, and Frans Kamsteeg, 139–55. London: Sage.

Mogendorff, Karen. 2010. "Doing Frogs and Elephants: Or How Atypical Moving Bodies Affect and Are Affected by Predominantly Able-Bodies." *Medische Antropologie* 22/2: 321–37.

Mosse, David. 2005. *Cultivating Development: An Ethnography of Aid Policy and Practice*. London: Pluto Press.

Mosse, David. 2006. "Anti-Social Anthropology? Objectivity, Objection, and the Ethnography of Public Policy and Professional Communities." *Journal of the Royal Anthropological Institute* 12/4: 935–56.

Mosse, George. 1975. *The Nationalization of the Masses*. New York: Howard Fertig.

Munro, Rolland. 2001. "Calling for Accounts: Numbers, Monsters and Membership." *Sociological Review* 49/4: 473–93.

Nader, Laura. 1972. "Up the Anthropologist—Perspectives Gained by Studying Up." In *Reinventing Anthropology*, edited by Dell H. Hymes, 284–311. New York: Vintage Books.

Nagel, Thomas. 1986. *The View from Nowhere*. New York: Oxford University Press.

Narayan, Kirin. 1993. "How Native Is a 'Native' Anthropologist?" *American Anthropologist* 95: 671–86.

Nencel, Lorraine and Yanow, Dvora. 2011. "Reconsidering Etic Outsiders, Emic Insiders, and Fieldwork Relationships: On Methodological Relics." Presented at the European Association of Social Anthropologists (Ljubljana, 26–30 August 2008), revised.

Nicolini, Davide. 2009. "Zooming In and Zooming Out: A Package of Method and Theory to Study Work Practices." In *Organizational Ethnography: Studying the Complexities of Everyday Organizational Life*, edited by Sierk Ybema, Dvora Yanow, Harry Wels, and Frans Kamsteeg, 120–38. London: Sage.

Norton, Anne. 2004. *95 Theses on Politics, Culture, and Method*. New Haven, CT: Yale University Press.

Oren, Ido. 2006a. "Can Political Science Emulate the Natural Sciences? The Problem of Self-Disconfirming Analysis." *Polity* 38/1: 72–100.

Oren, Ido. 2006b. "Political Science as History: A Reflexive Approach." In *Interpretation and Method: Empirical Research Methods and the Interpretive Turn*, edited by Dvora Yanow and Peregrine Schwartz-Shea, 215–27. Armonk, NY: M E Sharpe.

Oren, Ido and Kauffman, Robert. 2006. "Culture and Alliances: U.S. Portrayals of Saudi Arabia, Azerbaijan, and Kazakhstan Before and After September 11, 2001." In *The Limits of Culture: Islam and Foreign Policy*, edited by Brenda Shaffer, 111–65. Cambridge, MA: MIT Press.

Ortbals, Candice D. and Rincker, Meg E. 2009. "Fieldwork, Identities, and Intersectionality:

Negotiating Gender, Race, Class, Religion, Nationality, and Age in the Research Field Abroad." *PS: Political Science & Politics* 42/2: 287–328.

Pachirat, Timothy. 2006. "We Call It a Grain of Sand: The Interpretive Orientation and a Human Social Science." In *Interpretation and Method: Empirical Research Methods and the Interpretive Turn*, edited by Dvora Yanow and Peregrine Schwartz-Shea, 373–9. Armonk, NY: M E Sharpe.

Pachirat, Timothy. 2009a. "The Political in Political Ethnography: Dispatches from the Kill Floor." In *Political Ethnography: What Immersion Contributes to the Study of Power*, edited by Edward Schatz, 143–62. Chicago: University of Chicago Press.

Pachirat, Timonty. 2009b. "Shouts and Murmurs: The Ethnographer's Potion." *Qualitative and Multi-Method Research* [Newsletter of the American Political Science Association Organized Section for Qualitative and Multi-Method Research] 7/2: 41–4.

Pachirat, Timothy. 2011. *Every Twelve Seconds: Industrialized Slaughter and the Politics of Sight*. New Haven, CT: Yale University Press.

Paludi, Michele A., ed. 1996. *Sexual Harassment on College Campuses: Abusing the Ivory Power*, 2nd ed. Albany, NY: State University of New York Press.

Parsons, Wayne. 2002. "From Muddling Through to Muddling Up—Evidence Based Policy Making and the Modernization of British Government." *Public Policy and Administration* 17/3.

Pears, Iain. 1997. *An Instance of the Fingerpost*. London: Vintage.

Peattie, Lisa. 1970. "Drama and Advocacy Planning." *Journal of the American Institute of Planners* 36: 405–10.

Pierce, Jennifer. 1995. *Gender Trials: Emotional Lives in Contemporary Law Firms*. Berkeley: University of California Press.

Pike, Kenneth L. 1990. "On the Emics and Etics of Pike and Harris." In *Emics and Etics: The Insider/Outsider Debate*, edited by Thomas N. Headland, Kenneth L. Pike, and Marvin Harris, 28–47. Newbury Park, CA: Sage.

Pink, Sarah. 2008. "An Urban Tour: The Sensory Sociality of Ethnographic Place-Making." *Ethnography* 9/2: 175–96.

Piven, Frances Fox and Cloward, Richard A. 1977. *Poor People's Movements*. New York: Pantheon.

Polanyi, Michael. 1966. *The Tacit Dimension*. New York: Doubleday.

Polkinghorne, Donald E. 1983. *Methodology for the Human Sciences*. Albany, NY: SUNY Press.

Polkinghorne, Donald E. 1988. *Narrative Knowing and the Human Sciences*. Albany, NY: SUNY Press.

Poteete, Amy R. 2010. "Multiple Methods in Practice." *Qualitative and Multi-Method Research* [Newsletter of the American Political Science Association Organized Section for Qualitative and Multi-Method Research] 8/1: 28–35.

Poteete, Amy R., Jannsen, Marco A., and Ostrom, Elinor. 2010. *Working Together: Collective Action, the Commons, and Multiple Methods in Practice*. Princeton, NJ: Princeton University Press.

Prasad, Pushkala. 2005. *Crafting Qualitative Research*. Armonk, NY: M E Sharpe.

Prindeville, Diane-Michele. 2004. "Feminist Nations? A Study of Native American Women in Southwestern Tribal Politics." *Political Research Quarterly* 57/1: 101–12.

Putnam, Linda L. and Pacanowsky, Michael E., eds. 1983. *Communication and Organizations: An Interpretive Approach*. Beverly Hills, CA: Sage.

Rabinow, Paul and Sullivan, William M., eds. 1979, 1985. *Interpretive Social Science*, 1st and 2nd eds. Berkeley, CA: University of California Press.

Ragin, Charles C. 1997. "Turning the Tables: How Case-Oriented Research Challenges Variables-Oriented Research." *Comparative Social Research*, Vol. 16, 27–42. Greenwich, CT: JAI Press.

Ragin, Charles C. 2005. "The Challenge of Small (and Medium) N Research." Keynote address presented to the National Centre for Research Methods and ESRC Symposium on Small and Large-N Comparative Solutions, University of Sussex, Brighton, England (22–23 September).

Ragin, Charles C., Nagel, Joane, and White, Patricia. 2004. "Workshop on Scientific Foundations of Qualitative Research." Arlington, VA: National Science Foundation, Sociology Program, Methodology, Measurement and Statistics Program, Directorate for Social, Behavioral and Economic Sciences. www.nsf.gov/pubs/2004/nsf04219/nsf04219_1.pdf (accessed 2 February 2011).

Reinhardt, Gina Y. 2009. "I Don't Know Monica Lewinsky, and I'm Not in the CIA. Now How About That Interview?" *PS: Political Science & Politics* 42/2: 295–8.

Resnik, David B. 1998. *The Ethics of Science*. New York: Routledge.

Rhodes, R. A. W., 't Hart, Paul, and Noordegraaf, Mirko, eds. 2007. *Observing Government Elites: Up Close and Personal*. Houndmills, Basingstoke: Palgrave Macmillan.

Richardson, Laurel. 2000. "Writing: A Method of Inquiry." In *Handbook of Qualitative Research,* 2nd ed., edited by Norman K. Denzin and Yvonna S. Lincoln, 923–48. Thousand Oaks, CA: Sage Publications.

Ricoeur, Paul. 1971. "The Model of the Text." *Social Research* 38: 529–62.

Riddell, Sheila. 1989. "Exploiting the Exploited? The Ethics of Feminist Educational Research." In *The Ethics of Educational Research*, edited by Robert G. Burgess, 77–99. London: Routledge.

Riles, Annelise, ed. 2006. *Documents: Artifacts of Modern Knowledge*. Ann Arbor, MI: University of Michigan Press.

Robillard, Albert B. 1999. *Meaning of a Disability: The Lived Experience of Paralysis*. Philadelphia: Temple University Press.

Roethlisberger, Fritz J. 2001/1941. "The Hawthorne Experiments." In *Classics of Organization Theory*, 5th ed., edited by Jay M. Shafritz and J. Steven Ott, 158–66. Fort Worth, TX: Harcourt.

Rorty, Richard. 1967. *The Linguistic Turn*. Chicago: University of Chicago.

Rorty, Richard. 1979. *Philosophy and the Mirror of Nature*. Princeton, NJ: Princeton University Press.

Rosen, Michael. 1988. "You Asked for It: Christmas at the Bosses' Expense." *Journal of Management Studies* 25/5: 463–80.

Roy, Donald F. 1959. "Banana Time: Job Satisfaction and Informal Interaction." *Human Organization* 18/4: 158–68.

Rudolph, Susanne Hoeber. 2005. "The Imperialism of Categories: Situating Knowledge in a Globalizing World." *Perspectives on Politics* 3/1: 5–14.

Russell, Cherry, Touchard, Denise, and Porter, Maree. 2002. "What's Rapport Got to Do with It? The Practical Accomplishment of Fieldwork Relations between Young Female Researchers and Socially Marginalised Older Men." *The Qualitative Report* 7/1 (March). www.nova.edu/ssss/QR/QR7–1/russell.html (accessed 18 January 2011).

Sadiq, Kamal. 2009. *Paper Citizens: How Illegal Immigrants Acquire Citizenship in Developing Countries*. Oxford: Oxford University Press.

Sadiq, Kamal and Monroe, Kristen Renwick. 2010. "Unfulfilled International Agenda." *PS: Political Science & Politics* 43/4: 749–50.

Salemink, Oscar. 2003. "Introduction: Ethnography, Anthropology and Colonial Discourse." In *The Ethnography of Vietnam's Central Highlanders: A Historical Contextualization, 1850–1990*, 1–39. London: Routledge Curzon.

Sandberg, Jörgen and Alvesson, Mats. 2011. "Ways of Constructing Research Questions: Gap-Spotting or Problematization?" *Organization* 18/1: 23–44.

Sanjek, Roger. 1990. *Fieldnotes: The Makings of Anthropology*. Ithaca, NY: Cornell University Press.

Schaffer, Frederic C. 1998. *Democracy in Translation: Understanding Politics in an Unfamiliar Culture*. Ithaca, NY: Cornell University Press.

Schaffer, Frederic Charles. 2006. "Ordinary Language Interviewing." In *Interpretation and Method: Empirical Research Methods and the Interpretive Turn*, edited by Dvora Yanow and Peregrine Schwartz-Shea, 150–60. Armonk, NY: M E Sharpe.

Schatz, Edward, ed. 2009. *Political Ethnography: What Immersion Contributes to the Study of Power*. Chicago: University of Chicago Press.

Schatzki, Theodore R., Knorr-Cetina, Karin, and Savigny, Eike von, eds. 2001. *The Practice Turn in Contemporary Theory*. New York: Routledge.

Schatzman, Leonard and Strauss, Anselm L. 1973. *Field Research*. Englewood Cliffs, NJ: Prentice-Hall.

Schön, Donald A. 1983. *The Reflective Practitioner*. New York: Basic Books.

Schram, Sanford F. 2002. *Praxis for the Poor: Piven and Cloward and the Future of Social Science in Social Welfare*. New York: New York University Press.

Schwartz-Shea, Peregrine. 2002. "Theorizing Gender for Experimental Game Theory: Experiments with 'Sex Status' and 'Merit Status' in an Asymmetric Game." *Sex Roles* 47/7–8: 301–19.

Schwartz-Shea, Peregrine. 2003. "Is This the Curriculum We Want? Doctoral Requirements and Offerings in Methods and Methodology." *PS: Political Science & Politics* 36: 379–86.

Schwartz-Shea, Peregrine. 2006. "Judging Quality: Evaluative Criteria and Epistemic Communities." In *Interpretation and Method: Empirical Research Methods and the Interpretive Turn*, edited by Dvora Yanow and Peregrine Schwartz-Shea, 89–113. Armonk, NY: M E Sharpe.

Schwartz-Shea, Peregrine and Yanow, Dvora. 2002. "'Reading' 'Methods' 'Texts': How Research Methods Texts Construct Political Science." *Political Research Quarterly* 55: 457–86.

Schwartz-Shea, Peregrine and Yanow, Dvora. 2009. "Reading and Writing as Method: In Search of Trustworthy Texts." In *Organizational Ethnography: Studying the Complexities of Everyday Life*, edited by Sierk Ybema, Dvora Yanow, Harry Wels, and Frans Kamsteeg, 56–82. London: Sage.

Schwedler, Jillian. 2006. "The Third Gender: Western Female Researchers in the Middle East." *PS: Political Science & Politics* 39/3: 425–8.

Scott, James C. 1990. *Domination and the Arts of Resistance: Hidden Transcripts*. New Haven, CT: Yale University Press.

Shadish, William R. 2007. "Critical Thinking in Quasi-Experimentation." In *Critical Thinking in Psychology*, edited by Robert J. Sternberg, Henry L. Roediger III, and Diane F. Halpern, 37–53. New York: Cambridge University Press.

Shah, Sonali. 2006. "Sharing the World: The Researcher and the Researched." *Qualitative Research* 6: 207–20.

Shapiro, Ian. 2004. "Problems, Methods, and Theories in the Study of Politics, or: What's Wrong with Political Science and What to Do about It." In *Problems and Methods in the Study of Politics*, edited by Ian Shapiro, Rogers M. Smith, and Tarek E. Masoud, 19–41. New York: Cambridge University Press.

Shehata, Samer. 2006. "Ethnography, Identity, and the Production of Knowledge." In *Interpretation and Method: Empirical Research Methods and the Interpretive Turn*, edited by Dvora Yanow and Peregrine Schwartz-Shea, 244–63. Armonk, NY: M E Sharpe.

Shehata, Samer S. 2009. *Shop Floor Culture and Politics in Egypt*. Albany, NY: SUNY Press.

Shenhav, Shaul R. 2005. "Thin and Thick Narrative Analysis: On the Question of Defining and Analyzing Political Narratives." *Narrative Inquiry* 15/1: 75–99.

Shweder, Richard A. 2004. "Tuskegee Re-Examined." *Spiked-Essays* (8 January). www.spiked-online.com/Articles/0000000CA34A.htm (accessed 15 March 2008).

Shweder, Richard A. 2006. "Protecting Human Subjects and Preserving Academic Freedom: Prospects at the University of Chicago." *American Ethnologist* 33: 507–18.

Singleton, Royce A., Jr. and Straits, Bruce C. 1999. *Approaches to Social Research*, 3rd ed. Oxford: Oxford University Press.

Singleton, Royce A., Jr. and Straits, Bruce C. 2009. *Approaches to Social Research*, 5th ed. Oxford: Oxford University Press.

Snow, David A., Soule, Sarah Anne, and Hanspeter, Driesi. 2004. *The Blackwell Companion to Social Movements*. Malden, MA: Blackwell.

Soss, Joe. 2000. *Unwanted Claims: The Politics of Participation in the U.S. Welfare System*. Ann Arbor, MI: University of Michigan Press.

Soss, Joe. 2005. "Making Clients and Citizens: Welfare Policy as a Source of Status, Belief, and Action." In *Deserving and Entitled: Social Constructions and Public Policy*, edited by Anne L. Schneider and Helen M. Ingram, 291–328. Albany, NY: State University of New York.

Soss, Joe. 2006. "Talking Our Way to Meaningful Explanations: A Practice-Centered View of Interviewing for Interpretive Research." In *Interpretation and Method: Empirical Research Methods and the Interpretive Turn*, edited by Dvora Yanow and Peregrine Schwartz-Shea, 127–49. Armonk, NY: M E Sharpe.

Spradley, James P. 1979. *The Ethnographic Interview*. New York: Holt, Rinehart and Winston.

Stavrides, Stavros. 2001. "Navigating the Metropolitan Space: Walking as a Form of Negotiation with Otherness." *Journal of Psychogeography and Urban Research* 1/1. http://courses.arch.ntua.gr/stavrides.html (accessed 3 December 2009).

Strauss, Anselm and Corbin, Juliet. 1990. *Basics of Qualitative Research: Grounded Theory Procedures and Techniques*. Newbury Park, CA: Sage.

Super, Elizabeth H. 2010. "Constructing Credibility on the Doorstep: Thresholds, Networks, and Local Political Campaigners." 5th International Interpretive Policy Analysis Conference, Grenoble, France (23–25 June).

Swaffield, Simon. 1998. "Contextual Meanings in Policy Discourse: A Case Study of Language Use Concerning Resource Policy in the New Zealand High Country." *Policy Sciences* 31: 199–224.

Sykes, Chris and Treleaven, Lesley. 2009. "Critical Action Research and Organizational Ethnography." In *Organizational Ethnography: Studying the Complexities of Everyday Life*, edited by Sierk Ybema, Dvora Yanow, Harry Wells, and Frans Karmsteeg, 215–30. London: Sage.

Taber, Charles S. and Lodge, Milton. 2006. "Motivated Skepticism in the Evaluation of Political Beliefs." *American Journal of Political Science* 50/3: 755–69.

Tashakkori, Abbas and Creswell, John W. 2007a. "Editorial: The New Era of Mixed Methods." *Journal of Mixed Method Research* 1/1: 3–7.

Tashakkori, Abbas and Creswell, John W. 2007b. "Editorial: Exploring the Nature of Research Questions in Mixed Methods Research." *Journal of Mixed Method Research* 1/3: 207–11.

Tashakkori, Abbas and Teddlie, Charles B. 2003. *Handbook of Mixed Methods in Social and Behavioral Research*. Thousand Oaks, CA: Sage.

Taylor, Charles. 1971. "Interpretation and the Sciences of Man." *Review of Metaphysics* 25: 3–51. Reprinted in *Understanding and Social Inquiry*, edited by Fred R. Dallmayr and Thomas A. McCarthy, 101–31. Notre Dame, IN: University of Notre Dame Press, 1977; and in *Interpretive Social Science: A Reader*, edited by Paul Rabinow and William M. Sullivan, 25–71. Berkeley, CA: University of California Press, 1979.

Taylor, Charles. 1985. *Philosophy and the Human Sciences*. New York: Cambridge University Press.

Tessler, Mark and Jamal, Amaney. 2006. "Political Attitude Research in the Arab World." *PS: Political Science & Politics* 39/3: 433–7.

"The Evidence-Based Policy Movement." 2002. Special issue, *Public Policy and Administration* 17/3 (Autumn).

Thies, Cameron G. and Hogan, Robert E. 2005. "The State of Undergraduate Research Methods Training in Political Science." *PS: Political Science & Politics* 38: 293–7.

Traweek, Sharon. 1992. *Beamtimes and Lifetimes: The World of High Energy Physicists*. Cambridge, MA: Harvard.

Trinder, Liz, with Reynolds, Shirley. 2000. *Evidence-Based Practice: A Critical Appraisal*. Malden, MA: Blackwell Science.

Trope, Yaacov and Bassok, Miriam. 1982. "Confirmatory and Diagnosing Strategies in Social Information Gathering." *Journal of Personality and Social Psychology* 43/1: 22–34.

Tsoukas, Haridimos. 2009. "Craving for Generality and Small-N Studies: A Wittgensteinian Approach toward the Epistemology of the Particular in Organization and Management Studies." In *The Sage Handbook of Organizational Research Methods*, edited by David Buchanan and Alan Bryman, 285–301. London: Sage.

Van de Ven, Andrew. 2007. "Building a Theory." In *Engaged Scholarship: A Guide for Organizational and Social Research*, 100–42. New York: Oxford University Press.

van Hulst, Merlijn J. 2008a. *Town Hall Tales*. Delft: Eburon.

van Hulst, Merlijn J. 2008b. "Quite an Experience: Using Ethnography to Study Local Governance." *Critical Policy Analysis* 2/2: 143–59.

Van Maanen, John. 1978. "Observations on the Making of a Policeman." *Human Organization* 32: 407–18.

Van Maanen, John. 1988. *Tales of the Field: On Writing Ethnography*. Chicago: University of Chicago Press.

Van Maanen, John. 1996. "Commentary: On the Matter of Voice." *Journal of Management Inquiry* 5: 375–81.

Van Maanen, John. 2011. "Ethnography as Work: Some Rules of Engagement." *Journal of Management Studies* 48/1: 218–34.

Van Maanen, John, Sørensen, Jesper B., and Mitchell, Terence R. 2007. "The Interplay between Theory and Method." *Academy of Management Review* 32/4: 1145–54.

Venkatesh, Sudhir. 2008. *Gang Leader for a Day*. New York: Penguin.

Vickers, Sir Geoffrey. n.d. "On the Emperor's New Clothes." Cambridge, MA: Unpublished manuscript, Division for Study and Research in Education, MIT (ca. 1976).

Wacquant, Loïc. 2004. *Body & Soul: Notebooks of an Apprentice Boxer.* New York: Oxford University Press.

Walby, Kevin. 2010. "Interviews as Encounters: Issues of Sexuality and Reflexivity When Men Interview Men about Commercial Same Sex Relations." *Qualitative Research* 10/6: 639–57.

Walsh, Katherine Cramer. 2004. *Talking about Politics: Informal Groups and Social Identity in American Life.* Chicago: University of Chicago Press.

Walsh, Katherine Cramer. 2009. "Scholars as Citizens: Studying Public Opinion through Ethnography." In *Political Ethnography: What Immersion Contributes to the Study of Power,* edited by Edward Schatz, 165–82. Chicago: University of Chicago Press.

Warren, Dorian. 2005. "Wal-Mart Surrounded: Community Alliances and Labor Politics in Chicago." *New Labor Forum* 14/3: 17–23.

Wason, Peter C. 1960. "On the Failure to Eliminate Hypotheses in a Conceptual Task." *Quarterly Journal of Experimental Psychology* 12/3: 129–40.

Watson, Tony J. 2011. "Ethnography, Reality, and Truth: The Vital Need for Studies of 'How Things Work' in Organizations and Management." *Journal of Management Studies* 48/1: 202–17.

Webb, Eugene J., Campbell, Donald T., Schwartz, Richard D., and Sechrest, Lee. 1966. *Unobtrusive Measures: Nonreactive Research in the Social Sciences.* Chicago: Rand McNally.

Webb, Eugene J., Campbell, Donald T., Schwartz, Richard D., Sechrest, Lee, and Grove, Janet Belew. 1981. *Nonreactive Measures in the Social Sciences.* Boston, MA: Houghton Mifflin.

Weick, Karl E. 2005. "Organizing and Failures of Imagination." *International Public Management Journal* 8/3: 425–38.

Weiss, Robert S. 1994. *Learning from Strangers: The Art and Method of Qualitative Interview Studies.* New York: Free Press.

Weldes, Jutta. 2003. "Popular Culture, Science Fiction and World Politics: Exploring Intertextual Relations." In *To Seek Out New Worlds: Exploring Links between Science Fiction and World Politics,* edited by Jutta Weldes, 1–27. New York: Palgrave Macmillan.

Weldes, Jutta. 2006. "High Politics and Low Data: Globalization Discourses and Popular Culture." In *Interpretation and Method: Empirical Research Methods and the Interpretive Turn,* edited by Dvora Yanow and Peregrine Schwartz-Shea, 176–86. Armonk, NY: M E Sharpe.

Wendt, Alexander. 1998. "On Constitution and Causation in International Relations." In *The Eighty Years' Crisis: International Relations, 1919–1999,* edited by Tim Dunne, Michael Cox, and Ken Booth, 101–17. Cambridge: Cambridge University Press.

Wertz, Frederick J. 2005. "Phenomenological Research Methods for Counseling Psychology." *Journal of Counseling Psychology* 52/2: 167–77.

White, Jay D. 1992. "Taking Language Seriously: Toward a Narrative Theory of Knowledge for Administrative Research." *American Review of Public Administration* 22: 75–88.

White, Stephen K. 2004. "The Very Idea of a Critical Social Science: A Pragmatist Turn." In *The Cambridge Companion to Critical Theory,* edited by Fred Rush, 310–35. New York: Cambridge University Press.

Whitehead, Alfred North. 1997/1925. *Science and the Modern World.* New York: Free Press.

Whiteman, Gail. 2010. "Management Studies That Break Your Heart." *Journal of Management Inquiry* 19/4: 328–37.

Whyte, William Foote. 1955/1947. *Street Corner Society*, 2nd ed. Chicago: University of Chicago Press.

Wilkinson, Claire. 2008. "Positioning 'Security' and Securing One's Position: The Researcher's Role in Investigating 'Security' in Kyrgyzstan." In *Field Work in Difficult Environments: Discussing the Divergence between Theory and Practice*, edited by Caleb Wall and Peter Mollinga, 43–63. Berlin: Lit Verlag.

Williams, Malcolm. 2000. "Interpretivism and Generalisation." *Sociology* 34/2: 209–24.

Wingrove, Elizabeth. 2011. "Hearing Voices in the Archives." Western Political Science Association Annual Conference, San Antonio, TX (21–23 April).

Wolcott, Harry F. 2003/1973. *The Man in the Principal's Office: An Ethnography*. Walnut Creek, CA: AltaMira Press.

Wood, Elisabeth Jean. 2009. "Ethnographic Research in the Shadow of Civil War." In *Political Ethnography: What Immersion Contributes to the Study of Politics*, edited by Edward Schatz, 119–42. Chicago: University of Chicago Press.

Woolgar, Steve, Coopmans, Catelijne, and Neyland, Daniel, eds. 2009. "Does STS Mean Business?" Special Issue. *Organization* 16/1: 5–160.

Wylie, Alison. 2005. "The Promise and Perils of an Ethic of Stewardship." In *Embedding Ethics: Shifting Boundaries of the Anthropological Profession*, edited by Lynn Meskell and Peter Pels, 47–68. New York: Berg.

Yanow, Dvora. 1996. *How Does a Policy Mean? Interpreting Policy and Organizational Actions*. Washington, DC: Georgetown University Press.

Yanow, Dvora. 2000. *Conducting Interpretive Policy Analysis*. Newbury Park, CA: Sage.

Yanow, Dvora. 2001. "Learning in and from Improvising: Lessons from Theater for Organizational Learning." *Reflections* 2: 58–62.

Yanow, Dvora. 2003. *Constructing American "Race" and "Ethnicity": Category-Making in Public Policy and Administration*. Armonk, NY: M E Sharpe.

Yanow, Dvora. 2005. "In the House of 'Science,' There Are Many Rooms: Perestroika and the 'Science Studies' Turn." In *Perestroika! The Raucous Rebellion in Political Science*, edited by Kristen Renwick Monroe, 200–17. New Haven, CT: Yale University Press.

Yanow, Dvora. 2006a. "How Built Spaces Mean: A Semiotics of Space." In *Interpretation and Method: Empirical Research Methods and the Interpretive Turn*, edited by Dvora Yanow and Peregrine Schwartz-Shea, 349–66. Armonk, NY: M E Sharpe.

Yanow, Dvora. 2006b. "Neither Rigorous Nor Objective? Interrogating Criteria for Knowledge Claims in Interpretive Science." In *Interpretation and Method: Empirical Research Methods and the Interpretive Turn*, edited by Dvora Yanow and Peregrine Schwartz-Shea, 67–88. Armonk, NY: M E Sharpe.

Yanow, Dvora. 2009. "Dear Author, Dear Reader: The Third Hermeneutic in Writing and Reviewing Ethnography." In *Political Ethnography: What Immersion Brings to the Study of Politics*, edited by Edward Schatz, 275–302. Chicago: University of Chicago Press.

Yanow, Dvora and Schwartz-Shea, Peregrine, eds. 2006. *Interpretation and Method: Empirical Research Methods and the Interpretive Turn*. Armonk, NY: M E Sharpe.

Yanow, Dvora and Schwartz-Shea, Peregrine. 2008. "Reforming Institutional Review Board Policy: Issues in Implementation and Field Research." *PS: Political Science & Politics* 40/1: 483–94.

Yin, Robert K. 1989. *Case Study Research: Design and Methods*, rev. ed. Newbury Park, CA: Sage.

Yin, Robert K. 2009. *Case Study Research: Design and Methods*, 4th ed. Thousand Parks, CA: Sage.

Zabusky, Stacia E. 1995. *Launching Europe: An Ethnography of European Cooperation in Space Science*. Princeton, NJ: Princeton University Press.

Zaller, John R. 1992. *The Nature and Origins of Mass Opinion*. Cambridge: Cambridge University Press.

Zimmer, Carl. 2011. "It's Science, But Not Necessarily Right." *New York Times* (26 June, p. 12).

Zirakzadeh, Cyrus Ernesto. 2009. "When Nationalists Are Not Separatists: Discarding and Recovering Academic Theories While Doing Fieldwork in the Basque Region of Spain." In *Political Ethnography: What Immersion Contributes to the Study of Politics*, edited by Edward Schatz, 97–118. Chicago: University of Chicago Press.

INDEX